Making Connections:
Women's Studies, Women's Movements, Women's Lives

Edited by

Mary Kennedy, Cathy Lubelska and
Val Walsh

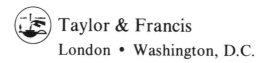

Taylor & Francis

London • Washington, D.C.

| UK | Taylor & Francis, 4 John St., London WC1N 2ET |
| USA | Taylor & Francis Inc., 1900 Frost Road, Suite 101, Bristol, PA 19007 |

First published 1993

A Catalogue Record for this book is available from the British Library

ISBN 0 74840 097 4
ISBN 0 74840 098 2 pbk

Library of Congress Cataloging-in-Publication Data are available on request

Cover design by Barking Dog Art. Based on a photograph by Val Walsh, 'Footprints in the Sand', which represents the movement and connection that is happening with respect to women.

Typeset in 10/12pt Bembo
by Graphicraft Typesetters Ltd., Hong Kong

Printed in Great Britain by Burgess Science Press, Basingstoke on paper which has a specified pH value on final paper manufacture of not less than 7.5 and is therefore 'acid free'.

Making Connections

Gender & Society:
Feminist Perspectives on the Past and Present

Series Editor: June Purvis
School of Social and Historical Studies,
University of Portsmouth, Milldam,
Portsmouth PO13AS, UK

This major new series will consist of scholarly texts written in an accessible style which promote and advance feminist research, thinking and debate. The series will range across disciplines such as sociology, history, social policy and cultural studies. Before submitting proposals, a copy of the guidelines for contributors to *Gender & Society* should be obtained from June Purvis at the address above.

Out of the Margins: Women's Studies in the Nineties
Edited by Jane Aaron, *University College of Wales*, and Sylvia Walby, *London School of Economics*.

Working Out: New Directions for Women's Studies
Edited by Hilary Hinds, *Fircroft College, Birmingham*; Ann Phoenix, *University of London*; and Jackie Stacey, *Lancaster University*.

Making Connections: Women's Studies, Women's Movements, Women's Lives
Edited by Mary Kennedy, *Birkbeck College, London*; Cathy Lubelska, *University of Central Lancashire*; and Val Walsh, *Edge Hill College, Lancashire*.

Mature Women Students: Separating or Connecting Family and Education
Rosalind Edwards, *South Bank University*

Gendered by Design?: Information Technology and Office Systems
Edited by Eileen Creen, Den Pain, *Sheffield Hallam University*; and Jenny Owen, *UMIST, Manchester*

Forthcoming

Women and Careers
Millicent Poole, *Queensland University of Technology*, and Janice Langan-Fox, *University of Melbourne*

Feminist Politics and Education Reform
Madeleine Arnot, *University of Cambridge*

Women and Modernism
Gabrielle Griffin, *Nene College, Northampton*

Feminism, Sexuality and Struggle
Margaret Jackson

Subjects and Objects: Gender and Schooling
Jenny Shaw, *University of Sussex*

Friendly Relations: Mothers and their Daughters-in-Law
Pamela Cotterill, *Staffordshire University (Stoke-on-Trent)*

AIDS: Gender and Society
Tamsin Wilton, *University of the West of England, Bristol*

Women in Britain 1914–1945
Edited by Sybil Oldfield, *University of Sussex*

This book is dedicated to
JO SPENCE-ROBERTS
(1934–1992)
activist/photographer/artist/teacher/friend . . .
who turned pain into politics and art, and
whose person, life and work continue to inspire us
in our activism and creativity.

Acknowledgment

Thanks to Comfort Jegede, Anthony Levings, Margaret Christie and Alison Waggitt for their sympathetic and speedy work on the production of this book. Despite the pressure of very tight deadlines, their interest in and responsiveness to, our ideas and wishes, extended and sustained the sense of collaboration which is so central to the themes and purposes of the book.

Contents

Contents

Making Connections: Women's Studies, Women's Movements, Women's Lives

Mary Kennedy, Cathy Lubelska and Val Walsh

> But essentially my relationship to theory is a very practical one. I'm not interested in abstractions, I'm interested in how you can use theory and who it's for and for what purpose. (Jo Spence, 1992)[1]

In recent years there has been a steady growth in feminist studies, not just in the UK. It is estimated that in 1992 there were over fifty-seven countries with Women's Studies research centres or allied courses (WISH Handbook, 1993).[2] In this collection we explore the value of our multiple identities — as women/ activists/academics — within Women's Studies, and the consequent process of renewing and reaffirming the connections.

Virginia Vargas and Nira Yuval-Davis, among others, provide evidence of the dangers of creating hierarchies amongst women, of stereotyping and forcing consensus and conformity on each other out of fear of plurality and difference. Challenging misogyny and sexism, hetero norms and homophobia, racism and assumptions based on able-bodiedness, requires us to prioritize connections and diversity, rather than difference and hierarchy. Perhaps Tamsin Wilton's concept of 'lesbian antennae' can be extended to suggest the activist consciousness we need as academics inside our institutions.

Feminists are producing new kinds of theory, grounded in our lives and experience, which reflexively refer to the lives and experiences of women (not just to our own) for confirmation that they are relevant and usable. Likewise, as Sylvia Walby points out, there has been a continuing tradition of women's history and scholarship from which we can learn. But this project is not simple, since Women's Studies combines the creation of knowledge and the politics of change, in academic contexts which perpetuate the idea of neutrality. As Nira Yuval-Davis says: 'Dialogue is crucial to the success of this epistemological approach'. In this spirit, seven of the fifteen chapters here are collaborations, and illustrate the relational and interactive methods of Women's Studies.

Section I: Identities and Feminisms

First they said I was too light
Then they said I was too dark
Then they said I was too different
Then they said I was too much the same
Then they said I was too young
Then they said I was too old
Then they said I was too interracial
Then they said I was too much a nationalist
Then they said I was too silly
Then they said I was too angry
Then they said I was too idealistic
Then they said I was too confusing altogether:
Make up your mind! They said. Are you militant
    or sweet? Are you vegetarian or meat? Are you straight
    or are you gay?
And I said, Hey! It's not about *my* mind. (Jordan, 1989)[3]

A politics based on identity tends to emphasize demarcation, difference and opposition, and can actually impede the crucial process of *identification*. As June Jordan recommended at a reading of her poems in Liverpool, in May 1992: 'We must organize, not around identity, but identification'. Only by activating and working with our necessarily multiple, developing identities and plurality of feminisms can we prevent these freezing into categories which can then be ranked for 'correctness'/importance/power. Nira Yuval-Davis suggests that our politics need to be coalition politics, 'without fixing the boundaries of this coalition in terms of "who" we are but in terms of what we want to achieve'. This is a crucial shift of priorities which, while recognizing our different but connected identities, loyalties and alliances, focuses on our 'common political situations'.

These papers provide evidence of Women's Studies as both feminist theory and politics. But this does not produce a pattern of neat connections. The concept of identity continues to be important for feminists, but along with other feminist ideas is challenged in new ways, for example in Celia Kitzinger and Sue Wilkinson's discussion of the precariousness of heterosexual female identities. Thus basic assumptions become newly complex questions: what do we mean by 'choice', 'identity', and the 'strength' and 'power' which accompany these imperatives? Joanna Liddle and Shirin Rai reconsider past and present attitudes to the 'other', the white/non-white relationship between women, in a timely discussion of the discourses of colonialization, in which they raise important questions about how we move beyond recognizing difference towards active coalition and a sense of mutuality. Even 'political choice' is not simply a matter of courage or sophistication alone, but may instead be a function of some kind of privilege or unacknowledged power over others.

The *feminist* identities which emerge here are linked to consciousness, and to political commitment to women. As important are the creative tensions between different kinds of feminisms in different political and historical contexts. For example, to what extent does lesbian possibility constitute a basic tenet of feminism? What can heterosexual feminists contribute to a politics of sexuality or power? How can we move from 'uncritical solidarity' (Nira Yuval-Davis), from notions of 'cultural differences' towards a concept of ethnicity which deconstructs oppression and domination?

Section II: Redefining Knowledge

The papers in this section all share a concern with the role of knowledge in the perpetuation of different and changing forms of patriarchal power and, therefore, of women's oppression. They all illustrate how feminist methodologies and historical understanding can expose the motives and workings of patriarchal knowledge and the ways in which this shapes discourses around women within the public domain. These discussions clearly demonstrate the defensive, insecure roots of such knowledge and strategies, and the implicit, often explicit, fear of women's own, inherently experiential, knowledge-as-power.

These themes are developed both by Stevi Jackson and by Lisa Isherwood and Dorothea McEwan. Stevi discusses the ways in which discourses around sexuality during the twentieth century have been reflected in constructions of romantic love, which have become 'central to the justification of women's material exploitation'. Here she explores the connections between reformulations of patriarchal knowledge and a defensive desire to regulate female sexuality. Lisa Isherwood and Dorothea McEwan demonstrate how feminist perspectives in theology, rooted in women's experiences, fundamentally challenge the patriarchal interpretations of the Church Fathers. They suggest, for example, that orthodox accounts of Eve the temptress were devised, in part, to outlaw and counter the perceived threat of women's knowledge, which is viewed as a loss of innocence or fall from grace.

Sylvia Walby's paper sees the role of patriarchy in the public sphere, as evinced, for example, by the impact of Thatcherite ideas upon the role of the state in women's lives, as characterizing the most recent 'backlash' against feminism. She argues that feminist scholarship is essential to both understanding and undermining this and other patriarchal devices which oppress women. This reminder resonates through the other papers: that in striving to redefine knowledge on our own terms and in developing appropriate epistemologies, Women's Studies is engaged in explicitly political projects which address the connections between our lives, experiences and activism.

Of particular importance is the significant extent to which the approaches and findings of all the authors reveal the threat — and potential power — generated by the validation of women's own experiences and knowledge. In redefining knowledge on their own terms, the writers here indicate the ways in which women's knowledge is the product of creative tensions generated by, for example, our experience of difference and our uneasy relationships with the Academy. Manifestations of these tensions and their role in the feminist research and practices through which knowledge is constituted, are honestly, sometimes agonizingly, discussed in the work of Julia Hallam and Annecka Marshall. An acknowledgment of, and willingness to work with, these and other tensions, make connections between women more possible, and provide pertinent and positive evidence of the centrality of both our consciousness and multiple identities in challenging the status quo.

Section III: Feminist Research and Education

These four case studies examine how research, teaching and learning intertwine and interact with autobiographical experience. They show how what is experi- enced — the experiential — is worked through in the institution, the class- room or the research area: theory in the making, being developed from reflexivity in research or teaching. All the writers here show how, in connection and interaction with students or research subjects, they can creatively learn to transform or re-form the curriculum or a research project. The tension between the 'objectivity' of the Academy and feminists' personal involvement can be creative, as well as a source of pressure.

At the heart of these tensions are power relations and the difficulties of empowering 'the other' in academic work. All the papers explore aspects of this crucial issue, but in different ways. Julie Matthews and Lynne Thompson share the personal experiences and growth in confidence of a disabled woman who became a mentor on a student-centred and student-managed Foundation Studies programme for mature students, showing how liberating this can be. Here we see a reversing of the usual relations between tutors and students, which demonstrates the importance of the contributions of disabled women to shared learning, and the integration of disability issues within Women's Studies.

Louise Morley's students, having worked through various participatory group learning experiences, felt confident enough to engage critically and constructively with course content and methodology, as well as with the limitations of a visiting lecturer. This provides a relevant model for practitioners and for students, showing how the processes of group learning can enhance a sense of self-identity. Both these studies show how we can create supportive contexts which empower both students and tutors. Part of the pleasure is the reversing, blurring, and equalizing of power relations between student and teacher, as we realize we are all students, all 'experts'.

In a similar vein, both Carrie Herbert and Gillian Reynolds show how vital it is in feminist research to learn from personal interaction with their research interviewees, and in the process modify the project. Carrie Herbert's working practice shows how she redesigned her research as a result of listening to and learning from her group of adolescent girls. She also draws some important conclusions for future research on sexual harassment. Gillian Reynolds's paper explores with painful honesty a common research dilemma for feminists: the complex contradictions around the gender imbalance in power relations between the woman as interviewer and the man as subject/ interviewee, in this case in the context of empowering the research subject in studies of disablement. This remains a serious difficulty, still seemingly un-acknowledged by higher education and research institutions.

Section IV: Feminists: In or Out of the Academy?

How do feminists in academia stay alive as functioning feminists? What are the risks and dangers? What are the opportunities? Is it worth getting in or staying out? This section provides some ideas in relation to these issues. Female academics who are not simply 'fascinated by the Master discourse' (Brodribb, 1992, p. x) find themselves subjected to, for example, ridicule, censure, anger.

We can see from the accounts here that maintaining our credibility in academia unavoidably creates contradictory pressures for feminists, confronted by the conflicting expectations of the Academy and our feminist principles. As Virginia Vargas observes, 'the segmentation of women's reality into specific themes . . . only made sense in the light of patriarchal categories', so that loosening the hold of these categories is central to the work of feminists, both inside and outside the Academy. Virginia writes as an activist from Latin America, coming out of an academic setting: she stresses the importance of our multiple identities and our diverse experiences, redefining these as a source of social and political strength.

Tamsin Wilton suggests we replace the notion of difference with an 'active engagement with the various oppressions of minority women and a transfor-mation of oppressive practices within feminism'. Feminist work in the Academy must do more than expose and oppose its values and practices. She argues for the importance of subjectivity in Women's Studies, over academic 'objectivity', as the latter disconnects knowledge from people's lives.

This active engagement with women's oppressions is evident in the chapter by Jennifer Marchbank, Chris Corrin and Sheila Brodie, as they trace the tensions between their lives and activism, and their work in education. These are activists who have chosen to come into academia, but not necessarily on a permanent basis. They testify to the pressures and pleasures of working as lesbians and as feminists, both inside and outside academia. Like Virginia Vargas, they provide evidence of the web of personal/political connections which sustain them, as they create spaces of safety and well-being for women, in what can be overtly hostile situations, which undermine the pedagogic and scholarly credibility of lesbians' work.

In the collaborative paper by Ruth Holliday, Gayle Letherby, Lezli Mann, Karen Ramsay and Gillian Reynolds, the academic space needed to support good research is conceived of in terms of the values of friendliness and friendship, in contrast to the taken-for-granted competitiveness of academia. Within this it is autonomy for each woman and mutual support which is highlighted. These postgraduate students create 'a collection of relationships' which facilitates their research process: their reflexivity is not only a strategy for survival, but vital to the development of their scholarly work.

Developing Connections

The themes in this collection show the range of work and thinking which connects Women's Studies to our lives and our politics. Through the development of consciousness and activism, women have turned subordination into knowledge, weakness into strength, vulnerability into power. As pedagogic and scholarly practice, Women's Studies can activate new ways of being in the Academy, new ways of knowing, new ways of organizing. Our experimentation and innovation are not for their own sakes but, like Jo Spence-Roberts, we judge them for their usefulness to our lives and work. These methods move us away from abstractions, towards a reflexivity which has epistemological as well as political ramifications.

The coherence of identity we claim is not a tidy, bounded, and fixed identity, but one which arises out of our purposes and our collectivity. As Jane Miller (1990, p. 164) has argued, 'Women must allow themselves complexity, doubleness, the strength of uncertainty'. Confidence in the uses of uncertainty opposes the Academy's emphasis on creating demarcations and fixed categories. Women's Studies, like women, has multiple identities: as feminism, activism, politics, and as epistemology, pedagogy, methodology. It challenges the compartmentalizing and fragmentation of the Academy, through its interdisciplinarity and the ways in which it defines what bell hooks calls 'the terms of engagement' (hooks, 1989, p. 53). Students confirm the importance of, and the interconnections between, our methods and the power relations pertaining to Women's Studies work:

> We had not expected academic knowledge to be so fragmented into specialisms, discourses, and disciplines. Nor had we expected academic knowledge to be so divorced or separated from *real* everyday life experiences. . . . Nor that . . . objectified knowledge would be so resistant to challenges and criticisms from women, and people other than academics. (Karach and Roach, 1992, p. 305)

Here, two students document the disempowerment of women students (including their own), not by the institution, but by female academics working in the context of Women's Studies. As feminists, we must continue to ask ourselves whether we are perpetuating the 'extremely narrow and constraining notion of intellectual achievement . . . not associated with the capacity to understand so much as with the capacity to demonstrate superiority to others' (Ramazanoglu, 1987, p. 67).

Because of our shared identifications and affinities, the concept of 'student-centred' education and pedagogy remains at the heart of Women's Studies. In its exercise, it constitutes part of the ethic of our work. Once again, an educational cliché, 'student-centred learning' (increasingly part of the rhetoric of management in higher education), becomes deepened, made more complex, through the presence and actions of women. A student-centred learning environment for Women's Studies students is like nothing that has gone before in its methods, or in its desire to remake the Academy with a 'feminine/feminist' face, because only this will make it 'human'.

We can see in this collection the importance of Black women writers, such as Audre Lorde, bell hooks, June Jordan, and Patricia Hill Collins, inspiring not only Black women towards a feminist politics. The work of Black feminists has been crucial in the reconceptualization of feminism and feminist politics. There is evidence, too, of the recent blossoming of a distinctive feminist disability perspective and its importance to feminists, not just as an extension of the experiential base of feminism and Women's Studies, but as contributing theoretical/political frameworks. And within these two perspectives, the vital contributions of lesbian writers and activists continue, both as intrinsic to these perspectives, and also as emergent within them. Challenging 'the enduring respectability of homophobia' (Tamsin Wilton), politicizing taken-for-granted heterosexuality or concepts of ethnicity and disability, are not merely academic concerns: they are issues for the wider society.

Taken together, the work in this collection amply demonstrates that making connections between our lives, our academic work, and our activism, is essential to the healthy development of a feminist Women's Studies of relevance to all women. The women here explore the processes through which this central aim is pursued. The importance of collaboration is emphasized; so too, is the continued need to challenge patriarchal knowledge and practices, which variously obstruct, oppress, expropriate or oppose our feminist aims and achievements. In highlighting the making of connections between women as central to both our consciousness and work inside and outside the Academy, a recurrent, if uncomfortable theme is the extent to which the existence of hierarchies and inequalities amongst women still qualify our sisterhood and threaten to depoliticize our endeavours. The acknowledgment of the ways in which women continue to oppress each other, through, for example, privilege or collusion, becomes a vital precondition of the recognition and validation of the identities voiced in these pages. Making connections means working with and learning from the creative tensions generated by our diversity, to develop a truly feminist Women's Studies.

Mary Kennedy, Cathy Lubelska and Val Walsh

Notes

1 Jo Spence, in extract of interview with David Hevey, taken from Chapter 8, 'Towards a Disability Imagery Currency. Part I: Cancer and the Marks of Struggle', of Hevey (1992), reproduced in *Women's Art Magazine*, 47, July/August 1992, just after Jo died in July.
2 Brown *et al.* (1993).
3 'A Short Note to My Very Critical and Well Beloved Friends and Comrades' in Jordan (1989).

References

BRODRIBB, SOMER (1992) *Nothing Mat(t)ers: A Feminist Critique of Postmodernism*, North Melbourne, Spinifex Press.

BROWN, LOULOU, COLLINS, HELEN, GREEN, PAT, HUMM, MAGGIE and LANDELLS, MEL (Eds) (1993) *The International Handbook of Women's Studies* (WISH), Hemel Hempstead, Harvester Wheatsheaf.

HEVEY, DAVID (1992) *The Creatures Time Forgot: Photography and Disability Imagery*, London, Routledge.

HOOKS, BELL (1989) *Talking Back: Thinking Feminist, Thinking Black*, London, Sheba.

KARACH, ANGELA and ROACH, DENISE (1992) 'Collaborative Writing, Consciousness-Raising, and Practical Feminist Ethics', *Women's Studies International Forum*, **15**, 2, 303–8.

JORDAN, JUNE (1989) *Lyrical Campaigns: Selected Poems*, London, Virago.

MILLER, JANE (1990) *Seductions: Studies in Reading and Culture*, London, Virago.

RAMAZANOGLU, CAROLINE (1987) 'Sex and Violence in Academic Life or You Can Keep a Good Woman Down', in HANMER, JALNA and MAYNARD, MARY (Eds) *Women, Violence and Social Control*, London, Macmillan.

Section I

Identities and Feminisms

Chapter 1

Beyond Difference:
Women and Coalition Politics

Nira Yuval-Davis

One of the effects of postmodernist deconstructionism on feminism has been the realization that 'everyone is different'. The first ones who were struggling to break the assumed homogeneity and the necessary commonality of interests among women within feminism have been Black feminists like bell hooks who claimed (1991, p. 29):

> The vision of sisterhood evoked by women's liberationists was based on the idea of common oppression . . . a false and corrupt platform disguising and mystifying the true nature of women's varied and complex social reality.

When this debate was taking place during the early 1980s, Floya Anthias and myself took a position that was then not too popular among either white or Black feminists (Anthias and Yuval-Davis, 1984). Although we welcomed Black feminists' attack on hegemonic feminism as exclusionary and racist we did not feel that the solution was to divide the feminist movement, or women in general, into dichotomous Black/white constituencies. We claimed that each woman has her own ethnicity — majority as well as minority women (except that hegemonic ethnicities have a power to 'naturalize' their world view and impose it on others as well). We also claimed that the 'Triple Oppression' approach which was then prevalent among British Black feminists in organizations such as OWAAD (Organization of Women of African and Asian Descent) was not theoretically valid as race, gender and class cannot be tagged on to each other mechanically for, as concrete social relations, they are enmeshed in each other and the particular intersections involved produce specific effects. Finally we claimed, and that brought upon our heads the wrath of some both Black and white feminists, that an exclusive focus on 'racism' fails to address the diversity of ethnic experiences of Black and other women, and that Black feminism, although suitable for certain political purposes, can be too wide or too narrow a category for specific feminist struggles, such as against racist and sexist immigration laws, domestic violence, certain cultural and religious customs etc.

Michele Barrett and Mary McIntosh (1985), while admitting the validity of our analysis, claimed that our deconstructionist approach is 'disabling to the large-scale political mobilizations'. Later postmodernist analyses developed the deconstructionist approach even more, developing the theme of the 'Inessential Woman' (Spelman, 1988) and in some absurd cases analyzing contemporary society as a 'semiotic society' with 'free floating signifiers' (Wexler, 1990).

Are effective politics and adequate sociological analysis, then, inherently contradictory to each other as Barrett and McIntosh and many others have claimed? My basic answer to this question is the same as that of Gayatri Chakravorty Spivak when she claimed (1991, p. 65):

> Deconstruction does not say anything against the usefulness of mobilizing unities. All it says is that because it is useful it ought not to be monumentalized as the way things really are.

Only such a political perspective of boundaries constructed of 'units' or 'unities' would keep our minds as well as our hearts open to continuous historical changes and could keep collectivity boundaries sufficiently open so as not to permit exclusionary practices. Concretely it means that we should see all feminist (and other forms of democratic) politics as a form of coalition politics in which the differences among women would be recognized and given a voice, without fixing the boundaries of this coalition in terms of 'who' we are but in terms of what we want to achieve.

This realization has already dawned upon some American feminists and Women's Studies scholars sometime ago. While reading for this paper, I came across the volume produced after the 1990 conference of the American Women's Studies Association. In the forward to the volume (Albrecht and Brewer, 1990, p. vi), Caryn McTighe Musil says:

> If the seventies were dominated by the exhilaration of discovering and naming ourselves as women, bound together in sisterhood, the eighties have been dominated by the discovery and definition of our differences as women. . . . The challenge of the nineties is to hold on simultaneously to these two contradictory truths: as women, we are the same and we are different. The bridges, power, alliances and social change possible will be determined by how well we define ourselves through a matrix that encompasses our gendered particularities while not losing sight of our unity.

The question, of course, is how to go about this task concretely. I shall now look critically at several approaches which attempted to develop this kind of politics: two which, although creative and thoughtful in many ways, have, I believe, some major flaws; and two which, although very different from each other, might point out the way for effectively tackling the problem.

The first approach has been described in the article by Gail Pheterson in the *Bridges of Power* collection (Pheterson, 1990). It describes an experiment in Holland in which three mixed women's groups (more or less in half and half proportions) were constructed — one of Black and white women, one of Jews and Gentiles and one of lesbian and heterosexual women. The groups operated very much within the usual pattern of the feminist consciousness-raising tradition. Pheterson (p. 3) found that:

> in every group, past experiences with oppression and domination distorted the participants' perceptions of the present and blocked their identification with people in common political situations who did not share their history.

She talks about the need to recognize and interrupt how we internalize both oppression and domination in order to create successful alliances. Such a position adds an important dimension to ethnicity — of oppression and domination and not just of 'cultural difference'. She also shows that women can experience internalized oppression and domination simultaneously as a result of different experiences: people are not just unidimensional. On the other hand this implies that there is such a thing as an 'objective truth' rather than a constructed one. I would say that rather than using a discourse of 'distortion', one should use a discourse of ideological positioning — and I will come back to this point later.

The discourse of 'distortion' creates its own distortions. Pheterson discusses, for instance, the reluctance of some women (Black women born in the colonies rather than in Holland; Jewish women who have only one Jewish parent) to identify with their groups and sees it as a distortion and 'blocked identifications'. Such a perspective assumes essentialist homogeneity in each category such as 'Blacks', 'Jews' etc. and refuses to accept that these women are genuinely located in a different positioning than other members of these groups. Moreover, it assumes that the centrality and significance of these categories would be the same to different women members and disregards differences of class, age and other social dimensions among the participants as inherently irrelevant for the group.

Such an approach is typical of 'identity politics' which have been very central in Western feminist politics. The whole consciousness-raising technique assumes as a basis for political action a reality that has to be discovered and then changed, rather than a reality which is being created and re-created when practised and discussed. Moreover, this reality is assumed to be shared by all members of the social category within which the consciousness-raising movement operates. They are perceived as constituting basically homogeneous social groupings and as sharing the same interests. Individual identity has become

equated with collective identity whereas differences, rather than being acknowledged, have been interpreted by those holding the hegemonic power
within the movement as mainly reflections of different stages of raised consciousness. Although to a large extent this has been acknowledged by the
Women's Movement in recent years, the solution has often been to develop
essentialist notions of difference, such as, for example, between Black and
white women, or middle-class and working-class women. And within each of
these prototypes, the previous assumptions about discovered homogeneous
reality usually continue to operate.

As I have elaborated elsewhere (Yuval-Davis, 1984; forthcoming), such
politics are very problematic when it comes to questions of representation.
Representation, firstly, of the grouping or 'the community' which belongs
to a specific category of identity politics, thus assuming the commonality of
experiences and interests of all members in a very unidimensional way and
with an ahistorical fixity of the boundaries of the category or grouping. Given
such assumptions, anyone who can claim to be a member of the grouping can
claim to represent it to outside agencies and benefit from it, no matter how
different s/he is in terms of class, power, gender etc. from the majority of the
people claimed to be represented.

Secondly, and linked to the first issue, is the problematics of the cultural
representation of specific communities or groupings. 'Culture', in such an
approach, is often perceived as, again, ahistorical, as essential and as equally
shared — or supposed to be shared — by all members. Such an approach has
been adopted by multi-culturalist policies which further assume that all these
cultures have an essence which is mutually exclusive from other cultures, but
at the same time is also mutually compatible (Anthias, Yuval-Davis and Cain,
1992, ch. 6).

Fundamentalist leaderships have benefited from the adoption of multi-
culturalist norms (Sahgal and Yuval-Davis, 1992). Within the multi-culturalist
logic, their presumptions about being the keepers of the 'true' religious way
of life for the members of their 'community' are unanswerable. External
dissent is labelled as racist and internal dissent as deviance (if not sheer
pathology, as in the case of 'self-hating Jews'). In the politics of identity and
representation they are perceived as the most 'authentic' 'Others'. At the same
time, they are also perceived as a threat, and their 'difference' as a basis for
racist discourse. Unlike older versions of 'multi-culturalism', fundamentalist
activists refuse to respect the 'limits of multi-culturalism' which would confine
'ethnic cultures' to a private domain or some limited community cultural activity sphere.

An attempt at a more sophisticated type of identity politics was theorized
by Rosalind Brunt in the influential collection *New Times* (1989). Brunt (p.
150) argues that:

> Unless the question of identity is at the heart of any transformatory
> project, then not only will the political agenda be inadequately

'rethought' but more to the point, our politics aren't going to make much headway beyond the Left's own circles.

Reflecting upon one's own identity, the return to the 'subjective' does not imply for Brunt withdrawal from politics, but rather the opposite — locating grids of power and resistance in the Foucauldian way (Foucault, 1980), which are horizontal and not just vertical, while keeping political frameworks of action heterogeneous and floating. She rejects the logic of 'broad democratic alliances' and 'rainbow coalitions' because, she argues, political action should be based on 'unity in diversity' which should be founded not on common denominators but on

> a whole variety of heterogeneous, possibly antagonistic, maybe magnificently diverse, identities and circumstances . . . the politics of identity recognizes that there will be many struggles, and perhaps a few celebrations, and writes into all of them a welcome to contradiction and complexity. (Brunt, 1989, p. 158)

As a positive example for this type of political struggle Brunt points to the support activities which surrounded the miners' strike in 1984–5. This is, however, an unfortunate example, because the strike ended in such a crushing defeat, not only of the miners and of the trade union movement, but of the anti-Thatcherite movement as a whole.

Real politics aside, Brunt's model of politics seems very seductive: it incorporates theoretical insights of highly sophisticated social analysis, and is flexible, dynamic and totally inclusive. However, it is in this last point that the danger lies. What ultimately lies behind Brunt's approach is a naive populist assumption that in spite of contradictions and conflicts, in the last instance all popular struggles are inherently progressive. She shares with other multiculturalists the belief about the inner compatibility and boundaries of difference which has been precisely the source of the space that has encouraged the rise of fundamentalist leaderships.

The next example which I want to discuss is that of Women Against Fundamentalism (WAF), which got organized in London in the wake of the Rushdie affair to struggle precisely against such fundamentalist leaderships of all religions as well as against expressions of racism which covered themselves up as anti-fundamentalist.

WAF includes women from a variety of religious and ethnic origins (Christians, Jews, Muslims, Sikhs, Hindus etc.). Many of the members also belong to other campaigning organizations, often with a more specific ethnic affiliation, such as the Southall Black Sisters (SBS), the Jewish Socialist Group, and the Irish Abortion Support Group. However, except for SBS which has had an organizational and ideological initiatory role in establishing WAF, women come there as individuals rather than as representatives of any group or ethnic category. On the other hand, there is no attempt to 'assimilate' the women who come from the different backgrounds. Differences in ethnicity and points of view — and the resulting different agendas — are recognized and respected. But what is celebrated is the common political stance of WAF members, as advocating 'the Third Way' against fundamentalism and against racism.

Patricia Hill Collins in her book on *Black Feminist Thought* (1990, p. 236) discusses the importance of recognizing the different positioning from which different groupings view reality. Her analysis echoes exactly the agenda which has been guiding the members of WAF:

> Each group speaks from its own standpoint and shares its own par-
> tial, situated knowledge. But because each group perceives its own
> truth as partial, its knowledge is unfinished [to differentiate from
> invalid — N.Y.-D.]. . . . Partiality and not universality is the condition
> of being heard; individuals and groups forwarding knowledge claims
> without owning their position are deemed less credible than those
> who do. Dialogue is critical to the success of this epistemological
> approach. . . .

The last example I want to discuss is also based on dialogue. A dialogue that was developed by Italian feminists from the movement Women In Black — especially the Women's Centres in Bologna and Turin — while working with feminists who are members of conflicting national groups, like the Serbs and the Croats, but especially Palestinian and Israeli Jewish women.

On the face of it, such a dialogue does not seem very different from the more common 'identity politics' type of dialogue such as was described by Gail Pheterson. However, several important differences exist.

The boundaries of the categories are not determined by an essentialist notion of difference, but by a concrete and material political reality. Also, the women involved in the different groups are not perceived simplistically as representatives of their groupings. While their different positionings and backgrounds — including the differential power relations inherent in their corresponding affiliations as members of the Occupier and the Occupied collectivities — are recognized and respected, all the women who were sought and invited to participate in the dialogue are committed to 'refuse to partici-pate unconsciously in the reproduction of the existing power relations' and are 'committed to finding a fair solution to the conflict' (Italian letter of invita-tion, December, 1991).

The basic perspective of the dialogue is very similar to that of Patricia Hill Collins. The terminology is somewhat different. The Italian women, especially Raffaella Lamberti from Bologna, use as key words the terms 'root-ing' and 'shifting'. The idea is that each participant brings with her the rooting in her own membership and identity, but at the same time tries to shift in order to put herself in a situation of exchange with women who have a differ-ent membership and identity. They call it 'transversalism' — to differentiate from 'universalism', which by assuming a homogeneous point of departure ends up being exclusive instead of inclusive.

Two things are vital in developing the transversal perspective. Firstly, that the process of shifting would not involve self-decentring, i.e. losing one's own rooting and set of values. It is vital in any form of coalition and solidarity politics to keep one's own perspective on things while empathizing and respecting the others as well as being open to change and growth as a result of the encounter. In the multi-culturalist type of solidarity politics there can be a risk of uncritical solidarity. This was very prevalent, for instance, in the politics of some sections of the Left around the Iranian revolution or the Rushdie affair. They saw it as 'imperialist' and 'racist' to intervene in 'internal community matters'. Women are often the victims of such a perspective which allows the so-called representatives and leaders of 'the community' to determine policies concerning women.

Secondly, and following from the first point — the process of shifting should not homogenize the 'other'. In the same way that there are diverse positions and points of view among people who are similarly rooted, so are there among the members of the other group. The transversal coming together should not be with the members of the other group 'en bloc', but with those who, in their different rooting, share compatible values and goals to one's own.

If empowerment of women, as many feminists have defined it (e.g. Hartsock, 1981; Bookman and Morgen, 1988; Antrobus, 1989; Ackelsberg, 1991; Bystydzienski, 1992), involves the power of self-knowledge and autonomy (rather than power over others), it is perhaps wise to end this paper with Gill Bottomley's warning (1992, p. 10):

> The dualistic approach of a unitary Us vs a unitary Them continues to mystify the interpenetration and intermeshing of such powerful constructs as race, class and gender and to weaken attempts at reflexivity. . . . Both the subjective and the objective dimensions of experience need to be addressed as well as the thorny issue of the extent to which observers remain within the discourses they seek to criticise.

The transversal pathway may be full of thorns, but at least it leads in the right direction — to the kind of feminist coalition politics which does not fall into some of the more common traps 'sisterhood' has tended to fall into in the past.

References

ACKELSBERG, MARTHA (1991) *Free Women of Spain*, Bloomington and Indianapolis, Indiana University Press.

ALBRECHT, LISA and BREWER, ROSE M. (Eds) (1990) *Bridges of Power: Women's Multicultural Alliances*, Philadelphia, New Society Publishers.

ANTHIAS, FLOYA and YUVAL-DAVIS, NIRA (1984) 'Contextualizing Feminism: Gender, Ethnic and Class Divisions', *Feminist Review*, 15.

ANTHIAS, FLOYA and YUVAL-DAVIS, NIRA (in association with CAIN, HARRIET) (1992) *Racialized Boundaries: Race, Nation, Gender, Colour and Class and the Anti-Racist Struggle*, London, Routledge.

ANTROBUS, PEGGY (1989) 'The Empowerment of Women', in GALLIN, R.S., ARONOFF, M. and FEGUSON, A. (Eds) *The Women and International Development Annual*, Vol. 1, Boulder, Colorado, Westview Press, pp. 189–207.

BARRETT, MICHELE and MCINTOSH, MARY (1985) 'Ethnocentrism in Socialist Feminist Theory', *Feminist Review*, 20.

BOOKMAN, ANN and MORGEN, SANDRA (Eds) (1988) *Women and the Politics of Empowerment*, Philadelphia, Temple University Press.

BOTTOMLEY, GILL (1992) 'Culture, Ethnicity and the Politics/Poetics of Representation', *Diaspora*, Summer.

BRUNT, ROSALIND (1989) 'The Politics of Identity', in HALL, S. and JACQUES, M. (Eds) *New Times*, London, Lawrence and Wishart.

BYSTYDZIENSKI, JILL M. (Ed.) (1992) *Women Transforming Politics: Worldwide Strategies for Empowerment*, Indiana University Press.

COLLINS, PATRICIA HILL (1990) *Black Feminist Thought: Knowledge, Consciousness and the Politics of Empowerment*, Boston and London, Unwin Hyman.

FOUCAULT, MICHEL (1980) 'Truth and Power', in GORDON, COLIN (Ed.) *Power/Knowledge: Selected Interviews and Other Writings 1972–1977*, Brighton, Harvester Press.

HARTSOCK, N. (1981) 'Political Change: Two Perspectives on Power', in BUNCH, CHARLOTTE *et al.* (Eds) *Building Feminist Theory: Essays from Quest*, New York, Longman Press.

HOOKS, BELL (1991) 'Sisterhood: Political Solidarity Between Women', in GUNEW, SNEJA (Ed.) *A Reader in Feminist Knowledge*, London, Routledge, pp. 27–41.

PHETERSON, GAIL (1990) 'Alliances Between Women — Overcoming Internalized Oppression and Internalized Domination', in ALBRECHT, LISA and BREWER, ROSE M. (Eds) *Bridges of Power: Women's Multicultural Alliances*, Philadelphia, New Society Publishers, pp. 34–48.

SAHGAL, GITA and YUVAL-DAVIS, NIRA (Eds) (1992) *Refusing Holy Orders: Women and Fundamentalism in Britain*, London, Virago.

SPELMAN, ELIZABETH (1988) *The Inessential Woman*, London, The Women's Press.

SPIVAK, GAYATRI CHAKRAVORTY (1991) 'Reflections on Cultural Studies in the Post-Colonial Conjuncture', *Critical Studies*, 3, 1, special issue on *Cultural Studies: Crossing Borders*, pp. 63–78.

WEXLER, PHILIP (1990) 'Citizenship in a Semiotic Society', in TURNER, B. (Ed.) *Theories of Modernity and Postmodernity*, London, Sage Publications.

YUVAL-DAVIS, NIRA (1984) 'Zionism, Anti-Semitism, and the Struggle against Racism', *Spare Rib*, September, pp. 18–22.

YUVAL-DAVIS, NIRA (forthcoming) 'Identity Politics and Women's Ethnicity', in MOGHADAM, VAL (Ed.) *Women and Identity Politics*, Oxford, Clarendon Press.

Chapter 2

Between Feminism and Orientalism

Joanna Liddle and Shirin M. Rai

Debates between Black and white feminists regarding the questions of race, power, and 'imperialism' during the eighties have concentrated our minds on the developing diversity of the feminist discourse. These debates, in challenging certainties of earlier feminism, have allowed both the movement and the discourse to become self-critical and therefore more aware of its own rootedness in the structures of power in society. Most of these debates, however, have focused on the relationship of Black and white women in the Western world. The inclusion of the 'Third World' has occurred in very particular ways. This article hopes to address the question of the relationship of the feminist movement of the West with that of the Third World. It argues that Western feminism has related to the 'East' in ways that can be called 'Orientalist'. This is due to the fact that Western feminists have continued to depend upon Orientalist literature for their understanding of the East. Further, because of their participation in the international hierarchies of knowledges and power, Western Black women have continued to speak for their sisters of the Third World.

This chapter is divided into three sections. The first is a critique of Western women's writings on India and Indian women. The second is an analysis of the current debates around the relationship between white and Black, East and West. In the third, we make an appeal for a 'world' public conversation amongst feminists so that the feminist discourse can begin to get beyond its present emphasis on recognizing difference but not on seeking ways to bridge it.

Orientalism, History and Legitimation

In his book *Orientalism* (1979), Edward Said explained the concept of Orientalism: first, that Orientalism was 'almost a European invention'; second, that it was a way Europe came to terms with its colonies in the Orient — through a European experience of them; third, that the construction of the

Orient was the most important image of the Other, of Europe's most significant 'cultural contestant'. All this, argues Said, made Orientalism a concept
fundamental to the identity of the European 'self'. However, cautions Said,
Orientalism was not simply an imaginative construct, but part of the materiality
of Western civilization. Its hold, therefore, was on both the idea of the Orient
and its material inclusion into Western civilization in particular ways. Orientalism was a *style* of writing about the Orient; it was also an academic tradition and career. It was a discourse. However, this discourse was not simply
the product of the sixteenth and seventeenth-century European academics
and colonialists.

> A field like Orientalism has a cumulative and corporate identity, one
> that is particularly strong given its associations with traditional learn-
> ing (the classics, the Bible, philology), public institutions (govern-
> ments, trading companies, geographical societies, universities), and
> generally determined writing (travel books, books of exploration,
> fantasy, exotic description). (Said, 1979, p. 202)

The result was a powerful consensus that has spanned many generations and
various media of communication, and, perhaps most importantly, has created
a universal imagination where the Orient is concerned.

The power of this universal image of the Orient was such that the people
of the Orient were themselves influenced by it. This was primarily through
the writings of the emerging Westernized intelligentsia in the first half of the
nineteenth century. Western academics had created a history for the Orient,
which they 'gave back' to the Orientals. This 'organised knowledge of the
past' (Williams, 1983, p. 146) not only rearranged what *had* been in the lands
that were now colonies, it also thought that process indicated the signs of the
future for these lands. If history can be seen as a continuous movement in
time, then this reconstruction of Oriental history took over both the past and
the future of the Orient by dominating its present. The intelligentsia in the
Orient found this reconstructed past appealing.

> This intelligentsia could regard itself as a product of an 'exhausted'
> culture but optimistic that despite the present circumstances they were
> representatives of a culture which had been organically disrupted by
> historical circumstance but was capable of revitalisation. (Chakravarti,
> 1989, p. 32)

The historical image that the Orientalists had created for the Orient was a
complex one. On the one hand, there was the recognition of the 'lost glory'
of the ancient cultures of the Orient, an acknowledgment of the debt that the
West owed to the East. On the other hand, and overlaying this more positive
image, was an image of decline. The 'bulk of colonial writing in India focussed

on demonstrating the peculiarities of Hindu civilisation, and the barbaric practices pertaining to women' (*ibid.*, p. 34). This re-created history explained the fall of Oriental cultures, as well as legitimizing continued colonial rule. What becomes clear from the above discussion is that 'in discussions of the Orient, the Orient is absent whereas one feels the Orientalist and what he [sic] says as presence' (Said, 1979, p. 208).

What emerges from a study of the Orientalist discourse is not simply the re-creation of a people's history by those who are 'outside' of it. It also points to the hierarchies of knowledge and power that have been established through this process. These hierarchies point to the success of the insidious nature and operations of power during the colonial period. The fact that the colonial intellectuals not only participated in validating these knowledges but also in invalidating their own, points to the position of enormous power that the colonists occupied. To be made in the image of the colonial rulers seemed the appropriate way forward. The philosophical, scientific, technological, literary and even artistic traditions of the West came to be regarded as naturally progressive and rational. For those fighting the colonial state this was a dilemma that was never really resolved and it is epitomized in the way the Indian state emerged from a movement. The Gandhian alternative of mass mobilization against the organized power of the state was acceptable, but not his agenda for an alternative for India's economic and political development. One could be regarded as part of the wider rational political discourse, the other could not. The parameters of that rationality were, however, not drawn either by Gandhi or by other nationalist leaders. Like knowledges, rationalities were also straitjacketed in the bindweed of colonial intellectual supremacy.

The legitimation of colonial rule found its easiest target in the position of women in the colonial countries. In his *History of India,* John Stuart Mill wrote: 'The condition of women is one of the most remarkable circumstances in the manner of nations. Among rude people the women are generally degraded, among civilized people they are exalted' (quoted in Sinha, 1987, p. 218). The Orientalist discourse was essentially a male discourse. Both the Western and the colonial historians who engaged in creating and legitimizing this discourse were men. Their concerns with power and powerlessness, with subjection and subjugation, with legitimation and protest were translated in a language that spoke of women and for them in contexts and ways that were alien to the women they were talking about. Attitudes towards the sexuality of Indian women, the openness regarding sexual matters in Indian households, the 'sexual licentiousness and brutality of the Indian male', against which the Indian woman had to be protected, were not simply evidence of racism of the Orientalist writers but were also used to justify the continued rule of the British in India: 'If Western education cannot bring the Bengali race into line with civilization, what force can possibly accomplish the desirable end?' (*Pioneer,* quoted in Sinha, 1987, p. 229). Women of the Orient remained absent in this discourse that so cynically used them to legitimize itself. For feminists this was an indicator not simply of the power of colonialism but also of patriarchy.

During the colonial period many women travellers and activists went to India and wrote their impressions. Two of these were Katherine Mayo and Eleanor Rathbone, both of whom were highly influential in bringing Indian women to the attention of the West.

In 1927, at the height of the Indian struggle for independence, a controversial book called *Mother India*, written by the American Katherine Mayo, documented the failings of Indian civilization from a Western perspective. The book attributes India's political subjugation and 'slave mentality' to the biological deterioration of the Indian stock, caused largely by abuses against women such as child marriage, child widowhood, premature consummation and pregnancy, destructive methods of midwifery, excessive childbearing, purdah and prostitution. She also discusses other areas of Indian life such as the caste system, Hindu/Muslim antagonism and the inadequacies of Indian medicine. Mayo argues that these failings, characterizing the India of the past and the present, explain why the Indian people 'are poor and sick and dying and why their hands are too weak, too fluttering, to seize or to hold the reins of government' (Mayo, 1927, p. 38).

Mayo rightly criticizes the customs and practices which have made child marriage a necessity, and details some of the horrific effects on women and girls, including examples of child sexual abuse. But in justifying foreign rule through the attack on child marriage, she also represents Indian women in an Orientalist manner.

Mayo constructs a unitary view of Indian culture and people as uncivilized and barbaric, and of Indian women as backward and ignorant. This view is reinforced by Mayo's exclusive focus on women as victims. There is no reference to the Indian women's movement, which had been campaigning against purdah, child marriage and the conditions of widowhood, and in favour of female education and the vote. Further, Mayo refuses to allow Indian women to represent themselves. Almost two-thirds of her sources are Government or other official reports, and publications by Western men and women. One-third are statements by Indian men, either from Legislative Assembly debates, or from published writing. Only one source by an Indian woman is used (Mayo, 1927, pp. 77, 81).

From Mayo's focus on women's oppression, one might expect a feminist approach to the matter of Indian culture and civilization. But the aim of this book is not to campaign against Indian patriarchy. It is to defend British colonialism. Mayo does not adopt a gendered analysis, and there is no examination of the cause of women's oppression except to locate it in the barbarity of the Indian people.

Mayo's approach is explicitly imperialist, not feminist. Her book exploits Indian women's oppression to confirm Western cultural superiority and to demonstrate that Indians are unfit for independence. *Mother India* is also a deeply racist book, for it argues that the colonized peoples of the East lack 'the power to grasp the spirit of democracy' (*ibid.*, p. 181) and that the idea of representing a constituency 'is as yet too gauzy a figment, too abstract a theory, too *non-oriental a conception* to figure as an influence in their minds' (*ibid.*, p. 269, emphasis added). As a review in the *New Statesman* (July 1927) proclaimed: 'Katherine Mayo makes the claims for Swaraj [self-rule] seem nonsense and the will to grant it almost a crime.'

In contrast to Mayo, Eleanor Rathbone was a committed feminist, a British suffragette and later a Member of Parliament. In 1934, fired by *Mother India*, she wrote *Child Marriage: The Indian Minotaur*. Rathbone's approach to the question of women's subordination in India is very different from Mayo's. She does not express the contempt towards the Indian people revealed in Mayo's book, and she supports Indian self-government and female suffrage. Indeed, one of her two main strategies for eliminating child marriage is to give women the vote and thereby 'the means of freeing themselves' (Rathbone, 1934, p. 16). Rathbone does not present a negative universalized image of the Indian woman as victim. But her sources are still heavily biased in favour of British authorities: 75 per cent consist of Government or other official reports plus individual British men and women authors. Another 17 per cent are Indian male sources. Only three (8 per cent) of the references quoted are by Indian women themselves: Muthulakshmi Reddy, Pandiata Ramabai and Dr Rukhmabai. These do at least show that Indian women were concerned about the condition of Indian womanhood, but they do not suggest more than token representation within the pages of Rathbone's book, and there is no indication that Rathbone consulted the Indian women's movement over the question of child marriage during her visit to India.

Although Rathbone is in favour of Indian independence and female suffrage, she campaigns for the British Government's position rather than the policies supported by the Indian nationalist movement and the Indian women's organizations. On votes for women she supports a compromise proposal which would enfranchise approximately 5 per cent of Indian women, although the All India Women's Conference and the Indian National Congress were demanding universal adult suffrage. Rathbone gives advice to the Indian women's movement based on her experience of the women's movement in Britain, without any recognition of the differences between them stemming from the colonial relationship. She never once refers directly to what Indian women who are campaigning on women's issues think is the best strategy to pursue, so there is never any possibility of open dialogue on matters about which they and she are divided. There is one oblique reference to what Indian women who disagree with her may think: 'I may be told, again, by Indian women themselves, that the time for such a campaign is not yet; that they have a more immediate task to do in helping their men to free India from foreign rule' (*ibid.*, p. 113). But the women activists with whom she disagrees are never allowed to put their own case. The overall impression from reading *Child Marriage* is, to change the pronoun in Said's phrase, 'the Orient is absent, whereas one feels the Orientalist and what she says as presence' (Said, 1979, p. 208).

Rathbone's approach to colonialism is ambiguous at best. Although she does not mount the kind of sustained defence of the British Raj which Mayo presents, and she supports Swaraj in principle, in practice she argues for a limited and conditional form of home rule, pressing the British Government's case for restricted political representation against Congress's demands for full-scale independence. She questions Congress methods of non-cooperation, favouring collaboration and working within the system. She believes that India should *earn the right* to Swaraj by improving social conditions, rather than believing that every people has the unconditional right to self-determination and freedom from foreign rule (Rathbone, 1934, pp. 113–14). Moreover, she criticizes Indians for lacking the spirit to achieve democracy:

> The engine of democracy can remove a mountain by tunnelling through it more effectively than a volcano which merely blows the top off. It can; but *when it does not,* it is either because the engine is not big enough, or because *the spirit that gives it driving-force is not behind it.'* (*ibid.*, p. 105, emphasis added)

This is very close to Katherine Mayo's argument: that the Indian people lack the spirit to achieve democracy and self-rule, even when they are in the midst of struggling for it.

Thus whilst Rathbone's *aims* were feminist, the *image* she presented was little different from those overtly Orientalist texts which used women's subordination as a defence of the British Raj. Eleanor Rathbone is a prime example of how Western feminism has related to the East in ways which can only be called Orientalist, drawing upon the Orientalist literature from the past, and creating for the present and the future a universal image of the Orient and the Oriental woman.

Imperial Feminism and its Critics

Our brief study of Western women's and first-wave feminist writing on India has indicated the power of the Orientalist image. Did these writings influence later Western feminist views of the East? Have second-wave feminist discourses been able to free themselves from the influence of Orientalism? What were and are the hierarchies of concerns, debate, and recognition established within the developing discourse of women's rights, movements, and of Women's Studies? How far did the feminism of the white women of the West build upon the position of power given to them by the history of Western colonialism? How was this historical collusion dealt with in the feminist discourse emerging in the seventies and the eighties? Some of these questions were first raised by Black feminists challenging 'imperial feminism'.

Black feminists began to 'identify the ways in which a particular tradition, white, Eurocentric, and Western, has sought to establish itself as the only legitimate feminism in current political practice' (Amos and Parmar,

1984, p. 3). Black feminists pointed to the feminist agenda drawn up by white women as indicative of another oppressive consensus that negated the particular issues faced by women of colour. This consensus included both the priorities of an essentially white middle-class feminist movement as well as a passive image of Black women. Marx had written of the colonial peoples in the Eighteenth Brumaire of Louis Bonaparte: 'They cannot represent themselves; they must be represented'. White feminists were doing exactly that; representing their Black sisters in mainstream feminist struggles assuming both their consent and their concerns. The norm continued to remain the white norm-the Woman a white woman. Otherness continued to embody Black women thus including the element of deviance in the construction of both 'Black-ness' and the 'woman-ness' of the non-white. A critique of both radical feminist texts and socialist feminism, indeed of all white feminism, was made by Black feminists increasingly alarmed at this new 'colonial' discourse. The Orientalism of the feminist discourse seemed not simply colourblind, it came dangerously close to being racist in the way it constructed not only oriental patriarchy, but the developing world itself.

In Mary Daly's book *Gyn/Ecology* the story of an Orientalist discourse as a continuing subtext of Western feminist writing is clearly visible. Daly discusses the Hindu ritual of *suttee* to 'dis-cover the global dimensions of its [the patriarchal myth's] gynocidal re-enactments' (Daly, 1979, p. 112). In doing so she obliterates many lines that form the complex network of the cultural and social life that is the lived experience of the Hindu woman. What emerges from this 'dis-covering' of the workings of patriarchy are many messages — of outrage at the ritual itself and all that it symbolized, but also of an arrogant ignorance that could only be sustained by a complete disregard of another culture, another people. More worrying is the fact that the way Daly sets about 'dis-covering' patriarchy in India leads her to construct an image of the Indian (as opposed to Hindu in the case of *suttee*) woman as *victim*. There is no 'dis-covering' of the resistance that Hindu women offered to this horrifying ritual. The flight/resistance of women is let slide past in order to concentrate on their actual annihilation on the husband's pyre. In a text full of examples to show the horror, the pain, and the misery of *suttee* we are not once invited to see how women did resist. The odds were overwhelmingly against them but they did muster the strength to say no. We get no evidence of this from Daly. In the only instance in the chapter where we do encounter a woman actively trying to escape her fate, Daly chooses not to comment (p. 117).

The sources that Daly uses in her essay form a significant part of the story of the power of Orientalism, and the hierarchy of knowledge that this establishes. *All* the sources used by her in constructing the history of *suttee* in India and its justification, and acceptance by the Hindu culture, are Western sources; furthermore, all except one are male. While Daly challenges the male version of cultural history, she does not do the same with the Orientalist construction of a religion and people. Indeed, she acquiesces in that construction and thus validates it. The sole female source used by Daly is Katherine Mayo's *Mother India*. Daly not only presents Mayo's work uncritically, but defends her from the attacks of both Western and Indian critics, and advises feminists to 'search out and claim such sisters as Katherine Mayo' (*ibid.*, p. 129).

Eleanor Rathbone was at least aware of Indian women's response to the Orientalist discourses presented by feminist and non-feminist Western authors when representing Indian women, despite her minimization of the problems of the colonial relationship. She was also aware of the existence and activities of the Indian women's movement. Mary Daly is oblivious to these concerns. All that remains of those debates in her writing is the Orientalist construction of Indian women, still firmly embedded in the cognitive structures of 'second-wave' feminism, and given added legitimacy through its reproduction in a modern feminist text.

The political fallout of such writing was great. First, it gave to a section of the Western readership a confirmation of the 'rudeness' of the Indian/Hindu society of which Mill had spoken. Second, it put Black feminists in a very difficult position. How could they let this one-dimensional representation of their countries of origin pass without contesting this strategy of challenging global patriarchy? There was a clash of multiple identities in Black feminists — something that Daly's writing failed to acknowledge. As a result we see a defence of 'culture' which in many instances did its own rewriting of history. The purdah, and the system of arranged marriages, where all the patriarchal forces of the male-headed family, religion and caste came into play, were redefined to show that they were and are not as oppressive of the Muslim or Hindu woman as feminist critics like Daly would have us believe: 'Today's arranged marriage system is qualitatively different from that of yesteryear and given that the choices open to Asian women are limited, some actually do support the practice' (Trivedi, 1984, p. 47). There was a closing of ranks that disallowed an openness of critique. The collusion that Said writes of in describing oriental intellectuals can be witnessed yet again but this time within the feminist movement. Women of colour reinterpreted rituals and restriction upon themselves by traditional patriarchal cultures as defence against the racism that they perceived in the insensitive handling of cultural difference within the feminist movement. However, in doing so they did challenge the 'imperial feminism' that arose out of the globalist approach to questions of patriarchy.

The challenges posed by Black feminist writing in the eighties were powerful critiques of second-wave feminism and helped enormously in directing the feminist movement to issues of difference, language and culture, and of multiple identities. The result was a widening and sharpening of the intellectual edge of feminist theory, and a gradual unpacking of terms that had been constructed with a careless sense of universality. 'Woman' herself was deconstructed, revealing different layers of consciousness and identity based upon sex, race and class, religion, culture and language, history and historical development. In trying to re-energize feminism intellectually and politically, while at the same time acknowledging and responding to the challenge that Black feminists had made, Western feminism adopted different strategies.

First, there was a strong critique of universalism — especially of the concept of global sisterhood. Women of the world were united in their oppression by and opposition to patriarchy, but the nature of patriarchy, of oppression and therefore of oppositions to it varied as did the actual lived experience of the women of different colours and cultures. The intellectual meeting of one strand of feminist discourse with poststructuralism contributed to a recognition of the need to deconstruct the grand theory of early feminism to allow the multiple realities of women to be projected. Second, there was a conscious attempt to give voice to Black feminists within the feminist movement, and in Women's Studies courses and establishments, through recognition and active recruitment. How this was done revealed real differences in the stages of consciousness and critique in mainstream white feminist discourse.

These strategies, however, had their own problems. The recognition of difference led white feminists to take the view that they were not in any position to speak for their sisters from other cultures. They looked to Black women in the West for an understanding about Black women of the world. This has put a great burden on Black women in the West. They are not only trying to make sense of their own position in societies unsympathetic to them, and fighting their own battles against the various forces of patriarchy, they also have to represent the experiences of women of the Third World. While the Black women of the West make contact with two worlds — of their present existence and of their countries of origin (through religion for example) — they are primarily rooted in their lived experience in the West. They cannot be moulded into a unity of 'the Black' covering millions of women of fundamentally different lived realities.

Such an approach to the question of Black feminism also allowed an uncritical acceptance of the 'recognized' Black feminist voices as authentic in their representation of women and issues for women from their countries of origin. This meant that the diversity of views, languages, cultures, religions, and economic and political institutions with which women of the countries of the Third World had to interact, and which has been represented in the diversity in their writing, art forms and struggles, did not become part of the 'public conversation' of the feminist discourse which remained largely Western focused. If 'articulation of experience (in myriad ways) is among the hallmarks of a self-determining individual or community' (Lugones and Spelman, 1986, p. 20) then Third World women have been denied empowerment even within the feminist discourse. While one unity of Woman was rejected in the creating of the new dichotomy of Black/white two unities were created! This has resulted in another denial of difference among these two categories. 'Difference *within* categories — here black and white — are underplayed in order to establish it *between* them' (Aziz, 1991, p. 300).

Further, by taking the view that 'knowledge is constructed by human subjects who are socially constituted to the conclusion that those who are differently located socially can never attain *some* understanding of [the other's] experience or *some* sympathy with [their] cause' (Narayan, 1989, p. 264) relativism began to creep into feminism. The choice seemed to lie between *being* the same and speaking for the women of 'other' cultures or to be disengaged from the 'others'' experience, languages, and, therefore, logically, from their struggles. This disengagement is disempowering of Third World women in two ways. First, politically, it does not give them the option to represent their own lived experience in a self-written text while at the same time linking up in resistance with an informed, sympathetic support base outside that experience. Second, the likelihood of Third World women making any intellectual and theoretical contribution to debates within feminism — which continue to be dominated by Western discourses — is greatly reduced in such a context. Disengagement is cutting loose; Western feminism does therefore have to confront the dilemma of including difference in a developing discourse while also continuing to recognize that difference.

Here we have to consider how Women's Studies, as an academic institution in the West, is situated in the networks of official discourses, of regimes of power, and therefore how it is privileged by these. This is important not only for the question of representation and validation raised above, but also of marginalization. It is evident that the developing discourses of resistance and of feminist critique in the Third World remain marginalized and particularized in the Women's Studies courses and feminist journals of the West. When we add to this intellectual position the reality of publishing and packaging, the situation seems even worse. Who gets published and by whom determines the readership of texts. The accessibility to the international networks of publishing houses is one area where Western feminists — both white and Black, to different degrees — are greatly privileged as compared to women from the Third World. And if a published (and therefore distributable) text is important to the development of a feminist 'public conversation', the disempowered position of the women with greatly limited access to that published world becomes clear. Further, the packaging of Third World women's writings also raises important issues for Women's Studies. In Women's Studies catalogues (see Sage, 1992) there are separate sections on, say, domestic violence, media, sexuality, work, health and politics, together with one special section on 'Women and the Third World'. Do women of the Third World have nothing to contribute to the general analysis of issues of domestic violence, work, politics, health etc.? Why are there no separate sections on women from Europe, from North America, from Australia? Is the Western or white experience the only 'generalizable' experience in a public discourse on domestic violence? If the Irish women's experience of their relations with the Irish state can form part of the discourse on women and the state together with state policy towards women in the Reagan era (Dahlerup, 1986) why can't the experience of Indian or Bangladeshi women's relations with their states? The point we are making here concerns not only the structures of power (as demonstrated in publishing and distribution networks and Western-dominated international markets) that Women's Studies departments support by accepting such divisions, but also Women's Studies courses themselves. How often do we find issues of imperialism, race, ethnicity, and the Third World packaged in the same way as the above-mentioned catalogue? Parallel conversations continue in Women's Studies departments and theoretical and political developments of Third World women do not become part of the mainstream courses. In such circumstances it becomes easier to ignore, forget, or marginalize issues emerging from women's experience in the developing world. The Third World remains a tame supplement to the white world within mainstream feminism.

Conversing and Listening

So, where do we move from this critique? Given the complex diversity of women's lived experience in different geographical, cultural, historical, political and demographic contexts can we move *beyond* recognizing these differences? Indeed, should we aspire towards such a goal at all? Are we advocating a new 'grand theory' of feminism that would speak for most women while recognizing the differences among them? One of the great strengths of post-structuralist feminism has been its insistence on plurality and its valuing of difference. However, built into this strength is the fatal weakness of relativism, of imbuing, actually or potentially, all accounts with the same validity. This leads to both nihilism and apathy (see Hawkesworth, 1989, p. 554). If there is no truth, the question arises: how are we to signify our experiences, make sense of them, relate to the other? Perhaps one of the most disempowering states is the state of not knowing. If we cannot validate our lived experience as our truth, however partial, any move towards praxis is impossible. Praxis must surely emerge from knowing, and then from doing. For most Third World women, however, retreat is not an option. Engagement not only with their own reality but also with the realities of others around them and of the power that constrains those realities is the only way forward. There has to be a continuous seeking of support across individual boundaries for these women if they are to survive as themselves and in all the social roles that are given them or that they take upon themselves. In this seeking of support, perhaps, we can find our answer to the question of going beyond difference.

One of the first ways of bridging differences that divide has to be to give voice to those differences. This, as we have seen, has already been attempted. However, giving voice becomes meaningless if that voice is not listened to. Practices of listening have therefore to be established within the feminist movement if the different voices are to be validated within its boundaries. However, all too often we find that these voices come to be 'regarded only as informative ethnographic specimens, suitable for the limited attention of experts and area specialists' (Said, 1992, p. 19). That feminists concerned with the politics of coalitions among women can also fall victim to this attitude is evidence of the pervasiveness of this approach to diversity. In an otherwise sensitively written piece on 'Making Common Cause: Diversity and Coalitions' Charlotte Bunch writes: 'Quite specifically, in 1985, white women can look to the growing women of color movement in the West and to feminism in the Third World as sources of both insight and information' (Bunch, 1990, p. 51). Black and Third World experience thus becomes a source of information that might enrich Western ideas of women. The main conversation remains the same — the Western woman still retains primacy on the feminist intellectual stage. This results in marginalization of certain voices from the mainstream conversation. Who is sidelined depends very much on the existing international structures of power which feminist institutions cannot transcend. They can, however, be more or less aware of their position in these hierarchies of power and work to subvert them.

One way of doing this, writes Said, is through the concept of *worldliness* which he describes thus: 'By linking works to each other we bring them out of the neglect and secondariness to which for all kinds of political and ideological reasons they had previously been condemned' (Said, 1992). Worldliness therefore is 'a restoration that can only be accomplished by an appreciation not of some tiny, defensively constituted corner of the world, but of the large, many-windowed house of human culture as a whole' (*ibid.*). Such inclusion of different voices — distinct, clear, yet part of a chorus — is what a 'feasible feminism' can move towards. The impulse towards such coming together can arise out of what we already experience in our individual lives — sympathy and friendship. Acceptance of differences of language and culture does not prevent us from forming lasting friendships that provide critical support in our individual lives; why can this not be aspired to in our social existence? Attuning our ears to the nuances of narratives, with sympathy that allows us to support the other without taking over the other's experience as our own, can bridge the differences that divide us. This would come with *understanding* the other's experience without needing to *live* it. Once we do this we can take the next step: to start an international feminist dialogue that is critical, incomplete but continuously developing.

References

AMOS, VALERIE and PARMAR, PRATIBHA (1984) 'Challenging Imperial Feminism', *Feminist Review*, 17, Autumn.
AZIZ, RAZIA (1991) 'Feminism and the Challenge of Racism: Deviance or Difference?', in CROWLEY, HELEN and HIMMELWEIT, SUSAN (Eds) *Knowing Women*, Cambridge, Polity Press.
BUNCH, CHARLOTTE (1990) 'Making Common Cause: Diversity and Coalitions', in ALBRECHT, LISA and BREWER, ROSE M. (Eds) *Bridges of Power: Women's Multicultural Alliances*, Philadelphia, New Society Publishers.
CHAKRAVARTI, UMA (1989) 'Whatever Happened to the Vedic *Dasi*? Orientalism,

Nationalism, and a Script for the Past', in SANGARI, KUMKUM and VAID, SUDESH (Eds) *Recasting Women: Essays in Colonial History*, New Delhi, Kali for Women.

DAHLERUP, DRUDE (Ed.) (1986) *The New Women's Movement: Feminism and Political Power in Europe and the USA*, London and Beverly Hills, Sage.

DALY, MARY (1979) *Gyn/Ecology: The Metaethics of Radical Feminism*, London, Women's Press.

HAWKESWORTH, MARY C. (1989) 'Knowers, Knowing, Known: Feminist Theory and Claims of Truth', *Signs*, **14**, 3, Spring.

LORDE, AUDRE (1981) 'An Open Letter to Mary Daly', in MORAGA, CHERRIE and ANZALDUA, GLORIA (Eds) *This Bridge Called My Back: Writings of Radical Women of Color*, Watertown, Mass., Persephone Press.

LUGONES, MARIA C. and SPELMAN, ELIZABETH V. (1986) 'Have We Got a Theory for You! Feminist Theory, Cultural Imperialism and the Demand for "The Woman's Voice"', in PEARSALL, MARILYN (Ed.) *Women and Values: Readings in Recent Feminist Philosophy*, Belmont, Calif., Wadsworth Publishing Company.

MAYO, KATHERINE (1927) *Mother India*, London, Jonathan Cape.

MOHANTY, CHANDRA T., RUSSO, ANN and TORRES, LOURDES (Eds) (1991) *Third World Women and the Politics of Feminism*, Bloomington, Indiana University Press.

NARAYAN, UMA (1989) 'The Project of Feminist Epistemology: Perspectives from a Nonwestern Feminist', in JAGGAR, ALISON M. and BORDO, SUSAN R. (Eds) *Gender/Body/Knowledge: Feminist Reconstructions of Being and Knowing* London, Rutgers University Press.

NEW STATESMAN (1927) 'India As It Is', 16 July.

RATHBONE, ELEANOR (1934) *Child Marriage: The Indian Minotaur*, London, George Allen and Unwin.

SAGE (1992) Catalogue on Gender Studies.

SAID, EDWARD (1979) *Orientalism*, New York, Vintage Books.

SAID, EDWARD (1992) 'Cultures and Vultures', *The Times Higher Education Supplement*, January 24.

SINHA, MRINALINI (1987) 'Race and Gender', in KIMMEL, M. (Ed.) *Changing Men*, London, Sage.

TRIVEDI, PARITA (1984) 'To Deny Our Fullness: Asian Women in the Making of History', *Feminist Review*, 17, Autumn.

WILLIAMS, RAYMOND (1983) *Keywords*, Glasgow, Flamingo.

Chapter 3

The Precariousness of Heterosexual Feminist Identities

Celia Kitzinger and Sue Wilkinson

It is a curious fact that feminists who live heterosexual lifestyles — who are happily married to, living with or having sex with men — often find it difficult or impossible to accept the identity 'heterosexual'. We became forcibly aware of this when we started to compile a list of 'heterosexual feminists' who might be willing to write for a 'Heterosexuality' special issue of the journal *Feminism and Psychology* (Kitzinger *et al.*, 1992), and for its subsequent expansion into an edited book (Wilkinson and Kitzinger, 1993). Not only did it quickly strike us how rare such a public identification is — and, indeed, how much easier it would have been to compile a list of self-identified 'lesbian feminists' — but we were surprised to find that in response to personal letters inviting contributions from women who (as far as we knew) had never identified themselves as anything other than heterosexual, we received anxious or angry letters, demanding to know how we *knew* they were heterosexual, and indeed, how *they* could tell whether they were heterosexual or not, and just what *is* a 'heterosexual' anyway?

'Why address me so categorically as a heterosexual?' writes the feminist psychologist Mary Gergen (widely known to be married to the social-constructionist psychologist, Kenneth Gergen):

> Why was anyone so sure? Because I am married? Or because my husband seems 'straight'? Is it about my hairdo or my shoes or the things I have said, or not said? . . . How did the heteros get picked out? (Gergen, 1992, p. 447)

Unwilling to accept 'heterosexual' identities, several feminists decided against contributing, saying, 'I have a strong ambivalence about accepting the label "heterosexual" ', or:

> While I do identify as a feminist, I don't have any sense of identity as a 'heterosexual feminist' and indeed would reject that label. For me

feminist politics is inspired by a sense of solidarity with other women and I would find it difficult to set myself apart from other women by applying such a label to myself.

Others, such as Rosalind Gill and Rebecca Walker (1992, p. 453) commented that they 'found it difficult to think about ourselves *as* straight feminists', and found 'writing this to be an educative process'. Robyn Rowland (1992, p. 459) clearly states at the outset:

> I don't go about saying 'I am heterosexual' and do not feel I am particularly identified as heterosexual . . . I would not call myself heterosexual, but rather say that I am in a heterosexual relationship.

Feminist psychologist Mary Crawford (1992, p. 429) describes her monogamous marriage, but identifies herself not as heterosexual but as 'a woman-identified person who, because of a decision to enter into a long-term affectional and sexual relationship with a man, is situated in a largely heterosexual social context'. More forcefully still, Sandra Bem (1992, p. 436) states: 'Although I have lived monogamously with a man I love for over twenty-six years, I am not now and never have been a "heterosexual".'

These feminists' discomfort with or denial of 'heterosexual' identities is in marked contrast to *lesbian* feminists' insistence on and celebration of 'lesbian' identities. It is hard to imagine a contemporary feminist declaring, in parallel with Robyn Rowland, that she would not call herself lesbian, but rather say that she is in a lesbian relationship; or claiming, with Sandra Bem, that although she has lived monogamously with a woman she loves for over twenty-six years, she is not now and never has been a *lesbian*. Such statements are, of course, fairly common from lesbians who are *not* feminists (cf. Kitzinger, 1987). Under hetero-patriarchal oppression, many lesbians are unhappy with and deny or conceal their lesbianism, and others express identities in which their lesbianism is diffused and diluted as much as possible (e.g. 'I've fallen in love with this *person* who happens to be a woman' or 'Being lesbian is just a tiny part of who I am; I'm a *person* first and foremost'). But for lesbian *feminists*, lesbian identities are proudly embraced, asserted, and (sometimes) incorporated into the very definition of feminism itself. While we could list many well-known *lesbian* feminists whose lesbianism is a core part of their feminism, and who consciously write from a '*lesbian* feminist' perspective (e.g. Allen, 1990; Frye, 1990; Hoagland, 1988; Penelope, 1986; Wittig, 1992), it is much harder to think of (or even to imagine what would be meant by) consciously, and as part of a feminist commitment, writing from a *heterosexual* perspective. The qualifier 'heterosexual' is, at best, an embarrassing adjunct to 'feminist'; at worst, it seems a contradiction in terms.

Many feminists, both heterosexual and lesbian, have debated whether all feminists should become lesbian (e.g. in the edited collection by Onlywomen

Press, 1981). It is not our intention to continue that debate here. Rather, we begin from the position that many feminists, for a variety of reasons, *are* engaged in heterosexual activities, and living heterosexual lives, but, nevertheless, do not have 'heterosexual feminist' identities. We ask *why* heterosexual feminists apparently find it so hard to claim a 'heterosexual' identity for themselves, and why heterosexual feminist identities are apparently so precarious.

We address these questions in terms of (1) the perceived negative consequences of heterosexuality for women, which makes it hard for heterosexual feminists to reconcile their political analyses with their chosen life-styles; (2) their experience of 'sexual fluidity' which (particularly given the political problems of (1) above) makes them reluctant to 'categorize' or 'label' their shifting sexual interests as 'heterosexual'; (3) the way in which, for most heterosexual feminists, heterosexuality was adopted as the taken-for-granted default assumption rather than actively chosen or constructed as an identity in its own right; and (4) the problems for feminists of an identity which remains largely unpoliticized even within feminism itself. We show how each of these four factors makes it difficult for heterosexual feminists to identify themselves *as* heterosexual, and address the consequences for feminism of the precariousness of heterosexual identity.

1 Glad to be Heterosexual?

In our Call for Contributions to the journal special issue (Kitzinger *et al.*, 1992), we deliberately posed a 'positive' question about the *benefits* of heterosexuality from a feminist perspective. We did not *ask* for misery. Yet what we received stands in bleak contrast to the celebratory tone of all those special issues and edited volumes on *lesbian* identities. Lesbians, under pressure to 'justify' lesbianism, frequently resort to protestations of happiness, having been 'pushed into years of shouting almost banal slogans such as "Glad to be Gay" ' (Parker, 1987, p. 141). By contrast, it seems that on the rare occasions when heterosexual feminists are challenged about their heterosexuality, they tend to describe how miserable they are, compared to the (presumed) happiness of lesbians. Our contributors write of 'unrelenting tension' (Lips and Freedman, 1992), 'unbalanced struggles and compromises' (Ramazanoglu, 1992), 'painful contradictions' (Gill and Walker, 1992) and the 'toll on my self-esteem' (Jacklin, 1992). Although criticism of heterosexuality is (it seems) less acceptable when it comes from lesbians, 'heterosexual women generally make no bones whatever about criticising heterosexual relationships, in depth, in detail, and with considerable passion and bitterness' (Onlywomen Press, 1981, p. 56).

We shouldn't really have been surprised. The reasons for heterosexual women's misery have been well documented. For example, despite pioneering studies on the politics of housework going all the way back to Charlotte

Perkins Gilman (1898) in first-wave feminism, and developed by Pat Mainardi (1970) and Ann Oakley (1974) in early second-wave feminism, a 1985 survey found that, while *un*married women in the USA do an average of 14.9 hours of housework per week, the burden of housework is half as much again for married women (22.4 hours), while married men average only 8.8 hours per week (cited in French, 1992, pp. 187–8). In an earlier issue of *Feminism and Psychology*, Rose Croghan (1991) documented the huge discrepancies between male and female labour in the home after the birth of the first child, and here she reflects on its implications for heterosexual feminists, while Carol Nagy Jacklin (1992) points out the financial benefits that accrue to men as a consequence of their wives' labour.

Not only is heterosexuality exhausting for women, it is also dangerous. Many feminists (lesbian *and* heterosexual) have pointed out that a great deal of violence against women takes place within, or is associated with, heterosexual institutions. Women who date men, or voluntarily have sex with or marry them, are disproportionately at risk for violence, rape and murder from those men. Each year in the US, 30 per cent of all women murdered are killed by their husbands or male lovers — about 1,500 women each year — and men's violence against their wives is well documented (Mayne, 1992). More than 40 per cent of all battered wives report having been raped by their husbands (Russell, 1990); and about half of these are subjected to anal rape, and are hit, kicked, or burned as part of the rape (Campbell and Alford, 1989). According to a survey of a random sample of nearly a thousand women in the USA, 14 per cent of all married women have been raped by their husbands (Russell, 1990), and date rape is increasingly coming to the fore as a serious problem for women (Muehlenhard and Linton, 1987; Johnson *et al.*, 1992). When male college students are asked if they would rape if assured they would not be caught and punished, more than a third say they would (34 per cent — Briere and Mulamuth, 1983; 37 per cent — Tieger, 1981). Add to this problems of dangerous contraception and unwanted pregnancies, and the rape of children by their mothers' husbands or male lovers, from all of which heterosexual women are disproportionately at risk.

No wonder, then, that psychologists have repeatedly found that heterosexuality is not very good for women. The classic study by Gove (1972) revealed that marriage is good for men's psychological health and bad for women's: there are much higher rates of mental illness among married women than among married men, but no significant sex differences in mental illness rates for the divorced, widowed, or never married. Standard psychological tests administered to both heterosexual women and lesbians reveal that, compared with lesbians, heterosexual women score *higher* on neuroticism (Wilson and Green, 1971; Siegelman, 1972), tension (Hopkins, 1969), anxiety (Ohlson and Wilson, 1974) and depression (Siegelman, 1972); and that they score *lower* than lesbians on scales designed to measure 'capacity for status', 'good impression', 'intellectual efficiency', 'endurance' (Wilson and Green, 1971), 'goal-direction', 'self-acceptance' (Siegelman, 1972), 'alertness', 'responsibility' and 'self-confidence' (Ohlson and Wilson, 1974).

'Lesbians might be oppressed in the public domain, but heterosexual women . . . enter unequal partnerships in which sexist norms and power relations prevail', says Nira Yuval-Davis (1992), adding that lesbians enjoy 'the comforts of the ghetto experience' and the 'luxury' of 'doing away with men' (would it were that easy!). For Rose Croghan (1992) whose research arises out of the 'stress [she] experienced as a mother within a heterosexual relationship', it is to lesbian mothers 'that heterosexual feminists look in the hope of finding a model of equality which can eventually be applied to our relationships with men'. Hilary Lips and Susan Freedman (1992) write of 'luxuriating' in the space afforded them at feminist gatherings:

> Despite our sidestepping our (hetero)sexuality on these occasions, it sometimes seems, paradoxically, that the tone of these gatherings, the sense that this is OUR time, is set by the lesbians who attend.

Attributing comfort, luxury, equality, and happiness to lesbians, heterosexual women write of the painful conflicts and compromises with the men in their lives. Most poignant is Sandra Lee Bartky (1992) who has 'often wished that I could love women erotically': she appeals to feminist psychologists to 'invent a therapeutic technique for releasing the heterosexual woman . . . from the prisonhouse of necessity into the free space of choice'.

For some heterosexual feminists, then, the contradictions between political ideology and lived personal experience are acute and painful, and involve constant compromise. As Carol Nagy Jacklin (1992) puts it, 'heterosexual feminists live, work, and may be in love relationships with the "enemy" '; they experience feminism as 'something that threatens our closest relationships' (Lips and Freedman, 1992). Their feminist consciousness is 'critical of our most intimate being and entails at least some resistance to close relationships with our nearest and dearest men' (Ramazanoglu, 1992). No wonder, then, that the identity 'heterosexual' is hard to sustain.

The *behaviours* commonly known as 'heterosexuality' are commonplace amongst our feminist contributors: they are married, have sex with their husbands and/or other men, and bring up children with the fathers of those children. The *identity* of 'heterosexual' (a sense that they are accurately described by that label) is much rarer. We refer to heterosexual identity as 'precarious' in part as a way of signifying the difficulty women have in claiming the label 'heterosexual' as their own — hard to do when it stands, in so much feminist theory, as synonymous with oppression. Many women find their own feminist analyses of heterosexuality difficult to reconcile with their heterosexual life-styles. Heterosexual identities are precarious, despite the ubiquity of heterosexual behaviour, because who *would* be heterosexual, really, if they had a choice?

2 Sexual Fluidity

Some heterosexual feminists resolve this dilemma by claiming not to have had a choice: Sandra Lee Bartky (1992), for example, says that she has 'been heterosexual the way some homosexuals say they have been homosexual, for ever'. Born-that-way heterosexuals have the least doubts about their own heterosexual identities. For many others, though, their heterosexual identities remain precarious in part, they say, because of the fluidity of female sexuality:

> Saying 'I am heterosexual' implies that my sexual preference is an unchanging and essential personal attribute. It is, however, certainly not clear that one's sexual preference is either unchanging or an essential attribute. . . . Sexuality is complex. . . . (Jacklin, 1992, p. 420)

> Sexual identity is much too fluid, and behaviour much too variable, to be so neatly categorised. . . . There are many women whom I love for their bodies, their minds, their quirks, their brilliant individualities, and their ways of being in the world. I recognise my sexual attraction to particular women, and to particular men other than my life partner, though I choose not to act on it (Crawford, 1992, p. 429)

Nira Yuval-Davis (1992, p. 438) comments that many women, 'Like me, who have had most, or even all, of their meaningful sexual relationships (and one-night stands) with men, refuse to call themselves heterosexuals . . .' in part, she says, because 'we all have, to a lesser or greater extent, bisexual desires'.

There is a marked contrast here between 'heterosexual' and 'lesbian' identities. Lesbian identities can apparently survive not just bisexual desires and heterosexual attractions, but even ongoing, long-term, heterosexual involvements. Although none of the non-lesbian feminists who wrote for us reported sexual relationships with women, most (though far from all) lesbians have experienced sex with men, some have enjoyed it, and some speak of their current sexual attractions to men without ever for one moment doubting their 'lesbian' identities:

> Some men I find sexually attractive, but I don't think I'd ever sleep with them, because, having got involved in feminism, I get very angry at the way men treat women at a very general level, and so, although physically I might be attracted to them, mentally I don't want to. . . . ('Samantha', in Kitzinger, 1987, p. 135)

> I think possibly I can imagine that if I was in a healthier society, where men were not brainwashed into being such subhuman creatures, I could possibly enjoy things a bit more with men. Because, I

mean, it's not as though men have such monstrous bodies. They're not terribly interesting physically, but I mean, they're not *awful*. If they were a bit nicer in their *heads*, then you could have relationships with them. (Shân, in Kitzinger, 1987, p. 136)

When feminists assert 'lesbian' identities, it is not (necessarily) because we never enjoyed sex with men (although some of us didn't); not (necessarily) because we are never sexually attracted to men (although some of us aren't); not because we experience our sexuality as a 'rigid', 'fixed', 'essential personal attribute', but because, while acknowledging the contradictions, we are making a *political* statement. A 'lesbian' identity occupies a key position within many women's feminism, and, indeed, comes to constitute that feminism to such an extent that even a change in the gender of sexual partners sometimes cannot shift 'lesbian' identities.

There have always been women who apparently 'choose' sexual involvements with men, while claiming a lesbian identity. The lesbian fiction writer, Jan Clausen (1991), for example, in now in a sexual relationship with a man, but refuses a heterosexual identity and continues to march in Lesbian and Gay Pride marches. 'Alice' (cited in Bart, 1993), has lived for the last decade with a male partner, but identified as lesbian and was sexually involved with women for ten years before entering her current heterosexual relationship. On the basis of those past sexual involvements, 'Alice' rejects both a 'heterosexual' and a 'bisexual' identity, saying 'I don't feel that I'm straight . . . I have a gay consciousness'. The 'tenaciousness' (Bart, 1993) of lesbian identities is further illustrated by a feminist support group at a major US university called 'Lesbians Who Just Happen to be in Relationships with Politically Correct Men' (Taylor and Whittier, 1992).

The asymmetry here should be clear. *Heterosexual* feminist identities are denied by women in long-term, exclusive, sexual relationships with men, on the basis of past, present, or possible future sexual attractions to and involvements with women. By contrast, *lesbian* feminist identities are eagerly claimed — even *with* past or present sexual attractions to and involvements with men. The apparent tenaciousness of lesbian identity (even with exclusively heterosexual involvements) contrasts with the precariousness of heterosexual identity (even with exclusively heterosexual involvements). It is almost as though some heterosexual feminists, recognizing the contradictions of their heterosexuality, are leaving open an escape hatch — escaping the necessity of addressing the inherent political contradictions and theoretical difficulties of 'heterosexual feminist' identities by seeking to dissolve such identities altogether in favour of a universal bisexuality or multiplicity of shifting sexual desires.

This heterosexual refusal of the principle of fixed dichotomized identities ('lesbian' and 'heterosexual') in favour of a continuum model or deconstructionist version of sexuality is often presented in feminist terms. According to this argument, 'dualism' and 'polarized categories' are typical of male patriarchal thought; women are supposed to celebrate 'fluidity', flux and change (see, for example, the debate in Hall *et al.*, 1992). However, the dissolution of the categories of 'lesbian' and 'heterosexual' started long before second-wave feminism began to address these issues. It was Kinsey and his fellow researchers in the late 1940s who invented the 'heterosexual-homosexual continuum' and initiated the recognition of everyone's alleged 'bisexual potential'. Far from polarizing 'lesbians' and 'heterosexual women' into two dichotomous and exclusive categories, male researchers have for decades emphasized the essential similarities between us (cf. Gagnon and Simon, 1973; Bell and Weinberg, 1978). The denial of lesbianism (and heterosexuality) as distinct states of being, and the characterization of lesbians as basically just the same as heterosexual women, is one of the most pervasive themes of liberal discourse on lesbianism (cf. Kitzinger, 1987). One of the functions served by arguments against the existence of 'categories' is to obscure the oppressions suffered by lesbians *as a category*, just as a claim such as 'we're all middle-class now' obscures the fact that one end of this supposed middle-class spectrum suffers housing conditions, inequalities in health care, restrictions of job opportunities and so on, that the other end of this 'continuum' would not endure for one minute. Categories of oppressed people are not well served by denying the existence of the categories to which they belong: at the very least, such denial refuses a name for the oppressed and militates against effective collective resistance.

3 Heterosexuality as a Default Identity

For heterosexual women this denial of categorical identities often feels perfectly legitimate because, unlike lesbians, they have never had (in the context of their *sexual* identities) to confront Otherness. A lesbian identity is usually achieved at great cost and after considerable struggle. For most women, it means claiming an identity we were taught to despise. Lesbian coming out stories (e.g. Stanley and Wolfe, 1980) rehearse tales of gradual dawning realization, or sudden sharp awareness; but in all there is a 'moment of truth', a time of self-discovery and self-naming. By contrast, the 'discovery' of one's own heterosexual identity is not, for the vast majority of people, a moment of particular salience. Like discovering that one speaks in prose, it simply names what one was (doing) all along. Heterosexual identity is assumed by default, because it never occurs to many women to be anything else. (This very fact indicates, of course, the enormous power of the institution of compulsory heterosexuality: it is often not necessary explicitly to coerce women into heterosexuality — they are able to 'choose' it 'of their own free will'.)

Living in a predominantly heterosexual society means that one's sexuality is generally assumed to be 'straight' (by oneself as well as others) unless proven otherwise, and few of us therefore ever stop to question why we are heterosexual. For me, then, this is a story which is ill-rehearsed: as far as becoming heterosexual is concerned, I can honestly say that it never occurred to me to be anything else. . . . (Thomas, 1993)

After leaving school most of my energy was directed towards finding my imaginary prince. I never once considered becoming a lesbian, even though almost all my friends were women rather than men. (Brown, 1993)

I never planned to be heterosexual, of course . . . I just *was*. A child of patriarchy, I was shaped by it. (S. Kitzinger, 1992, p. 440)

Whereas lesbians (whether feminist or not) have typically given a great deal of thought to the question of *why* they are lesbian, what it means to be lesbian, and how it affects our lives, most heterosexuals (even heterosexual feminists) have given sparse consideration to parallel questions about the nature and meaning of heterosexuality:

Of the many influences I have tried to find for my ideas and my work, my heterosexuality has not come to mind before . . . The status of heterosexual is a safe one and so has remained simply latent. (Beloff, 1992, pp. 424–5)

The very taken-for-granted nature of heterosexuality (even within feminism) is, as Shulamit Reinharz points out, a key to its importance:

Since I have neither read much nor thought much about this question, I assume it must be important and that some sort of silencing must be going on. That idea is essential to my notion of feminist research — pay attention to what you have not been paying attention to. (Reinharz, 1992: 450)

Having adopted heterosexuality as a default option, a life-style entered into without conscious consideration of the alternatives, heterosexual feminists have not made a deliberate commitment to heterosexuality paralleling lesbians' commitment to lesbianism. 'Default' identities like these, which constitute the 'normal natural way to be' ('white', 'able-bodied', 'male' etc.) are always less well theorized, less articulated, less self-conscious, than are oppositional or oppressed identities; lack of reflectiveness is the privilege of power. Whatever the problems and difficulties associated with heterosexuality for women (see section 1 of this chapter), it is the normal taken-for-grantedness of heterosexuality *per se* which makes it, as Kadiatu Kanneh (1992) says, a 'safe' and 'uncontested' identity.

4 Heterosexuality: A Non-Politicized Identity

Lesbianism is a *politicized* identity. That is, feminists have, for decades, consciously chosen lesbianism as an identity in accordance with feminist politics, and have at their disposal theoretical frameworks for analyzing the importance of lesbianism in achieving feminist goals. For many lesbian feminists, accepting the label 'lesbian' is a defiant act of self-naming, in which we assert our refusal of the hetero-patriarchal order, and our commitment to women and lesbians.

By contrast, there are no corresponding heterosexual feminist identities, political *by virtue of* their heterosexuality. 'We feel guilty about our heterosexuality', say Ros Gill and Rebecca Walker (1992), 'which is not "lived" as a political identity. . . . Who would want to mobilize around being straight?!' Or, as Caroline Ramazanoglu (1992) laments, 'there is no "politically correct" feminist way of bringing the men out of our closets'.

Of course, many women become feminists as a direct result of their heterosexuality (e.g. Thomas, 1993), becoming conscious of patriarchal oppression through the minute and particular details of their male partners' behaviour, just as many women become feminists as a direct result of their lesbianism, becoming conscious of hetero-patriarchal oppression through the experience of anti-lesbianism. In stating that there are no intrinsically politicized heterosexual identities, we do not mean to discount these experiences. Rather, we mean, while acknowledging them, to refer here to their inverse: few (if any) feminists have stated publicly that they chose heterosexuality as an identity in accordance with their feminist politics, nor have they produced the theoretical writings which might support such a choice.

'Heterosexual' and 'lesbian' are *not* opposite ends of the same continuum. Because 'lesbian' is an intrinsically politicized identity, and heterosexuality is not, the two terms are not commensurate, do not belong in the same conceptual space. Lesbian feminists have available a whole set of explicitly political meanings (cf. Onlywomen Press, 1981) — and in assimilating the term 'lesbian' into a heterosexual-lesbian continuum, or in emphasizing 'sexual fluidity' and personal flux, these meanings are lost. Membership of an oppressed group needs to be claimed, and tenaciously too, despite the contradictions. We would suggest that what is needed is not the depoliticization of lesbianism (through the adoption of continua and the like — e.g. Rich, 1981), but the politicization of the category 'heterosexual'. Despite the heterogeneity of heterosexuality (across cultures and intraculturally), there is a homogeneity about it (cf. (charles), 1993) which derives from its largely unquestioned status as the 'non-pretended' form of sexuality, from which all other forms are deviations. The problem for heterosexual feminists is, to quote Kadiatu Kanneh's (1992) question, 'how is it possible to inscribe a safe, uncontested identity as a purposeful political stance?'

Conclusion

The precariousness of heterosexual feminist identity has meant, in effect, an inability or refusal adequately to theorize heterosexuality. It could even be argued that the precariousness of heterosexual identity is functionally useful to heterosexual feminists precisely in so far as it apparently obviates the need for such theorizing. Claiming not 'really' to be heterosexual, feminists feel able to engage in heterosexual activity with political immunity. As radical feminists, we would argue that of course no women are 'really' heterosexual (in the sense of having been born with innate predetermined predispositions towards exclusive sexual activity with men). But we would also point out that many women appear to be engaged in exclusive heterosexual activity, and/or to be unproblematically identified by others as taken-for-granted heterosexuals. Not all of this heterosexuality is explicitly coerced or externally enforced: some (e.g. ex-lesbians, and many of the contributors to our book) appear to be making and/or remaking heterosexual *'choices'*. We call upon heterosexual feminists publicly to acknowledge this, and to develop theory to support these 'choices', rather than simply emphasizing their provisional, tentative and precarious nature. In a world in which heterosexuality is still so dominant as to make lesbianism virtually invisible, we consider it essential to the future of feminist theory and politics that heterosexual feminists claim and theorize their heterosexuality as a politicized identity.

References

ALLEN, JEFFNER (Ed.) (1990) *Lesbian Philosophies and Cultures*, New York, State University of New York Press.

BART, PAULINE (1993) 'Protean Woman: The Liquidity of Female Sexuality and the Tenaciousness of Lesbian Identity', in WILKINSON, SUE and KITZINGER, CELIA (Eds) *Heterosexuality: a 'Feminism and Psychology' Reader*, London, Sage.

BARTKY, SANDRA LEE (1992) 'Hypatia Unbound: A Confession', in KITZINGER, CELIA, WILKINSON, SUE and PERKINS, RACHEL (Eds) *Special Issue of 'Feminism and Psychology' on Heterosexuality*, **2**, 3, London, Sage.

BELL, ALAN P. and WEINBERG, MARTIN S. (1978) *Homosexualities: A Study of Diversity Among Men and Women*, London, Mitchell Beazley.

BELOFF, HALLA (1992) 'On Being Ordinary', in KITZINGER, CELIA, WILKINSON, SUE and PERKINS, RACHEL (Eds) *Special Issue of 'Feminism and Psychology' on Heterosexuality*, **2**, 3, London, Sage.

BEM, SANDRA (1992) 'On the Inadequacy of our Sexual Categories: A Personal Perspective', in KITZINGER, CELIA, WILKINSON, SUE and PERKINS, RACHEL (Eds) *Special Issue of 'Feminism and Psychology' on Heterosexuality*, **2**, 3, London, Sage.

BRIERE, JOHN and MULAMUTH, NEIL (1983) 'Self-Reported Likelihood of Sexually Aggressive Behavior', *Journal of Research in Personality*, **17**, 315–23.

BROWN, LOULOU (1993) 'Heterosexual Celibacy', in WILKINSON, SUE and KITZINGER, CELIA (Eds) *Heterosexuality: a 'Feminism and Psychology' Reader*, London, Sage.

CAMPBELL, J.C. and ALFORD, P. (1989) 'The Dark Consequences of Marital Rape', *American Journal of Nursing*, **89**, 7, 946–9.

(CHARLES), HELEN (1993) 'A Homogeneous Habit: Heterosexual Display in the English

Holiday Camp', in WILKINSON, SUE and KITZINGER, CELIA (Eds) *Heterosexuality: A 'Feminism and Psychology' Reader*, London, Sage.

CLAUSEN, JAN (1991) 'My Interesting Condition', *Out/Look: National Lesbian and Gay Quarterly*, 7, 10–21.

CRAWFORD, MARY (1992) 'Identity, "Passing" and Subversion', in KITZINGER, CELIA, WILKINSON, SUE and PERKINS, RACHEL (Eds) *Special Issue of 'Feminism and Psychology' on Heterosexuality*, 2, 3, London, Sage.

CROGHAN, ROSE (1991) 'First-Time Mothers' Accounts of Inequality in the Division of Labour', *Feminism and Psychology*, 2, 2, 265–8.

CROGHAN, ROSE (1992) 'Sleeping with the Enemy: Mothers in Heterosexual Relationships', in KITZINGER, CELIA, WILKINSON, SUE and PERKINS, RACHEL (Eds) *Special Issue of 'Feminism and Psychology', on Heterosexuality*, 2, 3, London, Sage.

FRENCH, MARILYN (1992) *The War Against Women*, London, Hamish Hamilton.

FRYE, MARILYN (1990) 'Do You Have to Be a Lesbian to be a Feminist?', *Off Our Backs*, **XX**, 8, 21–3.

GAGNON, JOHN and SIMON, WILLIAM (1973) *Sexual Conduct*, New York, Aldine.

GERGEN, MARY (1992) 'Unbundling Our Binaries — Genders, Sexualities, Desires', in KITZINGER, CELIA, WILKINSON, SUE and PERKINS, RACHEL (Eds) *Special Issue of 'Feminism and Psychology' on Heterosexuality*, 2, 3, London, Sage.

GILL, ROSALIND and WALKER, REBECCA (1992) 'Heterosexuality, Feminism, Contradiction: On Being Young, White, Heterosexual Feminists in the 1990s', in KITZINGER, CELIA, WILKINSON, SUE and PERKINS, RACHEL (Eds) *Special Issue of 'Feminism and Psychology' on Heterosexuality*, 2, 3, London, Sage.

GILMAN, CHARLOTTE PERKINS (1898) *Women and Economics*, New York, Harper and Row.

GOVE, W.R. (1972) 'The Relationship between Sex Roles, Marital Status, and Mental Illness', *Social Forces*, **51**, 1, 34–44.

HALL, MARNY, KITZINGER, CELIA, LOULAN, JOANN and PERKINS, RACHEL (1992) 'Lesbian Psychology, Lesbian Politics', *Feminism and Psychology*, 2, 1, 7–26.

HOAGLAND, SARAH LUCIA (1988) *Lesbian Ethics: Toward New Value*, Palo Alto, Calif., Institute of Lesbian Studies.

HOPKINS, JUNE (1969) 'The Lesbian Personality', *British Journal of Psychiatry*, 115, 1433–6.

JACKLIN, CAROL NAGY (1992) 'How My Heterosexuality Affects My Feminist Politics', in KITZINGER, CELIA, WILKINSON, SUE and PERKINS, RACHEL (Eds) *Special Issue of 'Feminism and Psychology' on Heterosexuality*, 2, 3, London, Sage.

JOHNSON, G. DAVID, PALILEO, GLORIA J. and GRAY, NORMA B. (1992) ' "Date Rape" on a Southern Campus', *Sociology and Social Research*, **76**, 2, 37–44.

KANNEH, KADIATU (1992) 'Sisters Under the Skin: A Politics of Heterosexuality', in KITZINGER, CELIA, WILKINSON, SUE and PERKINS, RACHEL (Eds) *Special Issue of 'Feminism and Psychology' on Heterosexuality*, 2, 3, London, Sage.

KINSEY, A.C., POMEROY, W.B. and MARTIN, C.E. (1948) *Sexual Behavior in the Human Male*, Philadelphia, Pa., W.B. Saunders.

KINSEY, A.C., POMEROY, W.B., MARTIN, C.B. and GEBHARD, P.H. (1953) *Sexual Behavior in the Human Female*, Philadelphia, Fa., W.B. Saunders.

KITZINGER, CELIA (1987) *The Social Construction of Lesbianism*, London, Sage.

KITZINGER, CELIA, WILKINSON, SUE and PERKINS, RACHEL (Eds) (1992) *Special Issue of 'Feminism and Psychology' on Heterosexuality*, 2, 3, London, Sage.

KITZINGER, SHEILA (1992) 'Heterosexuality: Challenge and Opportunity', in KITZINGER, CELIA, WILKINSON, SUE and PERKINS, RACHEL (Eds) *Special Issue of 'Feminism and Psychology' on Heterosexuality*, 2, 3, London, Sage.

LIPS, HILARY and FREEDMAN, SUSAN (1992) 'Heterosexual Feminist Identities: Private Boundaries and Shifting Centers', in KITZINGER, CELIA, WILKINSON, SUE and PERKINS, RACHEL (Eds) *Special Issue of 'Feminism and Psychology' on Heterosexuality*, 2, 3, London Sage.

MAINARDI, PAT (1970) 'The Politics of Housework', in MORGAN, ROBIN (Ed.) *Sisterhood is Powerful*, New York, Vintage Books.

MAYNE, ANN (1992) Book Review of *Battered Women as Survivors* by Lee Ann Hoff, in KITZINGER, CELIA, WILKINSON, SUE and PERKINS, RACHEL (Eds) *Special Issue of 'Feminism and Psychology' on Heterosexuality*, **2**, 3, London, Sage.

MUEHLENHARD, CHARLENE L. and LINTON, MELANEY A. (1987) 'Date Rape and Sexual Aggression in Dating Situations: Incidence and Risk Factors', *Journal of Counseling Psychology*, **34**, 186–96.

OAKLEY, ANN (1974) *The Sociology of Housework*, Oxford, Martin Robertson.

OHLSON, E. and WILSON, M. (1974) 'Differentiating Female Homosexuals from Female Heterosexuality by the Use of the MMPI', *Journal of Sex Research*, **10**, 4, 308–15.

ONLYWOMEN PRESS (Ed.) (1981) *Love Your Enemy: The Debate between Heterosexual Feminism and Political Lesbianism*, London, Onlywomen Press.

PARKER, JAN (1987) 'The Tables Need Turning', in HANSCOMBE, GILLIAN and HUMPHRIES, MARTIN (Eds) *Heterosexuality*, London, Gay Men's Press.

PENELOPE, JULIA (1986) 'The Mystery of Lesbians II', *Gossip: A Journal of Lesbian Feminist Ethics*, **2**, 16–68.

RAMAZANOGLU, CAROLINE (1992) 'Love and the Politics of Heterosexuality', in KITZINGER, CELIA, WILKINSON, SUE and PERKINS, RACHEL (Eds) *Special Issue of 'Feminism and Psychology' on Heterosexuality*, **2**, 3, London, Sage.

REINHARZ, SHULAMIT (1992) 'How My Heterosexuality Contributes to My Feminism and Vice Versa', in KITZINGER, CELIA, WILKINSON, SUE and PERKINS, RACHEL (Eds) *Special Issue of 'Feminism and Psychology' on Heterosexuality*, **2**, 3, London, Sage.

RICH, ADRIENNE (1980) 'Compulsory Heterosexuality and Lesbian Existence', *Signs*, **5**, 4, 631–60.

RICH, ADRIENNE (1981) Letter to Ann Snitow, Christine Stansell and Sharon Thompson, reprinted in RICHARDSON, LAUREL and TAYLOR, VERTA (Eds) *Feminist Frontiers II: Rethinking Sex, Gender and Society*, New York, Random House.

ROWLAND, ROBYN (1992) 'Radical Feminist Heterosexuality', in KITZINGER, CELIA, WILKINSON, SUE and PERKINS, RACHEL (Eds) *Special Issue of 'Feminism and Psychology' on Heterosexuality*, **2**, 3, London, Sage.

RUSSELL, DIANA (1990) *Rape in marriage*, Bloomington and Indianapolis, University of Indiana Press.

SIEGELMAN, MARVIN (1972) 'Adjustment of Homosexual and Heterosexual Women', *British Journal of Psychiatry*, **120**, 477–81.

STANLEY, JULIA PENELOPE and WOLFE, SUSAN (1980) *The Coming Out Stories*, Trumansburg, N.J., The Crossing Press.

TAYLOR, VERTA and WHITTIER, NANCY (1992) 'Collective Identity in Social Movement Communities: Lesbian Feminist Mobilization', in MORRIS, ALDEN and MUELLER, CAROL (Eds) *Frontiers in Social Movement Theory*, New Haven, Yale University Press.

THOMAS, ALISON (1993) 'The Heterosexual Feminist: A Paradoxical Identity?', in WILKINSON, SUE and KITZINGER, CELIA (Eds) *Heterosexuality: A 'Feminism and Psychology' Reader*, London, Sage.

TIEGER, TODD (1981) 'Self-Rated Likelihood of Raping and Social Perception of Rape', *Journal of Research in Personality*, **15**, 147–58.

WILKINSON, SUE and KITZINGER, CELIA (Eds) (1993) *Heterosexuality: A 'Feminism and Psychology' Reader*, London, Sage.

WILSON, M. and GREEN, R. (1971) 'Personality Chracteristics of Female Homosexuals', *Psychological Reports*, **28**, 407–12.

WITTIG, MONIQUE (1992) *The Straight Mind*, Boston, Beacon Press.

YUVAL-DAVIS, NIRA (1992) 'The (Dis)Comfort of being "Hetero" ', in KITZINGER, CELIA, WILKINSON, SUE and PERKINS, RACHEL (Eds) *Special Issue of 'Feminism and Psychology' on Heterosexuality*, **2**, 3, London, Sage.

Section II
Redefining Knowledge

Chapter 4

Love and Romance as Objects of Feminist Knowledge

Stevi Jackson

In recent years feminists have had far more to say about romantic fiction than about romantic love as such. A satisfactory account of women's interest in romance, however, itself requires that we pay attention to the emotional resonances such fiction has for women, that we give greater consideration to romantic love as an emotion. I am not suggesting that there is something called 'love' that exists outside society and culture. Emotions are cultural constructs, not pre-social essences: they are socially ordered, linguistically mediated and culturally specific (Jaggar, 1989; Hochschild, 1983; Rosaldo, 1984).

The critiques of love which emerged in the early years of second-wave feminism began to explore love as a socially constructed emotion, but these analyses have not been built upon substantially in recent feminist scholarship. I want to look again at this earlier work which, while limited by its particular historical context, offered insights which are worth recovering. I will then explore possible means of developing a theorization of romantic love drawing on more recent feminist perspectives on romance, subjectivity and sexuality.

Early Feminist Critiques of Love

Feminist scepticism about love has a long history. First-wave feminists only rarely questioned the naturalness of love between men and women, but some tentatively began to explore the ways in which it was shaped by relations of dominance and subordination. For example, Cicely Hamilton, in *Marriage as a Trade*, first published in 1909, argued that since marriage was for most women an economic and social necessity, they could not afford to be wholeheartedly romantic (Hamilton, 1981, p. 28). In many respects Hamilton anticipates later feminist critiques of marriage and of compulsory heterosexuality — although she champions the cause of celibacy rather than lesbianism. In arguing that men are far more romantic than women, however, her analysis differs from that of second-wave feminists who tended to see love as the bait which trapped women into marriage.

An alternative perspective, closer to later socialist feminist analyses, is that of the Russian revolutionary Alexandra Kollontai. She argued that the extreme individualism of capitalism produces an 'inescapable loneliness' which we try to remedy through love (1972, p. 4). In seeking this route to personal happiness we show little consideration for the one we love: rather we make absolute claims on them. This is exacerbated by the idea of possessing the partner, establishing ownership of the other's physical and emotional self, and excluding all others. Kollontai was well aware that double standards of sexual morality restricted women far more than men, that women became possessions on marriage in a way that men did not. She envisaged, however, a new morality arising from ideals of working-class solidarity which would undermine individualism, possessiveness and patriarchal values. Whereas Hamilton speculated that liberation from compulsion might lead to many women eschewing heterosexual relations altogether, Kollontai's vision is of 'deeper and more joyful' relationships between women and men entered into in a spirit of freedom and equality (*ibid.*, p. 13).

The publication of de Beauvoir's *The Second Sex* in 1949 paved the way for second-wave feminist analyses which saw love as a means of gaining women's acquiescence to their submission. For de Beauvoir women's self-abnegation through love not only reinforced their subordination but resulted from a subjectivity constituted through that subordination.

> There is no other way out for her but to lose herself, body and soul, in him who is represented to her as absolute, as the essential. . . . She chooses to desire her enslavement so ardently that it will seem to her the expression of her liberty . . . she will humble herself to nothingness before him. Love becomes for her a religion. (de Beauvoir, 1972, p. 653)

Love and its discontents were on the agenda of second-wave feminism in its early years as an aspect of wider debates about the politics of sexuality.[1] Love was seen as an ideology which justified our exploitation by men and simultaneously ensnared us into oppressive relationships with them. As the slogan put it: 'It starts when you sink into his arms and ends with your arms in his sink.'

Love made women vulnerable not only to exploitation, but also to being hurt by men. As de Beauvoir said, 'the word love has by no means the same meaning for both sexes' (1972, p. 652), a view endorsed by Firestone. Both of these theorists argued that women invest more in love and that they give more affection to men than they receive in return. Firestone asserted that 'love, perhaps even more than childbearing, is the pivot of women's oppression today' (1972, p. 121). What was so dangerous about love was, as de Beauvoir had noted, women's tendency to immerse ourselves totally in it. Becoming so obsessed with love diverted energies from other possible achievements. Moreover, making one person the centre of one's emotional universe was taken as symptomatic of emotional impoverishment elsewhere — a point which Kollontai had also made. The exclusivity of love meant quantifying and confining our emotions. As Lee Comer expressed it: 'Like so much butter, romantic love must be spread thickly on one slice of bread; to spread it over several is to spread it "thinly" ' (1974, p. 219). Hence we concentrate passion on one partner, taking jealousy as the proof of love rather than as 'an excrescence on our emotions' (*ibid.*, p. 220). Similarly, Firestone asks: 'Why has all the joy and excitement been concentrated, driven into one narrow, difficult-to-find human experience, and all the rest laid waste?' (1972, p. 147).

Underlying these critiques was a belief in the possibility of a less exclusive and possessive form of love, freed from power relationships and bourgeois institutions. Again we hear echoes of Kollontai's earlier utopian vision. Firestone argues for the rediffusion of 'sexual joy and excitement . . . over . . . the spectrum of our lives' (*ibid.*, p. 147). For Comer romantic love is symptomatic of our fragmented emotional lives, but 'In rare moments, when the external categories which fragment our emotions fall away, we do glimpse the possibilities of whole feelings' (Comer, 1974, p. 219). These 'whole feelings' involve a plurality of loves directed towards a multiplicity of others.

Compared with more recent feminist analyses of subjectivity, much of this may sound naive. The very possibility of 'whole feelings' now seems questionable, as does the notion of a 'purer' love uncontaminated by cultural and social structures. These early feminist accounts recognized that romantic love was not a constant feature of human nature, but were over-optimistic about the possibility of change. The tone of much second-wave writing implied that, once the illusion of romantic love was 'seen through', all we needed was an effort of will to break free from its shackles. This effectively precluded the possibility of confronting the potency of this emotion and seeking for an explanation of it. Once the oppressive nature of heterosexual love had been exposed, to try to explore it further seemed at best frivolous and at worst ideologically unsound.

Another shortcoming of the writings of this period was their unproblematized heterosexual focus. Some of the general points raised could apply to any exclusive romantic attachment, whether lesbian or heterosexual, but the heterosexual nature of love was taken as given. These analyses of love did, of course, contain within them an implicit critique of heterosexuality, but this was not their explicit object. By the time more telling critiques of heterosexuality emerged in the late seventies and early eighties (Rich, 1980; Wittig, 1992) love as such had ceased to be a matter of much concern.

In what follows I will be dealing primarily with heterosexual love and romance, but I hope to do so in a way which makes heterosexuality problematic. The discourses through which we make sense of love have, I would argue, largely been framed within a patriarchal and heterosexual context and impinge also on those who, in Wittig's (1992) terms, are fugitives from compulsory heterosexuality. In re-examining romantic love I am not discounting the contributions of earlier feminists. Although flawed, their accounts raised questions which deserve further consideration in the light of more recent theoretical development. Their central theme — that love serves to bind us to our subordination — is one that still needs to be pursued.

Love's Mysteries

Romantic convention tells us that love is in essence indefinable and mysterious: 'fools give you reasons, wise men [sic] never try'. Emotions, in the sense of what is subjectively felt by individuals, are obviously not immediately observable, but this does not place them beyond explanation. Alison Jaggar observes that we 'have no access either to our own emotions or to those of others, independent of or unmediated by the discourse of our culture' (Jaggar, 1989, p. 148). There is thus no way of exploring love except through the ways in which it is talked and written about. Language, however, itself contributes to the cultural construction of emotions and is a means by which we participate in creating a shared sense of what emotions are. If the discourses of love and romance circulating within our culture help shape our experience and understanding of love, they can also be drawn upon in analyzing it.

I am particularly interested in the idea of being or falling 'in love'. The adjectives commonly used to describe this experience mark it as very different from other forms of love. Love for parents, children, siblings or friends is not usually thought of as mysterious, compelling, overwhelming, uncontrollable, inexplicable and ecstatic — nor even is love in long-term sexual relationships. A distinction is commonly made between loving someone and being in love with them. The latter is recognized as a more transient emotion, but the ideology of heterosexual romance tells us that falling in love is the prelude to a lasting, secure and stable conjugal union. This ideal, as Jacqueline Sarsby points out, is contradictory:

> Love is seen as the bolt from the blue against which one cannot struggle, the pre-ordained meeting of twin souls, the compulsion which allows one to break any of society's rules as long as one is faithful to the emotion itself. The extraordinary contradiction lies in the fact that love is the almost prescribed condition for marriage in most of Europe and the United States . . . millions of private, potentially socially disruptive, emotional dramas are virtually the only acceptable means of moving towards marriage. . . . (1983, pp. 5–6)

There is a further contradiction here in the ideal of romantic love as the basis of an affectionate and caring relationship. Feminists from Kollontai to Firestone have suggested that romantic love is not really about caring for another, but is self-centred and individualistic. To be in love is to make another the centre of your universe, but it also demands the same in return: that we should be the 'only one' for the other. Being 'in love' is not a gentle feeling: it is often characterized as violent, even ruthless (Bertilsson, 1986). 'More than wanting to cosset the beloved we may feel we want to eat them alive' (Goodison, 1983, pp. 51–2).

Within Western culture falling in love has often been described as a form of ecstasy akin to a mystical experience, as 'comparable in force and in momentum to a religious conversion' (Bertilsson, 1986, p. 28). Even feminist accounts, otherwise firmly grounded in material reality, sometimes slide towards mysticism. Frigga Haug, for example, asserts that through love we retrieve the 'buried and forgotten stirrings of the soul', that love reorganizes 'the forces of the soul' (Haug *et al.*, 1987, pp. 278–9). Casting love in such terms is problematic in that it seems to accord it a special legitimacy, placing it on some higher plane inaccessible to reason or explanation. It does, however, suggest that love is experienced as a deeply felt inner transformation.

There appears to be something about romantic love as described in feminist, social scientific, psychoanalytic and literary writings which suggests that it is the product of restriction and unattainability. The excitement of being in love is fuelled by 'compulsion and denial' and 'gratification destroys the compulsion little by little' (Wilson, 1983, p. 42). The chronic insecurity so often suffered by lovers is not, I think, merely a result of romantic passion but is fundamental to its continuance: being 'in love' appears to wear off once lovers feel secure with each other. Insecure and compulsive passion centred on a unique other can engender feelings of powerlessness, of being at the mercy of the beloved. It also, however, holds out the promise of power — of being the loved one, of ensnaring another into total psychic dependence. The attraction that love has for women may in part be because it is a means by which they can aspire to power over men. This is a central theme of romantic narrative (Modleski, 1984) — in both fairy-tales and romantic fiction love tames and transforms the beast.

The potency of romantic passion is not easily accounted for, yet it is patterned in ways which indicate that it is culturally constructed. It is also clearly deeply embedded in our subjectivities. It is an emotion to which both sceptics and romantics can succumb, which is felt by lesbians as well as by heterosexual women. It is much easier to refuse to participate in romantic rituals, to resist pressures towards conventional marriage, to be cynical about 'happy ever after' endings than it is to avoid falling in love.

Desire and Psychoanalysis

Psychoanalytic theory is often invoked to explain aspects of our subjectivities which are irrational or inconsistent, especially where sexuality is concerned. Psychoanalysis challenges the idea of a rational, unitary human subject and in theorizing desire it might seem to offer an explanation of how and why we fall in love. Hence its attraction for many feminists seeking to explain the pleasures of romantic fiction (e.g. Kaplan, 1986; Light, 1984; Radway, 1987). This approach is, however, problematic.

Janice Radway (1987) uses Chodorow's (1978) work in attempting to explain the appeal of romantic fiction to women, in particular to explain why women's emotional needs go unmet, leading them to seek vicarious satisfaction in romance. For Chodorow the fact that women mother produces gender differentiation, in particular women's nurturant capacities and men's inability to nurture. Femininity is developed through a girl's identification with her mother, while masculinity requires boys to break from the feminine and hence repress their nurturant capacities. In the process men's sense of self becomes more autonomous, that of women relational (Chodorow, 1978). This account is quite intelligible without its psychoanalytic trappings, but placed within the framework of psychoanalysis it becomes reductionist. All the complexities of our subjectivities are reduced to the early experience of being mothered. Such a perspective is also universalistic, assuming that this pattern occurs — albeit with variations — in all societies. Importantly, in the present context, desire is absent from Chodorow's analysis. It may explain women's need for warmth, affection and attention and men's incapacity to give women what they want, but it does not explain the force of being 'in love' nor the tendency for passion to subside once the lover feels secure. Radway is only able to apply Chodorow to her romance readers because of her failure to confront the fact that what the women are reading is as much about passion as it is about nurture (McRobbie, 1991).

The perspective deriving from the work of Lacan, which places desire at the centre of its concerns, appears more promising in this respect (Mitchell and Rose, 1982). Lacanians make a distinction between a need, which is capable of satisfaction, and desire, which is not (Rose, 1982). The idea of desire as a yearning for unattainable fulfilment does seem to accord with the various emotions and sensations experienced when 'in love'. The compulsion to possess the other totally, to be made whole by them, also finds a correspondence in the psychoanalytic theorization of desire constituted through lack. There are, however, a number of problems here. The lack which underpins desire is held to be a consequence of the series of splits and losses which accompany our entry into language and culture as language cuts us off for ever from direct experience of the 'real'. Becoming speaking subjects also means submitting to the Law (of the father/phallus) which comes between mother and child and which forces us to take up positions as gendered subjects. Entering language thus involves inevitable loss. The sequence of events through which desire is constituted is conceptualized in terms of entry into language and culture *per se*, not of entering a specific culture. Desire, by implication, is an essential part of human social nature. Lacanian psychoanalysis does not admit of the possibility of emotions being structured differently in different cultural settings and thus imagines the whole world to be beset by the same desire — an assumption that anthropologists would make us wary of (Rosaldo, 1984; Errington and Gewertz, 1987).

I am not convinced, either, that the Lacanian account can deal with the specifics of the ways in which language structures emotional and sexual experience even within Western culture. Emotions are not simply 'felt' as internal states provoked by the unconscious sense of lost infantile satisfactions — they are actively structured and understood through culturally specific discourses. These discourses differentiate between love as nurture, being 'in love', lust and sexual arousal — all of which are conflated in the psychoanalytic concept of desire. While accounts of being 'in love' produced from within our culture are congruent with 'desire' as something intrinsically incapable of satisfaction, such accounts also acknowledge levels of emotional and sexual feeling quite unlike this. For example 'desire' as used in common-sense parlance can mean a form of sexual arousal which is perfectly satiable. It is questionable whether 'desire' in any sense can be said to be constituted at the moment of our entry to language when we have barely begun to gain access to the discourses through which we make sense of emotion and sexuality (Jackson, 1983).

Lacanian psychoanalysis, while ostensibly an account of the cultural construction of emotion, locates 'desire' as an inner state and thus precludes the possibility of linking the experience of 'love' to specific cultural contexts and to the specific discourses and narratives which give shape to our emotions. Feminist accounts of the pleasures of romance reading within this type of psychoanalytic framework, for example Alison Light (1984) on *Rebecca* and Cora Kaplan (1986) on *The Thorn Birds*, seem to me to suggest that romantic fiction reflects, gives voice to or is constructed around a set of emotions which already exist. I would argue, on the contrary, that romantic narrative itself contributes to the cultural construction of love. I do not maintain, as some early critics of romance did, that it is simply a means of brainwashing women into subservience. Rather I am suggesting that this is but one of the resources from which we create a sense of what our emotions are. As Michelle Rosaldo argues, 'feelings are not substances to be discovered in our blood, but social practices organised by stories that we both enact and tell. They are structured by our forms of understanding' (Rosaldo, 1984, p. 243).

Tales of Love: Narratives of the Feminine Self

Our subjectivities, including that aspect of them we call emotions, are shaped by the social and cultural milieu we inhabit, through processes which involve our active engagement with sets of meanings available in our culture. We create for ourselves a sense of what our emotions are, of what being 'in love' is, through learning scripts, positioning ourselves within discourses, constructing narratives of self. 'The script for love has already been written and is being continually recycled in all the love songs and love stories of Western literature and contemporary media' (Brunt, 1988, p. 19).

When we fall in love it feels like 'getting to star in your own movie' (*ibid.*). What Ros Brunt is describing here is not a passive internalization of these scripts but an active locating of ourselves within them. We can identify with love stories not because they record some pre-existing emotion, but because our cultural tradition supplies us with narrative forms with which we begin to be familiarized in childhood and through which we learn what love is. Narratives are not only encountered in novels, plays and films — they are very much a part of everyday cultural competences. We constantly tell stories to ourselves and others and we continually construct and reconstruct our own biographies in narrative form. Hence subjectivity is in part constituted through narrative.

The narratives woven around love and romance are available to both women and men within our culture, but not equally so. Being constituted as feminine involves girls in discourses of feeling and emotion, and more specifically the culture of romance, from which boys are more often excluded or from which they exclude themselves in order to affirm their own maleness. It is through the idiom of sexual bravado and conquest, a discourse of sexual drives — and not the language of romance — that masculinity is asserted (Hollway, 1984; Wood, 1984).

Children learn the standard pattern of romance narrative very early in life from such sources as fairy-tales (see Davies, 1989). For girls this acculturation into romance is continued through reading matter marketed for their consumption. Through such sources, as well as through conversations with other girls and adult women, girls are learning nuances of meaning through which they make sense of emotions and relationships.[2] This is by no means a process of passive inculcation into romanticism, rather romance narrative is a resource girls use to make sense of their emotional and social world. As Christian-Smith (1991) found, young teenage readers may look to romance fiction as a means of learning about heterosexual relationships. This may be one of the few sources available to young women where sexual 'knowledge' connects with feelings and desires (see also Gilbert and Taylor, 1991; Thomson and Scott, 1991). Romance is a fictional form which girls learn to manipulate, employing its narrative devices to construct their own private fantasies (Thompson, 1989).

We should not assume that the reduction in the space given to romantic fiction in teenage magazines noted by McRobbie (1991) heralds the decline of the culture of romance. The features in many of these magazines, especially those concerning the stars of popular music, may well be providing the material for personal romantic fantasies which girls find preferable to the stilted photo-stories they are offered (Thompson, 1989). Moreover, the decline in the romance content of magazines should be balanced against the growth of 'teen fiction' formula romances noted in the American and Australian contexts (Christian-Smith, 1991; Gilbert and Taylor, 1991). The American versions are widely available in the UK and according to my younger students are avidly read and exchanged by girls in their early teens, along with Mills and Boon romances. Girls are certainly capable of being critical of romantic fiction (Frazer, 1987; Gilbert and Taylor, 1991), but its continued popularity makes it unwise to deny it any effectivity in the construction of feminine subjectivity.

What is being created and reproduced in these narratives as well as elsewhere in the feminine culture of girls and women is a certain form of emotional literacy which men rarely acquire. Women's dissatisfaction with men's emotional illiteracy is a noted source of dissatisfaction in heterosexual relationships (Hite, 1988; Mansfield and Collard, 1988), and is also central to Radway's (1987) account to the pleasures of reading romance. As well as satisfying unmet needs for nurturance, romance also redefines problematic aspects of masculinity: the emotionally cold 'spectacularly masculine' hero ultimately reveals himself as a tender, caring lover. There is a danger here, however, of conflating the two forms of love which those who inhabit our Western culture habitually distinguish between — caring affectionate love and romantic passion.

The romances which Radway describes do not simply represent the heroine as the recipient of affection, but as the object of uncontrollable passion. Often the hero rapes the heroine. This is constructed not as an act of violence but as the result of overwhelming desire. Radway suggests that women are thus enabled to deal with real fears about male violence without questioning the patriarchal culture which sustains it. While recognizing that this is an accommodation to patriarchy, Radway does not explore the interconnections between this eroticization of male power and women's subordination. That women find pleasure and excitement in male sexual violence *is* problematic, and evidence of it is not confined to Radway's research. It is also a feature of Helen Taylor's (1989) study of *Gone With The Wind* fans, many of whom found the scene in which Rhett rapes Scarlett highly erotic. They do not, however, generally describe this scene as a rape: rather Rhett is seen as 'driven mad' by his love for Scarlett and his actions are read as resulting from *her* power over him. The meaning of the quintessential male enactment of power over woman is thus reversed. Elizabeth Wilson comments that 'the magic of dominance and submission is written into romantic tales just as much as it is written into pornography' (1983, p. 43). Insofar as romance helps to construct a form of femininity which finds pleasure in submission, this is a very good reason why we should retain our critical stance on it.

Some recent accounts of women's consumption of romance and other popular fictions give me the uneasy feeling that romance is being rehabilitated. In moving beyond the straightforward dismissal of romance as a means of co-opting women into heterosexual monogamy — and in offering new perspectives which take women's pleasure in romance seriously — feminists like Radway have produced more sophisticated accounts of women's readings of romance. At the same time, this shift of emphasis risks blunting the edge of feminist critique. Recognizing the pleasure gained from reading romance should not prevent our being critical of it. As Tania Modleski has recently written, 'even the cultural analyst may sometimes be a "cultural dupe" . . . we all exist inside ideology . . . we are all victims, down to the very depth of our psyches, of political and cultural domination (even though we are never *only* victims)' (Modleski, 1991, p. 45).

Conclusion: The Material and the Emotional

I have suggested that narratives of self are something we actively construct through accessing certain discourses and narrative structures existing within our culture, that subjectivity is discursively constructed. Despite my scepticism about psychoanalysis I would not wish to rule out the possibility that certain felt emotional needs and desires are constituted through our early experiences of nurture and through our entry into a particular culture, nor would I rule out the role of unconscious processes. However, I prefer an account which recognizes the historical and cultural specificity of these experiences and which does not regard our emotional needs as essentially fixed at some point in childhood. It is also important to keep in mind the material power differences between women and men. Women's economic dependence and the emotional and physical labour they perform for men underpin romantic narratives and our experience of romantic attachments.

One of the strengths of early feminist critiques of love lay in the linkage between the emotional and the material: that romance ends with your arms in his sink. This connection may have been articulated rather crudely, but we should not ignore the material contexts in which our subjectivities are forged. I am not suggesting that emotions can be linked to the material in any simple reductionist sense, but rather that connections do exist and should be noted. The emotional labour women perform, for example, clearly is linked to other forms of labour, and love is central to the justification of women's material exploitation. Women's emotional impoverishment in the economy of love (Langford, 1992) parallels their relative material poverty in terms of the distribution of family resources. Similarly emotional dependence is not unconnected with material dependence. I do not believe that these correspondences between emotional and economic relations are accidental or merely coincidental. Precisely how we theorize such interconnections, however, is a difficult issue to resolve.

Notes

1   I have chosen to focus here on Lee Comer (1974) and Shulamith Firestone (1972) — a British socialist feminist and an American radical feminist — whose work gives a flavour of the range of views being discussed within the WLM in the early seventies.
2   This is certainly culturally specific. For a discussion of the gulf of understanding that separates a young Western woman from her counterpart in New Guinea see Errington and Gewertz, 1987, p. 128.

References

BEAUVOIR, S. DE (1972) *The Second Sex*, Harmondsworth, Penguin.

BERTILSSON, M. (1986) 'Love's Labour Lost? A sociological view', *Theory, Culture and Society*, **3**, 1, pp. 19–35.

BRUNT, R. (1988) 'Love is in the Air', *Marxism Today*, February, pp. 18–21.

CHODOROW, N. (1978) *The Reproduction of Mothering*, Berkeley, University of California Press.

CHRISTIAN-SMITH, L. (1991) *Becoming a Woman through Romance*, London, Routledge.

COMER, L. (1974) *Wedlocked Women*, Leeds, Feminist Books.

DAVIES, B. (1989) *Frogs and Snails and Feminist Tales*, Sydney, Allen and Unwin.

ERRINGTON, F. and GEWERTZ, D. (1987) *Cultural Alternatives and a Feminist Anthropology*, Cambridge, Cambridge University Press.

FIRESTONE, S. (1972) *The Dialectic of Sex*, London, Paladin.

FRAZER, E. (1987) 'Teenage girls reading *Jackie*', *Media, Culture and Society*, 9, pp. 407–25.

GILBERT, P. and TAYLOR, S. (1991) *Fashioning the Feminine*, Sydney, Allen and Unwin.

GOODISON, L. (1983) 'Really Being In Love Means Wanting to Live in a Different World', in CARTLEDGE, S. and RYAN, J. (Eds) *Sex and Love: New Thoughts on Old Contradictions*, London, Women's Press, pp. 48–66.

HAMILTON, C. (1981) *Marriage as a Trade*, London, The Women's Press.

HAUG, F. *et al.* (1987) *Female Sexualization*, London, Verso.

HITE, S. (1988) *Women and Love: A Cultural Revolution in Progress*, London, Viking.

HOCHSCHILD, A. (1983) *The Managed Heart*, Berkeley, University of California Press.

HOLLWAY, W. (1984) 'Gender Difference and the Production of Subjectivity', in HENRIQUES, J., HOLLWAY, W., URWIN, C., VENN, C. and WALKERDINE, V. *Changing the Subject*, London, Methuen, pp. 227–63.

JACKSON, S. (1983) 'The Desire for Freud: Psychoanalysis and Feminism', *Trouble and Strife*, 1, pp. 32–41.

JAGGAR, A. (1989) 'Love and Knowledge: Emotion in Feminist Epistemology', in JAGGAR, A. and BORDO, S. (Eds) *Gender/Body/Knowledge: Feminist Reconstructions of Being and Knowing*, New Brunswick, Rutgers University Press, pp. 145–71.

KAPLAN, C. (1986) *Sea Changes*, London, Verso.

KOLLONTAI, A. (1972) *Sexual Relations and the Class Struggle*, Bristol, Falling Wall Press.

LANGFORD, W. (1992) 'Gender, Power and Self-Esteem: Women's Poverty in the Economy of Love', The Women's Studies Network (UK) Conference.

LIGHT, A. (1984) ' "Returning to Manderley" — Romance Fiction, Female Sexuality and Class', *Feminist Review*, 16, pp. 7–25.

MANSFIELD, P. and COLLARD, J. (1988) *The Beginning of the Rest of Your Life*, London, Macmillan.

McROBBIE, A. (1991) *Feminism and Youth Culture*, London, Macmillan.

MITCHELL, J. and ROSE, J. (Eds) (1982) *Feminine Sexuality: Jacques Lacan and the école freudienne*, London, Macmillan.

MODLESKI, T. (1984) *Loving With a Vengeance*, London, Methuen.

MODLESKI, T. (1991) *Feminism Without Women*, New York, Routledge.

RADWAY, J. (1987) *Reading the Romance*, London, Verso.

RICH, A. (1980) 'Compulsory Heterosexuality and Lesbian Existence', *Signs: Journal of Women in Culture and Society*, **5**, 4, pp. 631–60.

ROSALDO, M. (1984) 'Toward an Anthropology of Self and Feeling', in SHWEDER, R.A. and LeVINE, R.A. (Eds) *Culture Theory*, Cambridge, Cambridge University Press, pp. 137–57.

ROSE, J. (1982) 'Introduction II', in MITCHELL, J. and ROSE, J. (Eds) *Feminine Sexuality: Jacques Lacan and the école freudienne*, London, Macmillan, pp. 27–57.

SARSBY, J. (1983) *Romantic Love and Society*, Harmondsworth, Penguin.

TAYLOR, H. (1989) *Scarlett's Women: Gone With The Wind and its Female Fans*, London, Virago.

THOMPSON, S. (1989) 'Search for Tomorrow: On Feminism and the Reconstruction of Teen Romance', in VANCE, C. (Ed.) *Pleasure and Danger: Exploring Female Sexuality*, London, Pandora, pp. 350–84.

THOMSON, R. and SCOTT, S. (1991) *Learning About Sex: Young Women and the Social Construction of Sexual Identity*, London, Tufnell Press.

WILSON, E. (1983) 'A New Romanticism?', in PHILLIPS, E. (Ed.) *The Left and the Erotic*, London, Lawrence and Wishart.

WITTIG, M. (1992) *The Straight Mind and Other Essays*, Hemel Hempstead, Harvester Wheatsheaf.

WOOD, J. (1984) 'Groping Towards Sexism: Boy's Sex Talk', in MCROBBIE, A. and NAVA, M. (Eds) *Gender and Generation*, London, Macmillan, pp. 54–84.

Chapter 5

In God's Image or in Man's Image: A Critique of Patriarchy in Christian Theology

Lisa Isherwood and Dorothea McEwan

Introduction

We have chosen to speak on feminist theology because we believe that

> Societal and ecclesiastical norms do not simply materialize from thin air, they are fashioned by deeply held convictions and prior circumstances. The norms of the Western world have been greatly influenced by its Judaeo-Christian heritage. . . . and they are still shaping our thoughts today. (Isherwood and McEwan, 1992, p. 30)

Our title plays on a phrase found in the Hebrew scriptures where we are told man was made in God's image. This phrase became the foundation for what we call patriarchal theology — a theology that is written by men for political reasons, patriarchy meaning the rule of the fathers, not only in the spiritual but also in the secular realm.

These ideas, assumptions and prescriptions leave us wondering in whose image we are made — are we merely spare ribs, plucked out as pale reflections of our original dwelling place, man(!?) Or are we autonomous, self-determining, equal, divine creations? The answer depends on many things. We will try and examine some of them.

If, as for many centuries, the scriptures are viewed as beyond the realm of questioning, then our investigation can go no further. God HAS indeed ordained that woman be inferior: the helpmate, the comforter, the brood mare. Many people may think that these biblical ideas have long ago been abandoned or do not inform our conscience any longer. Sadly this is not the case; we present you with the following randomly chosen examples to highlight the extent to which modern perceptions are still formed by stereotypes traced back to the interpretation of the biblical narratives.

Mary Macaulay, in saying that the question of rape in marriage would never be a question if women were more loving and giving of themselves, clearly shows that women's bodies are still considered not to belong to them (cf. Borrowdale, 1991). Nearer to our time the former Anglican Bishop of London, Dr Leonard Graham, likened the ordination of women to the priesthood to the Napoleonic invasion of this country: that is to say, women are thought of as enemies, bent on destroying the values on which a sexist church is built (Furlong, 1991, p. 90). An example from the Roman Catholic tradition would be the Pope addressing a large group of women, cleaning ladies in vicarages. He told them they should thank God daily for having been given the privilege of serving the clergy (Isherwood and McEwan, 1992, p. 20). From these randomly chosen examples we see that woman is still a sex object who is to be treated with caution, who has to be controlled, and above all should be grateful for the opportunity to serve men.

However, if we open our eyes and seek the knowledge that Adam was warned against, then the picture becomes quite a different one.

The Beginnings

Just a cursory look at the creation story in Genesis shows us that the Judaeo-Christian sources seek to explain the creation in a manner distinctly different from creation myths from other western Asiatic and northern African societies of the time. These are accounts of how the world came to be and they speak of a mystical fusion and joint workings of male and female deities (Sanday, 1981, p. 219). Creation would not be easily explicable, comprehensive or acceptable otherwise. These accounts also try to explain the riddle of the origin of the One and its diversification into many. The biblical agenda does not go as far, yet at the same time goes further. In the Genesis story the female agency is redacted out, God is firmly a 'He' who engenders offspring without active female participation. But while there is no female agency at work in the biblical creation, the accounts go on to explain how good and evil came into the world which was created a 'paradise' — a Persian word for walled garden — by a male God. Mary Daly notes in this context that 'paradise', an enclave, something walled in and self-contained, could not have been enough for Eve who would have wished to explore it further, since seeking knowledge through understanding one's environment is a human activity (Daly, 1987, p. 66). God as male is the mirror image of a patriarchal society in which the leaders of the tribes are men, who rule and judge. The context in which the creation account was written reflects the — male — priestly writers, and the political agenda of Jewish — male — monotheism spelt the domination of woman by man.

Rosalind Miles speaks of the limitations of monotheism as she perceives it not only as a religion but as a power relation: 'Any "One God" idea has a built-in notion of primacy and supremacy. . . . As a power-relation, then, monotheism inevitably creates a hierarchy' (1989, p. 92) and we might add, a male hierarchy, of course. When considering the God of Israel, we are introduced to a male God who has given woman a 'life sentence of second-order existence', because, in the words of Miles, 'If God was male and woman was not male, then whatever God was, woman was not' (Miles, 1989, p. 93). The power relation of monotheism is asymmetrical.

There are two creation stories in Genesis. The first account, in Genesis 1:26–27, says:

> Then God said, 'Let us make man in our image, after our likeness; and let them have dominion over the fish of the sea, and over the birds of the air, and over the cattle, and over all the earth, and over every creeping thing that creeps upon the earth.' So God created man in his own image, in the image of God he created him; male and female he created them.

The second account deals with the creation of man separately from the creation of the woman. We read in Genesis 2:21–23:

> So the Lord God caused a deep sleep to fall upon the man, and while he slept took one of his ribs and closed up its place with flesh; and the rib which the Lord God had taken from the man he made into a woman and brought her to the man. Then the man said, 'This at last is bone of my bones and flesh of my flesh; she shall be called Woman, because she was taken out of Man.'

The first account imputes no inferiority to the woman, but the second one does. It is no surprise that under male monotheism the story suggesting equal creation under God was quickly forgotten. It would have served no useful purpose for patriarchy to remember it.

The message of women's inferiority is threefold in the creation and Fall stories:

(a) God is solely male;

(b) Woman is created from man and therefore is secondary in human creation.

(c) The male God, having made the perfect world, has it shattered by disobedient woman.

From this interpretation springs a world of commentary, from the Jewish rabbis to the scholastics in the Middle Ages, in which it is taken for granted that women are essentially inferior to men. Woman is the temptress, the seductress, the polluter, and therefore in need of supervision by male masters.

The story of the creation and the Fall of man needs to be re-examined against the background struggle at the time between Goddess religion and the new male monotheism, which was trying to establish itself. Under Goddess religions women had more social acceptance and standing, because their ability to bring forth life was viewed with reverence. Consequently there was less undervaluing of females. It is important to note that woman and the snake, both central to the story of the Fall, were primary symbols and agents of the Goddess as both gave new life and wisdom. As such Eve (woman) and the snake had to be vilified. This is neatly done in Genesis by the snake tempting the woman, who in turn tempted the man and led him to disobedience which resulted in 'the Fall of Man'. Paradise is lost and God will eventually have to send his son as a blood sacrifice to atone for the evil in the world; the evil brought into the world by Eve (woman). Ambrose wrote many centuries later: 'Adam was led to sin by Eve, not Eve by Adam. It is just and right then, that women accept as Lord and Master him who she led to sin' (Ranelagh, 1985, p. 49).

This is strange logic since surely one is ill-advised to accept as one's master a character who is so easily led to sin. But more so, it overlooks the biblical evidence, in Genesis 3:16, that shows that men rule over women as a result of sin. Traditionally this passage, 'yet your desire shall be for your husband, and he shall rule over you', has been used to justify men's power over women. But for feminist theology this does not follow. The passage can equally be understood as the Fall causing the sin of sexism, the subjugation of woman, the 'individual degradation of one half of humanity on socio-biological grounds' (Illich, 1983, p. 34).

While woman is being blamed for being wicked, there is a further consequence and that is that the physical and spiritual realms are being split apart, life is understood as dualistic and the two human genders, which came to represent the split, are seen as complementary to each other. They are opposites, yet they complement each other, one is not possible without the other, like the two sides of a coin.

> In this lies the very root of women's inequality — for if males embody one set of characteristics, and if with characteristic modesty they arrogate to themselves all the strength and virtues, then women are necessarily opposite *and lesser* creatures: weak where men are strong, fearful where men are brave, and stupid where men are intelligent. (Miles, 1989, p. 100)

To this list we may add physical where men are spiritual, emotional where men are rational.

The biblical stories are 'myths'. They do not present a 'gospel truth', rather a particular way of truth, written for a semi-literate culture reading with their mouths and not with their eyes. Feminist theology views Genesis as a story of seeking knowledge, not a story of 'original sin', and prefers to see the murder of Abel as 'original sin', because it is the first story of a violent act committed by humans. This act signalled the destruction of mutuality. Christianity has chosen to overlook this breakdown in human relations as being the fundamental sin of humanity and has instead focused on a narrow interpretation of the Genesis story whereby original sin is declared as the sin of sex for which women are responsible. Whenever we deal with these stories we should remember that they carry a political agenda.

The Radical Message

The Christian message was something totally different. It was radical, it was new, an awareness of the worth of everybody and everything. The actions of Jesus gave new hope to women. Jesus grasped God's commitment to compassion and his treatment of women was not usual for his day. He cured them, even when they were considered ritually unclean (Matthew 9:18–23), he spoke with them, even when they were from a despised race (John 4:5–26) and he offered forgiveness, even if that meant challenging the law (John 9:1–11). Further, he defended them against criticism (John 12:1–9) and had them as close friends (John 11:1–4). The Christ was born to a woman (Luke 2:1–8) and made his first resurrection appearance to a woman (John 20), who, significantly, has in tradition been called a whore. Jesus' actions towards women do not suggest that he viewed them as insignificant. Traditionalists point to the fact that he did not have women disciples and so they feel this justifies an exclusively male ministry. However, within the context of the time it may not have been expedient for him to choose women for this role, although there has been speculation regarding the gender of the 'beloved disciple' mentioned in John. Some scholars have argued that this disciple is Mary Magdalene, thus explaining Jesus' appearance to her after the resurrection. They also attribute the writing of the gospel of John to her which would further explain the positive treatment of women found in its passages. Even if this appears unacceptable to many people, they cannot deny that Jesus' treatment of women did not suggest that he found them inferior and unworthy of spiritual dialogue and compassionate treatment.

Women disciples are mentioned in Acts as present with Mary at the birth of the Church at Pentecost. Women received the Holy Spirit equally with men and were prominent in the early Church. They were usually gentiles who actively spread the Good News from their own houses. Paul commended 'our sister Phoebe, a deaconess of the Church at Cenchreae', Prisca and Aquila 'my fellow workers in Christ Jesus . . . greet also the church in their house'. Five other women workers are mentioned in the same passage, as is the convert Lydia, a businesswoman in Philippi (Romans 16:1–5). In the social context of the time it is remarkable that women went to meetings, that they converted others, that they actively promoted the gospel and that they were publicly thanked for it. Paul, of course, had preached the equality of all in Christ:

For as many of you as were baptized into Christ, have put on Christ. There is neither Jew nor Greek, there is neither slave nor free, there is neither male nor female; for you are all one in Christ Jesus. (Galatians 3:27–28)

The Reduction of the Message

But despite this radical vision of equality in Christ regardless of one's race or sex, this position for women did not develop into a norm. There is the famous injunction for women to remain silent at meetings (1 Corinthians 14:33–5):

As in all the churches of the saints, the women should keep silence in the churches. For they are not permitted to speak, but should be subordinate, as even the law says. If there is anything they desire to know, let them ask their husbands at home. For it is shameful for a woman to speak in church.

Here we see the Law being quoted despite the fact that the message of Jesus is supposed to have moved beyond it and we also see an implicit understanding that if you keep knowledge from people then you keep them subordinate. What all this indicates is that women had obviously not kept quiet at meetings, had asked questions and had not kept in the background. Whether their questions were difficult for the men to answer or whether women actually questioned the creeping restrictions upon the freedom originally granted to them in baptism, the fact was that the charismatic freedom of the early Church was eroded quite quickly despite Christ's proclamation that he came to teach service, not domination, domination being the mainstay of patriarchal systems, be they religious or secular.

We need to keep in mind two developments. Even though the nascent Jesus movement crossed cultural and racial borders, 'through St Paul the Jewish tradition, savagely anti-feminist, was affirmed', as Simone de Beauvoir put it in her seminal work *The Second Sex* (1949, Picador edition 1988, p. 128), so that demands for inclusivity in Christ were soon eroded by the prevailing cultural context of misogyny. And these views as shown by Paul's advice to women, given to meet concrete situations, were soon turned into abstract law (cf. Fiorenza, 1988). That is why Christianity is correct in asserting that a metanoia, a turning around, is required by Christians. Spiritual assent it not sufficient, a new economic and social view becomes necessary. Domination is the old law, mutuality the new.

Paul's negative attitude towards sex (e.g. 1 Corinthians 6:18, 1 Corinthians 7:1–2) further reinforced the negative consequences for women, since it fed the already existant dualism. His lack of enthusiasm for personal relationships was due to his feeling of living in the 'end-time'. Christ was believed to be returning soon and so Paul felt it best to spend time preparing for this by spiritual pursuits rather than by becoming involved in relationships. Therefore, many of his sexually repressive statements should be understood in this context, as simply short-term measures. We may still wish to disagree with them, but perhaps we can understand his motivation a little better. Sadly, the Church Fathers, who lived in quite different times, took his words and used them to back up their own sexual neuroses (Brown, 1988).

Faith of Our Fathers

Gradually the Christian communities increased and the underground movement emerged triumphantly under Emperor Constantine. It was no longer a sect set in the Jewish culture, but firmly rooted in Graeco-Roman culture. Here, the position of woman was not on a par with that of man, but subservient to man. The Church reacted to its surroundings by reducing the role of women from active instructors in the faith to passive church visitors. The diaconate, the presbyterial and episcopal offices had developed into male preserves. Women must have fought this — the Council of Laodicea in 343 decreed that women might not be appointed as elders or presbyters in the Church. As we know from a fresco in the Catacomb of Priscilla in Rome, women were concelebrating the Eucharist as a matter of course, in this instance a group of virgins living together (Morris, 1988).

The world of the Roman Empire was deeply misogynistic. It had many ascetic sects which reacted to the excesses they believed had brought about the decline of the Roman world. Christianity was inevitably affected by these movements. This reinforced the notion that the material, the physical, led to decline and, again, this very notion was tragic news for women.

The primitive Church had disregarded the Jewish view on purity and impurity. But the established Church had succumbed to the ancient division and it naturally followed that women were excluded from cultic functions because of their so-called 'monthly impurity'.

Added to this, theologians like Augustine witnessed the fall of Rome to the barbarian Vandals and Goths, the uncivilized invaders, who had obliterated Roman sophistication. It is little wonder that he believed rational self-control was necessary, if man was not to be dragged towards decline. Christians were suffering from anxiety because Jesus had not returned and the world was crumbling. They began to view the world as a place where one did battle with the body in order to preserve the soul. The fourth-century bishop Ambrose was able to write 'Think of the soul rising free of the body having turned away from sexuality and the sweet pleasures of the flesh, and cast off the cares of this worldly life' (*De Isaac et anima* iii:8, 1897 edition).

The speculations of the Church Fathers which became church law resulted in centuries of religious abuse of women. Those who entered religious life were encouraged by male spiritual directors to negate themselves through extreme means. Men, even though they suffered martyrdom, were rarely advised to pursue the perverse practices which women were encouraged to, such as mutilating their breasts, starving themselves and drinking lepers' vomit. The two options for women, cloister or marriage, both placed them under the control of men. When the Reformation removed one option, cloister, it enforced the other with vigour. Luther, for example, declared that women should bear children until they died of it. Traditional patriarchal theology has not been the good news for women that we are told it should be.

Patriarchal theology with all its negativity about women has not only divided the world between spirit and matter, but also between private and public.

Gains for Men

Public edicts of morality move in two spheres, the private sphere and the public sphere. In both spheres the man has power over woman, even if it is conceded that in the private sphere the woman reigns supreme. The woman is here likened to the queen of the home, rather the queen bee, absorbed by the labours of reproduction. Added to these are the duties expected of and demanded from a wife and mother, housekeeper, nurturer, comforter, permanently on call. In fact, woman is reduced to a commodity, an object, facilitating the public work or work outside the home of the man. She is also told this is in her best interest, she breaks out at her peril, dangers untold lurk outside. The fear of rape is a potent mechanism in this way of arguing. The attitude that women deserve it is still prevalent in society. How can this be true if there is not an implicit belief that women belong at home, safe and owned? If they move away from the protection of their master, they become anybody's property.

We believe that public actions display more privately held beliefs and we find it a matter of great concern that these beliefs are generated by increasing numbers of fundamentalist Christians. Their private religious interpretations and phobias have been translated into public demands for removal of women from the workplace, restrictions upon women's rights to abortion, demands for the removal of aid for raped or battered women, all of which they euphemistically call promoting Christian family values.

Social Reality for Women

The secular is hardly different. In many countries around the globe women are cheap labour, doing hard work and long hours next to their work as housekeeper and mother. Added to the burden of reproduction is the burden of production.

Further, women know what it means to be excluded. Women have been excluded from decision-making processes in the public sphere until very recently, when they were fighting for universal suffrage — it is not true that they were given universal suffrage; the establishment would never have done so had the women not fought for it themselves. But with greater autonomy in society come the opportunities of education and profession and with it the guilt-trip: should the woman pursue a career or should she stay at home and have babies and look after them? If it is so much better for the children and by implication for the state, then why are not more women convinced of it any longer?

There are three issues which highlight why women are indeed no longer convinced by the arguments that patriarchy puts forward. These are abortion, celibacy and ordination of women to the priesthood. All three have in common that what the Church declares is linked to its dualistic, hierarchical mode of thought, i.e. its patriarchy.

On Abortion

While feminists do not argue against the sanctity of life, they do argue for women's choice in all areas of life, not least that of producing life. The decision should not be taken out of the hands of the parents, as the church advocates. The imposition of moral absolutes is fundamentally wrong and against the feminist theological understanding that each person must exercise his or her own rights. In the case of the Catholic Church, we find a fundamental contradiction: it has a doctrine of 'just war', but it could never contemplate such a thing as a just abortion. The only thing that is consistent in these two contradictory positions is that the Church gains power over people's lives.

On Celibacy

These days the idea is perpetuated that celibacy is useful because it frees people so that they can have more hours in the day to serve God through the Church. This is a piece of justification with hindsight and was never the theological motivation for the doctrine. Celibacy was introduced once again as a means of control, but more: in order to protect the 'clean' sex, i.e. men, from the fallen 'unclean' sex, i.e. women. By keeping themselves from women, celibate clergy occupy a very high position in society. Therefore the fundamental dualism that was introduced into Christianity under Greek influence, which stated that the spirit was superior to the flesh, served to create a clerical hierarchy and in so doing disadvantaged the laity in general and women in particular.

This is linked once again with notions of purity. Women are considered unclean and therefore not fit to represent Christ at the altar. The sinfulness of Eve and the maleness of Jesus have both been over-interpreted to stand in the way of a healthy understanding of the sexes.

If we realize that our original subjugation in religious texts was political, with all that this implies regarding societal control, financial control and control over our bodies, then reclaiming the image of the Divine for ourselves is not merely a 'nice' spiritual aspiration, it is a radical political act.

Method

Feminist theology has used the methodology of feminism by placing women's experience at the centre of creating theology. Do I experience myself as the devil's gateway, as the Church Father Tertullian said? If not, how do I see myself in relation to that which we may call God and all that is around me?

Much of what tradition calls 'theology' is supposed 'to happen from the neck up', to use rational arguments in order to organize thoughts about otherworldy, extra-creation divine power. What characterizes feminist theology is the awareness of our experiences, the inclusion of the rest of ourselves in the doing of theology. The real lives and lived experiences of women and men, their diversity and gifts, their differences and struggles, commit us 'to ask theological questions and to give feminist answers' (cf. Storkey, 1985, p. 85).

Basing theology in experience is not in itself a new departure. Human experience has always been the starting point for theological reflection and people tend to forget that scripture and tradition are only 'codified collective human experiences' (Ruether, 1983, p. 12). It is because of this forgetting that systems of authority and hierarchy are able to use this experience to control the behaviour of others. They do this by 'objectifying' this collective experience thereby suggesting that it is somehow received from beyond our experience. In this way the symbols as employed by hierarchy dictate to us what we can experience in the present and how that experience will be interpreted. Ruether points out that this is a delusion because the reality is opposite. 'If a symbol does not speak authentically to experience, it becomes dead or must be altered to provide a new meaning' (Ruether, 1983, p. 13).

The canon of scripture and the creeds are examples of how original human experience becomes sorted out. History shows that the consequences for not accepting these 'guidelines' have often been horrific — inquisition, 'holy wars', crusades, witch hunts. This is why feminist theologians, recognizing that all theology starts with claiming experience as the base for theological reflection, have started to claim women's experience as the base of theological reflection.

What Will This Mean?

Understood as a liberation movement, feminist theology has considerable political potential. The demand that everybody should be taken seriously, the demand of a right to personal development and autonomy, the demand to expand the radius of action for everybody so as to develop fully and find acceptance as an individual person, have political implications. They will generate analysis and findings which will question many an assumption in society and in churches: our behaviour towards each other, the behaviour of the state in the political arena and our attitude towards the exploitation of the earth's resources. A new paradigm of non-violence starting from our relationship of partnership with each other will result in a major rethink about politics.

The tradition of exclusion is our tradition, to date, but feminist theology sees tradition as 'a dynamic action of God's love which is to be passed on to others of all sexes and races' (Russell, 1974, p. 79). To overcome the Christian praxis of exclusion means shedding the claim of patriarchal theology to speak for all and for all times. The task is to create a new relationship of equals, a gentle relationship with nature, enabling everybody to become an agent in his or her own right, with full personhood and autonomy. In accepting divine revelation in nature and in human interaction, in what we as women and men can experience, patriarchal Christianity may be directed towards transformation.

Feminist theology has rejected the assumption of the sameness of human experience and of male values as normative values. Patriarchal prescriptions did away with doubt; the rationale for doubt was redacted out. Feminist theology is therefore engaged in freeing women's potential from adapting to a system to finding personal fulfilment, away from surviving a system to living a faith.

Where exactly should we start if we wish to offer a critique of patriarchal theology? How do we find the authority to carry out this task when we are so used to bowing to external authority and demands? We have seen that women's experience is a starting point but we need to narrow it down still further. We do not become conscious of our experience in abstract terms; our experience lies in our concrete reality, which we grasp through our bodies. Our first task then in offering our critique of patriarchal theology is to reclaim our bodies. 'All that patriarchal culture has named evil must be reclaimed as part of ourselves — sensuality, change, darkness, self-affirmation, nature, death, passion, woman' (Brock, 1988, p. 59).

The analysis of patriarchal culture by Brock gives us a framework in which to examine the issues of feminism more closely. This in turn sets the agenda for feminist theology if we put theology in lived experience.

We see from this that in reclaiming our bodies we are stating not only that the material, the physical, is a vehicle for the divine, but that change is holy, that passion is sacred and self-direction the path of divinity. How different this is from the picture of Eve in Eden! There is a further affirmation, that nature, the created world, the creation in its totality, is sacred. Therefore, when we as women claim our own bodies, not as objects to be harassed and mistrusted, but as sources of divinity to be freed and celebrated, we open up new realms in theology. This is where we start and where we should always return to find our motivation for doing theology. We should ask — what is happening to our bodies, the bodies of others and the body of the cosmos? If we see lack of love, nurture, respect and worship, then we must speak out; our critique is body-based and body-directed (cf. Isherwood and McEwan, 1992, pp. 113–16).

But can the knowledge and culture created by such action be viewed as Christian? To speak with Rosemary Radford Ruether, we should not any longer pose the question whether something is Christian in our political and social, personal and practical life, but pose the question whether it is healthy to us, the agents of our own history and destiny (talk, June 1988, London). If it does not produce an attitude of discrimination, if it fosters equality, if it puts us into an open relationship with those around us, if, most importantly, it transforms classism, racism and sexism, then we follow the command of the Apostle Paul who said that there is no discrimination in Christ.

Patriarchy stands in need of transformation; to follow its own high ideals it needs the insights formulated by those who have been harmed and hurt by it. Women will then be able to claim the image of God for themselves and in so doing bring to the fore new knowledge and the creation of a different reality.

References and Further Reading

Bible quotes are taken from the Revised Standard Version, Edinburgh, Nelson, 1966.

AMBROSE (1897) *De Issac et anima*, Ed. C. SCHENKL, CSEL 32, Vienna, Tempsky.
ARMSTRONG, K. (1986) *The Gospel According to Woman*, London, Pan.
BEAUVOIR, S. DE (1988) *The Second Sex*, London, Picador.
BORROWDALE, A. (1991) *Distorted Images: Christian Attitudes to Women, Men and Sex*, London, SPCK.
BROCK, R. (1988) *Journey By Heart: A Christology of Erotic Power*, New York, Crossroad.
BROWN, P. (1988) *The Body and Society: Men, Women and Sexual Renunciation in Early Christianity*, London, Faber.
CHRIST, C. and PLASKOW, J. (1979) *Womanspirit Rising*, San Francisco, Harper and Row.
CHRIST, C. and PLASKOW, J. (1989) *Weaving the Visions: New Patterns in Feminist Spirituality*, New York, Harper Collins.
COUNTRYMAN, W. (1988) *Dirt, Greed and Sex*, London, SCM.
DALY, M. (1973) *Beyond God the Father*, Boston, Beacon Press.
DALY, M. (1984) *Pure Lust: Elemental Feminist Philosophy*, London, Women's Press.
DALY, M. (1987) *Gyn/Ecology: The Metaethics of Radical Feminism*, London, Women's Press.
DOWELL, S. and HURCOMBE, L. (1981) *Dispossessed Daughters of Eve: Faith and Feminism*, London, SCM Press.
FIORENZA, E.S. (1988) *In Memory of Her*, London, SCM Press.

FURLONG, M. (1991) *A Dangerous Delight*, London, SPCK.

GILLIGAN, C. (1982) *In a Different Voice: Psychological Theory and Women's Development*, Cambridge, Mass., Harvard University Press.

GIMBUTAS, M. (1982) *The Goddesses and Gods of Old Europe 6500 to 3500 BC*, London, Thames and Hudson.

HARRISON, B. (1985) *Making Connections: Essays in Feminist Social Ethics*, Boston, Beacon Press.

HEYWARD, C. (1989) *Touching Our Strength: The Erotic as Power and The Love of God*, New York, Collins.

HUNT, M. (1991) *Fierce Tenderness: A Feminist Theology of Friendship*, New York, Crossroad.

ILLICH, I. (1983) *Gender*, London, Boyars.

ISHERWOOD, L. and McEWAN, D. (1992) *Introducing Feminist Theology*, Sheffield, Sheffield Academic Press.

MACAULAY, M. (1957) *The Art of Marriage*, Harmondsworth, Penguin.

McEWAN, D. (Ed.) (1991) *Women Experiencing Church: A Documentation of Alienation*, Leominster, Fowler Wright Books.

MILES, R. (1989) *The Women's History of the World*, London, Paladin.

MORRIS, J. (1988) *Occasional Paper*, reprinted in *Woman in Early Christian Priesthood*, Briefing Paper 1, Christian Women's Resource Centre, London, p. 4.

RANELAGH, E.L. (1985) *Men and Women*, London, Quartet.

RUETHER, R.R. (1983) *Sexism and God-Talk: Towards Feminist Theology*, London, SCM Press.

RUSSELL, L. (1974) *Human Liberation in a Feminist Perspective*, Philadelphia, Westminster Press.

SANDAY, P.R. (1981) *Female Power and Male Dominance: On the Origins of Sexual Inequality*, Cambridge, Cambridge University Press.

STORKEY, E. (1985) *What's Right with Feminism*, London, SPCK.

THISTLETHWAITE, S.B. (1990) *Sex, Race and God*, London, Geoffrey Chapman.

WOLLSTONECRAFT, M. (1992) *A Vindication of the Rights of Woman*, London, Penguin.

YOUNG, P.D. (1990) *Feminist Theology/Christian Theology: In Search of Method*, Minneapolis, Fortress Press.

Chapter 6

Layers of Difference: The Significance of a Self-Reflexive Research Practice for a Feminist Epistemological Project

Julia Hallam and Annecka Marshall

Introduction

> Change means growth, and growth can be painful. But we sharpen self-definition by exposing the self in work and struggle together with those whom we define as different from ourselves, although sharing the same goals. For Black and white, old and young, lesbian and heterosexual women alike, this can mean new paths to our survival. (Audre Lorde, 1984)

Constructing a feminist base to knowledge which is 'objective' and 'true' has been a major concern of feminists working in academia in the last twenty years or so. In recent years, Black feminists have pointed out that this project has perpetuated a white middle-class bias that has ignored or marginalized differences other than gender such as race, sexuality and class.[1]

'Objectivity' and 'truth', however, continue to be the hallmarks that guarantee and legitimize the production of knowledge in academia. As doctoral students undertaking traditional academic apprenticeships that will legitimize our own status as professional knowledge producers, we would like to propose that a degree of personal reflexiveness is an important part of the process of knowledge production. Many feminist knowledge producers have tried to base their research in women's experiences, but that experience has often been narrowly defined in terms of gender, and has tended to ignore other differences that are equally significant in the construction of subjectivity. Academe's demands for objectivity in the research process also means that it is difficult to account for the role and experience of the researcher, who shapes and moulds the experience of others into forms of knowledge. In this paper we take up a position that claims all knowledge is a form of cultural production, and that the 'truth' of any knowledge is therefore integrally connected both to the institution that produces it and to the particular historical moment in which it has been constructed. Rather than aspiring to the production of universalizing 'truths' that apply to all women, a stance which often masks the standpoint of the knowledge producer, we will argue that personal biographical factors play an important role in the production of knowledge.[2] It is this relationship, between personal biographies and knowledge production, that we seek to explore through a self-reflexive research practice. This means that our own research practice is a self-reflexive process where we try to situate ourselves and our work in open discursive frameworks. By this, we mean that the positions we take up are not fixed and unchanging but open to adjustment as we read and debate our work with others. We would like to suggest that feminist knowledge cannot become multivalent and multivocal until self-reflexive practices are more widely accepted.[3]

Diary Entries

Annecka

. . . My lack of power . . . I query the use of my research. Is it for Black women? I am weary of having to engage in a white and male-dominated intellectual framework. I am worried about my lack of control. I see myself from outside my own body. So, how do I deal with this dilemma? I will not do anything that contradicts my moral principles. I will make sure that I do not do research that is detrimental to Black womanhood or to Black people. I want to guarantee that my research benefits the women that I interview. . . . That I don't get lost. . . .

Julia

. . . The more I try to do this PhD, and the more I think about the process of doing it, the more it seems that I am involved in creating a kind of reality — translating my personal experience into a form that gives it not only personal meaning but political value. As I read the autobiographies of other women who spent their lives as nurses, I wonder why this form of self-writing has no value in knowledge terms. So what value will my research have? How does my position as a researcher make a difference? How will my story, refracted through their stories, count as knowledge? I can't pretend that I'm objective, that I've not experienced these things. . . .

Annecka

At the time I started doing my doctorate I felt alienated in a predominantly white, male, middle class and heterosexual academic setting, that failed to address the needs of those like me who do not conform to the image of a typical PhD student. For months I wondered whether my thesis could be considered to be 'an original contribution to knowledge', in view of the fact that epistemology is mainly defined by white scholars. Also, if my work was acceptable I feared that it would be the result of compromising my Black female identity. In this paper I want to discuss the ways in which these concerns influenced my experiences during my second year of research.

Julia

My reasons for doing this work are tied up with my own experiences, first of all as a nurse, and later as a mature undergraduate student with a growing sense that here was something in addition to nursing that I could do well. And it isn't seen pejoratively as 'woman's work', that was really important to me at the beginning. My research project, Nursing the Image, is concerned with how women have been represented as nurses and how, as nurses, they have represented themselves. I bring to this work a certain kind of 'insider' knowledge from my own experience as a nurse, but I am also aware that I am now an 'outsider', no longer a nurse but an academic researcher. Initially, I thought this position, of being both an insider and outsider, would be an advantage — it was a guarantee of the 'authenticity' of my objectivity. I had been there, therefore I could comment, I could judge. Increasingly, I have found the notion of objectivity problematic. How can I be objective when I have such a large emotional investment in the work?

Annecka

For a year before I started my research I considered the notion that a PhD should explore unknown territory in order to push the horizons forward. In relation to the experiences of Black women, so little is known about the complexity of our lives that I initially found it difficult to concentrate on one area. Since research on racism has tended to analyze a Black male viewpoint, and feminism has until quite recently focused on the interests of white middle-class women, there was an immense vacuum that needed to be filled. Knowing that there are few Black women who are privileged enough to be in a position to do research, and feeling accountable to the general needs of Black women, I deliberated over the selection of a research topic.

My research examines the ways in which Black female sexuality is stereotyped and the impact of this on Black women's lives. In brief, I examine how myths of Black women as animalistic, diseased and licentious, constitute a means whereby white men cope with their anxieties over their social control. For whites a secure definition of self is maintained by projecting the loss of sexual control onto Black women, who symbolize dirt, decay and unbridled sexuality. This categorization not only represents the transference of white ambivalence but also, my research indicates, vindicates the oppression of Black women. A review of the historical literature confirmed that since slavery Black women have been portrayed as creatures of sex. Under enslavement, the icon of the lascivious Black female not only effectively legitimized the maximum exploitation of her reproductive labour, but also exonerated white men who sexually abused her from guilt (see Davis, 1981; Gilman, 1985).

Julia

If we accept that the objectivity of traditional academic discourse extends the white Eurocentric masculine viewpoint and frame of reference to a general view of the world, then it is clear that much of the work undertaken by feminist researchers has been concerned with breaking down the authority of this unified viewpoint so that it can include others who are differently constituted as subjects — not male, not middle-class, and more recently not white, not Anglo-European.

The problem for me is how I do this in my own work: how do I find a place to speak from that does not assume an objective (masculinist) view, but at the same time does not reduce what I say to subjective relativism? Black feminists have pointed out in recent years how much feminist work in academia has excluded rather than included them. My research has revealed the exclusion of Black images from nursing recruitment literature, and the paucity of these images in all forms of popular fiction about nurses, in spite of the fact that during the period I am researching, Black nurses formed a significant proportion of the NHS workforce. Interviews with senior nurses responsible for recruitment have revealed how Black female labour was used to do the dirtiest work in the most difficult areas, and how the prestigious teaching hospitals resisted having 'too many Black faces on the wards'. One interviewee told me that a Chief Nursing Officer in charge of a large psychiatric hospital used to send for 'a boatful from Barbados' when nursing numbers got low.

I have to find a way to represent this experience in my work, whilst making it clear that I speak not on behalf of or for Black nurses, but from the point of view of someone who was trained in a teaching hospital and therefore worked in a position of comparative privilege — a privilege that only became apparent to me when I became an agency nurse and worked in one of the most poorly funded sectors of medicine, that of geriatrics, which is still mainly staffed by Black nurses. My analysis of this situation can only be that of an outsider, stating the facts as they appear to me to be. What worries me about this is that in interviewing Black nurses, I feel voyeuristic because I do not think my research will make any real difference to their situation. They are giving me their time, they are telling me about their experiences. I will write it up, and through this writing up can claim the authority of the knower, the expert. Such is the power of the traditional academic, to be able to re-present the experiences of others as knowledge of 'the other'. This particular knowledge is however 'outsider' knowledge, and is quite different to the kind of knowledge that might be produced by someone with 'inside' experience of racism and sexism. It would clearly be a very different proposition if these experiences were being researched by a Black woman researcher rather than white, middle-class me.

Annecka

As a Black woman doing research in a British university I often wish that I was in a supportive Black feminist arena. Most of my inspiration on Black feminist methodology and epistemology is gathered from American literature. Although this is relevant, there is a great need to develop Black British feminist frameworks. According to Patricia Hill Collins the process of conducting research is especially difficult for Black women because they occupy an 'outsider within' status (Collins, 1990). Thus Black women are marginalized by theories of knowledge that subjugate their subjectivity, while Black women academics simultaneously feel frustrated and empowered by the tension of struggling to articulate a unique Black feminist standpoint. It is imperative to legitimate the defiance of Black women's self-definitions. Similarly, I see my research as validating, affirming and strengthening my interviewees as well as myself. The situation of being both inside and outside the role of Black woman/researcher is a personal, academic and political concern. My rationalization for doing my research is that as a Black woman I have a specific awareness of the interface of racism, sexism, heterosexism and class oppression in Black women's lives, an understanding that white women and Black men are less likely to have. However, it is necessary to problematize the degree to which I have integrated into a white-dominated system, and to ask whether this assimilation makes me less Black, i.e. reduces my affinity and commitment to Black women. At the same time I feel anxious, isolated and misunderstood in academia. Historically defined as inferior, trying to prove myself is sometimes an exciting challenge, but mainly a draining process.

Julia

In doctoral research, the researcher undergoes a three-year apprenticeship. This acquaints the researcher with academic practice and socializes the individual into academia. This can be described as a 'process of incorporation' aimed at perpetuating the academic enterprise, that is to produce knowledge. In order to 'pass out' from this apprenticeship, the researcher has to show that they are cognizant with the major strands of Western thought which relate to their subject discipline, and that they can situate both themselves and their research within the thought frameworks that give the discipline its shape. This means that new knowledge is always built on old foundations — foundations which have deep roots in Greek thought. We know now that this system of thought was the product of a hierarchical and militaristic society which was built on slavery and deeply antagonistic to women (Harding, 1986). It is therefore extremely important that we ask ourselves, 'Why is this knowledge being produced? Who is producing it? And what kinds of feminist political effects is the work likely to have?'

As a white woman from working-class roots, I also worry about the degree to which I have been incorporated into a white male-dominated research system, a system that still has difficulty in perceiving differences of race, gender and sexuality even as it subjects others to its enquiring gaze. Within this system, I am having to learn to be objective, which means I have to try to be unemotional in my approach to my work. However, the concept of the objective researcher depends upon the notion that individuals can present themselves as a coherent unity. Recent academic work — particularly feminist work in psychoanalysis — denies this concept of the unity of the speaking subject, and has pointed out how we are fragmented individuals who are culturally constructed to think of ourselves as unified subjects.[4] Most people are an amalgam of differences, differences that consist of class, gender, race, sexuality, age, religion and nationality, to name but a few. My culturally constructed amalgam of identities must therefore be a factor in my self-presentation and practice as a researcher, but our training as researchers works to efface these differences in the interests of appearing as an authorial source of knowledge, as a 'knower'.

This image of the researcher as a coherent unity is difficult to square with the knowledge that we are not unitary subjects. As researchers, we have to find a place to speak from, a place that is grounded in our subject discipline. When we present our research, we have to find a unitary position, which means for some of us that we have to literally 'put ourselves together on paper' and find a coherent voice. The choices we make about how we do that are not objective, but shaped by our intellectual biographies, which are in turn shaped by factors like gender, race and sexuality. Female researchers are often faced with the difficult choice of adopting the apparently ungendered discourse of knowledge in the interests of producing work that will be recognized as significant by their peers, or of risking exclusion from the mainstream discourses of their disciplines if they insist on difference. In other words, as a female researcher I can choose to identify with a male view of the world and become a 'token man', or insist on my difference and risk relegation to the margins of academic life and knowledge production. This was clearly illustrated at a recent job interview, where I was asked if I intended to publish 'only for the feminist press'. The implication behind these remarks was that 'real' knowledge was produced and published elsewhere in the mainstream, and that the work that I am doing has low academic status to an employer because it is still viewed pejoratively as 'woman's work'. Sometimes I get the feeling I've been here before . . .

The above example clearly illustrates that questions of knowledge production are not just theoretical abstractions, but material practices in which oppositional stances are viewed with suspicion and distrust. As a material practice, knowledge production is not a neutral activity. It follows therefore that the methodologies used in research are not neutral either, but carry with them political and ideological implications. Because of this there has been a great deal of debate in recent years over whether there is or could be a specifically feminist methodology, and if there were, what that model might look like.[5] Some of the approaches to the ways and means of doing research and analyzing its results have been said to be more 'feminist' than others. For instance, quantitative research (or number crunching as it is sometimes derisively called) is seen as being problematic for feminists, whilst other approaches, like ethnography, are seen as more valid because they allow people to speak for themselves. But this emphasis on the political validity of self-speaking tends to overlook the mediating role of the researcher, who has shaped the context and the discourse in which that selected self-speaking may occur. We need to be aware that 'knowing which mode of analysis is appropriate in specific problem situations is an issue that feminist epistemology has not yet adequately addressed' (Hawkesworth, 1989).

I would argue that there is no single research methodology which is intrinsically feminist. Methodologies are tools that enable knowledge to take particular forms, some of which are more useful for achieving certain ends and results than others. For instance, the lack of quantitative information on the numbers of Black nurses who arrived from overseas to work in the health service in the fifties and sixties means that we shall probably never know just how many women came to Britain to be nurses, and it is now too late to gather the information. We will never know how many women stayed in nursing and how many of them left, or why they left. At that time, 'race' was not a quantifiable statistic. Research into the experiences of Black nurses in Britain only began in the late sixties. In much of this research those who experienced difficulties at work were seen as 'homesick' rather than the likely recipients of racial abuse both on a personal and institutional level. Difficulties were seen as the fault of individuals, as a failure to adjust; the institution was never called into question, and nor were those who managed it. This research and the methodologies that it used to 'prove' the problem was one of personal maladjustment have only recently been called into question by Black researchers and health workers.[6]

If there is no research methodology that is intrinsically feminist, what does it mean to be a feminist researcher? Different feminists will clearly have different answers to this question, but for me it means attempting to explore and analyze the relationship between the personal and the political, the private and the public. There follows from this a focus in my methodology on the role played by autobiographical factors in the research process. Research undertaken by Bob Burgess into autobiographical accounts of the research process at the University of Warwick confirms that most postgraduate researchers have some sort of direct autobiographical connection with their choice of research topic.[7] **In the writing-up of research, however, this relationship between intellectual biography and lived experience tends to be effaced in the interests of presenting knowledge that appears to be 'objective' and 'value-free'.**

Annecka

The search for a 'representative' sample, as well as the time and monetary constraints of being a self-financed part-time student, inevitably structure the choice of methodology employed in the research process. This led me to the selection of twenty-one Black women for interviewing, their ages ranging from 20 to 65. In terms of self-definitions of sexual identity, eighteen are heterosexual, two are bisexual and one is a lesbian. Three are nurses; three are students; two are housewives; and two are secretaries. The others include a machinist, a catering assistant, a temp, an unemployed woman, a teacher, a trainee solicitor, a trainee environmental health officer, a housing officer, a research worker, an office supervisor and an artist. When asked how they think that Black women are seen in British society, they said as sensuous, bestial, good in bed, loose, promiscuous, prostitutes, predatory and breeders. Whilst being interested in the degree to which this image prevails, my main concern is in the existence and social implications of racialized beliefs about sexuality, and their effects upon Black women's identity and relationships. To explore these issues I devised a semi-structured interview schedule which was based on open-ended probe questions. I asked for example:

> Do you think that race affects how you feel about your sexual experiences?

> In general, how do you think that Black women are seen sexually?

> Do you think that sexual images of Black women influence our lives?

The interviewees explain that Black women are often seen as aggressive and oversexed temptresses who bewitch, mesmerize and emasculate men.

Due to the onslaught of negative images and their institutionalization by the mass media, the welfare state, and employers, a fundamental form of resistance is the construction of positive self-images and self-definitions. Thus it is acknowledged that our sexuality is seen by white society as the threat of being potentially radical and subversive. Black women challenge these myths by creating alternative definitions of Black womanhood.[8] Hence Roseanne, a 22-year-old student, asserts the importance of self-determination:

> The white man is not going to understand why the Black woman is like she is sexually. The reason why she is what she is sexually is because of her history. She's an independent person and this transforms her sexually.

Zora, a 29-year-old temp, maintains that positive self-definitions are vital to wider strategies for Black women's liberation:

> It's to define yourself. I think that it is the most powerful thing that you can do is to define yourself; because so much definition has been done to us by other people; and then even our Black male counterparts can use you as something to define themselves against. None of that anymore. The time has come. If they don't like it, well tough. You've got to keep going and don't let anybody stand in your way. . . .

In my final year of undergraduate study I became so stressed out that for one course I was unable to write an assessed essay, and so opted to be fully examined. As I explained this to the lecturer, he told me about the white man's lust for the Black woman's body, and that if I was willing he would help me to relieve my tension. Needless to say I was not willing, and instead of getting the 2:1 that I had expected for that course, I got a third. That lecturer presently has an obsessive interest in my research. The way that he constantly tells me his views is a classic case of intellectual masturbation. Fortunately, the power relationship has since altered more to my favour since I have become a postgraduate and a part-time tutor. However, I want to actually fight against the reduction of Black women to our genitalia, rather than just be in a more comfortable position to deal with it. Therefore in my role as a PhD student and lecturer, I'm showing that Black women are not the stereotypically stupid and hypersexual being.

Nevertheless, I want to move beyond rejecting myths. The process of interviewing other Black women about the significance of racialized sexual images to their lives necessarily involves looking at the effects upon me. Last week, whilst I was marking assessed essays, I was disturbed by a phone call from a concerned friend. 'I want to discuss your problem,' she said. Since I was in one of my spells of depression because that day I had received two threatening letters — one from NatWest about my overdraft and the other from the university for failing to pay my fees and my rent, I thought that she meant my financial situation. However, the problem according to this woman was my relationship with a white man. How could I call myself a Black feminist when I was selling out? For an hour she explained why she thought that I was destroying the Black race. I was too angry and too tired to defend myself again. I tried to explain that narrow prescriptions of politically correct behaviour do not enhance revolutionary struggles. Instead of attacking Black women who do not adopt a code of ideologically sound behaviour (which is usually defined by Black men), we should try to understand and respect our differences, was my retort. Of course, this was seen as a cop-out and I was criticized for seeing myself as an individual, and not defending the common requirements of Black people. She mentioned three suitable Black men whom she thought could help me to see the error of my ways. I laughed, but I wondered for how long my pro-Blackness, feminism, class allegiance, anti-heterosexism etc. would be called into question.

A primary reason for embarking on my research is the fact that the racialization of the social construction of sexuality is largely ignored. When stereotypes of Black sexuality are discussed, this is usually subject to heterosexist bias. Thus debates on Black female sexuality tend to concentrate on heterosexual Black women and render Black lesbians invisible.[9] There is an emphasis upon the history of Black female availability to white men. In conjunction with these debates, the problems that this raises for relationships between Black men and women are discussed. Black lesbian feminists challenge such denials of their reality but, as with the argument that the issue of racism is not only pertinent to Black people, it is also necessary for heterosexual Black women to combat heterosexism. I am interested in the inter-relationship between racialized images of sexuality and homophobia. In particular I think that it is important to examine the ways in which Black people, bisexuals, lesbians and gay men are seen as possessing pathological, deviant and diseased sexualities. This concern leads me to assess the distinct oppression of Black lesbians. However, this has been a source of tension in the research process.

My subjective experience of being a heterosexual woman is a source of anxiety as I query the extent that I can fully appreciate the circumstances of lesbians and bisexual women. Whilst I reject notions of the objective researcher, I am aware of the potential dilemmas arising out of both my empathy with the interviewees on the basis of Black womanhood and my heterosexuality. How do I ensure that mine is not a heterosexist standpoint as opposed to a heterosexual one? My desire to include the views of lesbians and bisexuals could be interpreted as tokenistic, yet my personal and political commitment to fighting against homophobia negates this charge. Whilst my snowball technique of selecting a sample introduced me to fewer lesbians and bisexuals than I had hoped, I endeavour to highlight the interface of racism and heterosexism in their lives. I argue that it is encumbent for all Black women to tackle homophobia and to recognize lesbianism as a subversion of male definitions and control of our sexuality. Rather than seeing homosexuality as a 'white man's disease' that is detrimental to Black culture, it is vital to recognize that homophobia not only represses our sexual desires, but it is also divisive to Black liberation struggles.

Julia

My research is revealing that under the white starched respectability of nursing in Britain in the fifties and sixties, there were attitudes that can only be described as racist, sexist, and classist. The oppression of women by other women is a part of women's history that tends to remain hidden, but I think it is important that as feminists we try to deal with such issues. In a series of case studies of nurses' attitudes to their professional image conducted through open-ended semi-structured interviews, I have asked Black and white nurses to talk about their relationship to the professional image of the nurse. Whilst some white writers have written about the problems and personal discomfort that they have experienced in this interview situation, I have to admit that I am more worried about how I re-present that experience when I write up that section of the research. The decision not to exclude the experience of Black nurses, however, in spite of my own position as a white researcher (which leaves me open to criticism on a number of grounds), was made on the basis of the existing exclusion and invisibility of Black nurses in most of the (white) writing on images of nurses, both here and in the United States.

Like many people, I have often allowed myself to be intimidated by those who claim to know more than I do. For years, I didn't go to university because I thought I wouldn't be good enough, that I would fail. During those years I became a feminist. For me, the personal was (and still is) political, and I was quite convinced that as well as changing the world politically, women had to change themselves. Now in middle age, I am learning to be a researcher and an academic. For me at least, a more self-reflexive research practice which is clearer about the choices it makes and why it makes them serves a feminism which still abides by the notion that the personal is political. In that, I am a product of the forces that have shaped me as a feminist and this informs my research practice, rather than a researcher who is informed by academic feminist

knowledge. This difference, between feminists who have become academics and academics who have become feminists continues to be a productive tension in the construction of feminist knowledge.

Annecka

Given the difficulties that I have had to get this far I am afraid of life after the PhD. When I was looking for temporary employment after doing a master's, I was offered cleaning jobs. If my options are adopting a Black role as a maid or a white role as a lecturer, what is the point? Of course I want to transcend these roles, so that whether I end up in Women's Studies, Race Relations or Sociology, I ensure that the distinct position of Black women is recognized. Yet can I count on your full support?

Conclusions

In this paper we have discussed the necessity of a self-reflexive approach to research practice as well as some of the problems that this gives rise to. For those women who are excluded from feminist epistemological debates this is especially pertinent. Working-class women, lesbians and Black women, for example, problematize 'feminist standpoints' that either marginalize, misrepresent or completely ignore their experiences. Their struggles to develop and validate their claims to knowledge are often in isolation. As feminists, we need to support each other's epistemological projects. Our accountability to the empowerment of ourselves and other women is often only realized in gatherings such as the Women's Studies Network (UK) conference. We need to ensure that our research and teaching is always striving to create knowledges that not only are accessible to a feminist academic elite, but also speak of and to the great diversity of women's lives.

> We have chosen each other
> and the edge of each other's battles
> the war is the same
> if we lose
> someday women's blood will congeal
> upon a dead planet
> if we win
> there is no telling
> we seek beyond history
> for a new and more possible meeting.
> (Audre Lorde, 1984)

Notes

1 See for instance the work of Patricia Hill Collins, bell hooks, and Audre Lorde.
2 A good explication of this position is to be found in Stanley (1990).
3 By this, we mean that we would like to be part of developing a knowledge base which enables many voices to speak in different kinds of combinations.
4 See for instance Henriques *et al.* (1984).
5 See Harding (1987) and Stanley (1990).
6 For a summary of this work see Baxter (1988).
7 This is research in progress conducted by Bob Burgess, Head of the School of Graduate Studies, University of Warwick.
8 See, for instance, the article by Attille and Blackwood in Charlotte Brunsdon (Ed.) *Films for Women* and the film *Dreaming Rivers* (BFI 1988).
9 See for instance Audre Lorde and Cherril Clarke in Barbara Smith (1983).

References and Further Reading

ATTILLE, M. and BLACKWOOD, M. (1986) 'Black Women and Representation', in BRUNSDON, C. (Ed.) *Films for Women*, London, BFI.
AMOS, V. and PARMAR, P. (1984) 'Challenging Imperial Feminism', *Feminist Review*, 17.
BAXTER, C. (1988) *The Black Nurse: An Endangered Species*, Cambridge, Training in Health and Race.
BRUNSDON, C. (Ed.) (1986) *Films for Women*, British Film Institute.
CARBY, H. (1982) 'White Woman Listen! Black Feminism and the Boundaries of Sisterhood', in CENTRE FOR CONTEMPORARY CULTURAL STUDIES (Ed.) *The Empire Strikes Back*, London, Hutcheson.
CLARKE, C. (1983) 'The Failure to Transform: Homophobia in the Black Community', In SMITH, B. (Ed.) *Home Girls: A Black Feminist Anthology*, New York, Kitchen Table, Women of Color Press, pp. 197–209.
COLLINS, PATRICIA HILL (1990) *Black Feminist Thought: Knowledge, Consciousness and the Politics of Empowerment*, Boston and London, Unwin Hyman.
DAVIS, A. (1981) *Women, Race and Class*, London, Women's Press.
EDWARDS, R. (1990) 'Connecting Method and Epistemology: A White Woman Interviewing Black Women', *Women's Studies International Forum*, **13**, 5, pp. 477–90.
GILMAN, S.L. (1985) *Difference and Pathology: Stereotypes of Sexuality, Race, and Madness*, Ithaca and London, Cornell University Press.
HARDING, S. (1986) *The Science Question in Feminism*, Milton Keynes, Open University Press.
HARDING, S. (Ed.) (1987) *Feminism and Methodology: Social Science Issues*, Bloomington and Indianapolis, Indiana University Press/Milton Keynes, Open University Press.
HAWKESWORTH, M. (1989) 'Knowers, Knowing, Known: Feminist Theory and Claims of Truth', *Signs*, **14**, 3.
HENRIQUES, J., HOLLWAY, W., URWIN, C., VENN, C. and WALKERDINE, V. (1984) *Changing the Subject*, London, Methuen.
HOLLWAY, W. (1984) 'Gender Difference and the Production of Subjectivity' in HENRIQUES, J., HOLLWAY, W., URWIN, C., VENN, C. and WALKERDINE, V. *Changing the Subject*, London, Methuen.
HOOKS, B. (1991) *Yearning: Race, Gender and Cultural Politics*, London, Turnaround.
JORDAN, J. (1989) *Moving Towards Home: Political Essays*, London, Virago.
LORDE, A. (1984) *Sister Outsider: Essays and Speeches*, New York, Crossing Press.

REEVES, M. and HAMMOND, J. (1989) *Looking Beyond the Frame: Racism, Representation and Resistance*, Oxford, Links.

SMITH, B. (Ed.) (1983) *Home Girls: A Black Feminist Anthology*, New York, Kitchen Table, Women of Color Press.

SMITH, D.E. (1987) *The Everyday World as Problematic*, Milton Keynes, Open University Press.

STANLEY, L. (Ed.) (1990) *Feminist Praxis: Research, Theory and Epistemology in Feminist Sociology*, London, Routledge.

Chapter 7

'Backlash' in Historical Context

Sylvia Walby

Introduction

'Backlash' appears to be a recurring feature in the history of feminism. Feminist successes have often met, not only with resistance, but with renewed determination by patriarchal forces to maintain and increase the subordination of women. Gender politics includes not only the actions of women, but the reactions of men.

But is the form that backlash takes the same across different historical periods and different continents? Much recent feminist theory has emphasized the significance of diversity in women's experiences (Aaron and Walby, 1991; Barrett and Phillips, 1992; Begum, 1992; Brah, 1991; Spellman, 1988; Watt and Cook, 1991) and the difficulty of translation across historical periods (see Stanley, 1990). The postmodernist turn in feminist theory (Franklin, Lury and Stacey, 1991; Fraser and Nicholson, 1988) is modest in its claims, hesitating to generalize beyond a specific ethnic group or historical period, and focusing upon difference rather than commonality. However, this position sometimes underplays the significance of what can be learnt from the experiences of women in different times and cultures.

I shall address this question in the context of turn-of-the-century and contemporary feminism and compare the US and UK so as to illuminate our contemporary concern with 'backlash'. I shall argue that feminism does have a continuing tradition, varied across nation, ethnic group, social class, and time, but with enough commonalities to declare it a feminist tradition.

A second issue to be addressed is that of the conditions needed for women to be able to make effective political claims. Women have sometimes been criticized for political passivity and effectively blamed for their own oppression. This tends to underestimate the significance of patriarchal backlash, and the forms of men's oppositional and reactive patriarchal politics, especially in understanding the form and effectiveness of feminist movements (see Chafetz and Dworkin, 1987; Harrison, 1978; Kimmel, 1987; Walby, 1988). Chafetz and Dworkin (1987) note that feminism and other social movements have often been followed by a backlash; that the form, timing and extent of the backlash vary, according primarily to the strength and success of feminism; but that these will have a similar focus, namely the family. Kimmel (1987) however, suggests that there are different responses to the turn-of-the-century women's movement. So how do we understand backlash in historical context?

I will start with present concerns about backlash, then consider the backlash experiences of turn-of-the-century feminism. Finally I will return to the present, and consider differences between the US and the UK.

The Backlash

Faludi has written a well documented account of the contemporary form of backlash in the US (Faludi, 1991), which she has applied to the UK (Faludi, 1992). She argues that women in the UK and the US are seeing a reaction against the advances made by feminists in the last two decades. She suggests that backlash is not a new phenomenon, but that it occurs wherever feminists make advances.

One of the features of the contemporary backlash is that it works by reversal, in that the difficulties faced by women today are being falsely represented as the result of feminism. Feminism is blamed for the problems in women's lives. Faludi argues that in reality the problems are due to aspects of gender inequality which have not yet been removed. She provides many examples of the way the debate has been reversed, focusing primarily on those related to marriage and fertility. The following four examples are ones which Faludi herself headlines.

Firstly, there was a story about a man shortage in which a Harvard/Yale study was supposed to have shown that college-educated women were going to find it very difficult to marry if they delayed, as increasing numbers of women were in fact doing. They suggested they had statistical evidence that a college-educated unwed woman of 30 had a 20 per cent likelihood of marriage, at 35 a 5 per cent chance and at 40 1.3 per cent (Faludi, 1992, p. 21). This was not true, as was shown by later, more reliable studies and statistics, which the press did not publicize.

Secondly, there was the question of divorce, in particular of whether the new no-fault divorce laws hurt women. A piece of research by Weitzman (1985), then at Stanford, suggested that women suffered a decline of 73 per cent in their living standard on divorce, while men received a 42 per cent rise, and that the no-fault divorce laws had made it worse.

Faludi states that other studies show that these figures seriously exaggerated the decline in women's standard of living. Other larger sample surveys showed that after several years, rather than one year, women were better off after divorce. There were no actual data in Weitzman's book comparing the no-fault with fault-related divorce. Yet these criticisms of the thesis of the detrimental impact of divorce received little publicity.

Thirdly, there was the question of fertility decline. There was a story that fertility rates among women in their thirties were so low that women who were deferring having children were risking never having them — among women between 31 and 35, 39 per cent were claimed not to be able to conceive.

Again Faludi argues that the figures were unreliable, since the sample was very special and small. A larger study showed fertility was not a major problem with thirty-something women, but again this was not seriously reported. In fact younger women in their twenties were subject to a fall in fertility, largely due to diseases to which little attention had been given.

Fourthly, there were stories about burn-out. Women's mental health was alleged to be declining as a result of staying single and having stressful careers. In fact studies showed that single women had significantly better mental health than housewives who stayed home looking after children.

All these media stories suggested that women had better marry fast and early, stay married, have children early, rather than take high-powered jobs, if they wanted happy, fulfilled lives.

Faludi has hundreds of similar examples where the media picked up on poor academic studies to suggest that the change in the position of women was detrimental, whereas when better studies came to light to show that these findings were fallacious they were poorly reported. She continues with analyses of other media, including film, which she argues took a conservative turn in movies such as *Fatal Attraction*.

Faludi argues that this media distortion of research on gender and women is a backlash against feminism and the changes which feminism has wrought in women's lives. She states that they are trying to turn the clock back on women's advances.

I want to engage in a two-way comparison in order to assess Faludi's account, firstly by comparing the present with a backlash against an earlier feminist wave, and secondly by comparing Britain and the USA. In her section on earlier backlashes in the USA, and in the UK edition of her book, Faludi includes examples to parallel the US experience, thereby suggesting similarities. But are there also important differences?

Chafetz and Dworkin (1987) suggest that, although there are differences in the form of the backlash, depending largely on the strength of the feminist movement, there are no significant differences in content: 'The passage of nearly 100 years has apparently done little to change the ideological focus of the opponents of women's movements' (Chafetz and Dworkin, 1987, p. 52). Kimmel (1987), however, suggests that men's responses to turn-of-the-century feminism are diverse, including two quite different antagonistic stances. He suggests that there was an anti-feminist backlash, as evidenced in anti-suffrage organizations, such as the Man Suffrage Association and the Illinois Association Opposed to Women's Suffrage; as well as a masculinist reaction which did not see women as the enemy, but nevertheless opposed creeping cultural feminization, shown in organizations such as the Boy Scouts of America. He also identifies a third response among men, a pro-feminist response, which was less influential, instanced by the leaders of the newly opened women's colleges such as Matthew Vassar, the Socialist Party, and the sex radicals of Greenwich Village.

So there are disagreements here over whether the contemporary backlash is simply a repeat of previous examples of backlash. To explore this further I want to turn to examine why first-wave feminism ended, and the place of backlash in this.

Why Did First-Wave Feminism End?

A variety of reasons have been put forward as to why first-wave, or turn-of-the-century, feminism ended (if it did). I shall present three main reasons (with several sub-variants), then two versions of the argument that it did not in fact end.

They Were Successful

First-wave feminism ended because it achieved its objects. This view represents the movement as one in which the main goal was the winning of suffrage, with a secondary interest in equal rights, such as access to universities and to property rights. The majority of women in Britain won the vote in 1918, and the remainder of those between 21 and 30, and those without even minimal property, did so in 1928. At the end of the nineteenth century married women had won the right to possess property, and women had gained the right of entry to some universities; many other legal barriers were removed in the 1919 Sex Disqualification Removal Act (for instance, women were to be allowed to sit on juries). Hence it could be argued that turn-of-the-century feminism ceased because it had achieved its main aims.

This is probably the dominant historical interpretation of turn-of-the-century feminism. The problem with this account is that the demands of first-wave feminism were not in fact so narrow, and while these and indeed many other demands had been won by 1918, many had not. For instance, women had not obtained equal access to employment, equal pay, or freedom from men's violence and sexual abuse (Butler, 1896; Strachey, 1978).

Blame the Feminists

Failure of Internal Organization
While initially turn-of-the-century feminism was a broad movement with varied aims, by the early twentieth century it had narrowed down its goals, prioritizing suffrage. So when this was achieved, they had serious organizational difficulties in reorienting to the new circumstances, and failed: for

instance, the old suffrage organizations changed into new ones. The main suffrage organization in Britain, the National Union of Women's Suffrage Societies, became the National Union of Societies for Equal Citizenship in 1919, and then the Townswomen's Guilds. In the US a similar transformation occurred. In each case the new organization chose to focus on education rather than campaigning. They lost political focus and momentum, and ceased to be recognizably feminist organizations.

This view blames the feminists for bad political organization and strategy.

Internal Divisions Destroyed Them

Women split over different opinions on war and peace. This argument is also related to the issue of priorities and organizational form, but focuses on divisions. The women's movement split very badly over the Great War of 1914–18. One grouping, including some of the suffragettes with Christabel and Emmeline Pankhurst, supported the war as an essential patriotic event, and argued for the cessation of suffrage activities for its duration. Another group, including the socialist-oriented Sylvia Pankhurst, opposed the war and argued for pacifism. A large and effective women's peace movement was established (Wiltshire, 1985), but this split the feminist voice, and it was difficult to reconstitute some of the groupings and momentum after the war.

It is clear that this was a problem. However, it should not be over-stated. It is another version of the 'blame the feminists' argument.

They Were Co-Opted

Some women did acquire leadership positions in the early twentieth century, for instance as Members of Parliament and trade union leaders. Were these women simply co-opted by the dominant male structures? For instance, we see a series of amalgamations of women's trade unions with men's trade unions in the 1920s and 1930s. These might be regarded as strengthening women, since they acquired access to the reserves of the richer male unions, but they also involved the loss of autonomy of the women's unions and the loss of the voice of women trade union leaders on the national stage.

Instead of seeing this as a process of co-option, we should see this period as one in which the segregationist strategy of organized male labour was replaced by one in which women were included, but segregated. The worst of the exclusionary practices were prevented by these amalgamations, but at a price. This constituted a major shift in patriarchal strategy, so that it was no longer in direct confrontation with the feminist strategies, but developing new forms of subordination of women. It is unreasonable to blame the feminists of that period for insufficiently realizing the significance of these manoeuvres.

These last three explanations are variants of the theme of blaming women for the misfortunes that befall them. Greater attention needs to be placed on the next one — backlash.

Sylvia Walby

Backlash

They Were Smashed

The turn-of-the-century women's movement was smashed by the repressive powers of the state. The militant phase of the suffrage movement, which entailed actions such as the simultaneous smashing of all the windows in Regent Street, the burning of pillar boxes and the burning of 'votes for women' into golf courses, as well as more self-sacrificial gestures such as chaining themselves to the gates of Buckingham Palace, met with strong state repression. Demonstrations were broken up with police violence (Morrell, 1981); mob violence against suffrage demonstrators was not prevented; suffrage activists were imprisoned and, when they went on hunger strike, forcibly fed. When close to death they were let out only until they were well enough to be re-incarcerated under the notorious Cat and Mouse Act. This view maintains that the repressive power of the state was successful in deterring a reintroduction of the guerilla tactics of the militant suffragists after the war. These tactics had been essential in raising the profile of the movement, even though the majority of women in the movement did not engage in them.

Feminists Were Undermined by a Shift in Sexual Discourse

The second version of this argument focuses on the shift in sexual discourse which led to the portrayal of the husband-free women of the suffrage movement as unnatural because they did not engage in sex with men (Faderman, 1981; Jeffreys, 1985; Millett, 1977). 'Experts' on sexuality, such as Freud, introduced new ideas and norms about appropriate sexual conduct. The Freudianization of the understanding of sexuality made heterosexual sex appear to be necessary for a healthy life-style. Thus as women won demands on a political level, they were faced with increasing pressures to marry and engage with men at a sexual level, and this undercut the independence which women had been developing.

This argument accurately describes a change in sexual discourse. However, this new discourse also included some new freedoms and spaces for women to make demands within heterosexual relations, especially around the control of fertility.

These attempts variously explain the end of first-wave feminism as a vibrant political force: feminists were successful ushering in a postfeminist era; they made strategic and organizational mistakes; they met backlash. These explanations all engage with something significant, but I think the importance of backlash is underestimated in most historical accounts (except of course those which focus on it, such as that by Jeffreys). Turn-of-the-century feminism met an enormous backlash, both very directly in the repressive power of the state, and, only slightly less directly, in the cultural attack on the life-style and sexual identities of women not attached to men. There were attempts to incorporate women, especially at the level of the labour movement, and internal divisions led to organizational splintering, for example as a result of their differences over the First World War. But feminists did have enormous successes.

The historical accounts have tended to play down the significance of patriarchal opposition to feminism, preferring to blame women, for instance, for not getting their organization together.

They Continued

A very different interpretation is that first-wave feminism did not end in 1918, or even 1928, but has been a continuing force, as evidenced by numerous ensuing campaigns to improve women's position. Women have argued for health care, especially for mothers and children. Women have fought for access to contraception and abortion. Women continued to fight for school meals for children, for free school milk. We have campaigned for the same grounds for divorce as men, and for easier grounds for divorce. The political actions of women were crucial in building the foundations of what we used to call the welfare state. The welfare state was not an achievement of an ungendered labour movement, represented as a male labour movement, but an alliance between feminism and the labour movement (see Banks, 1981; Middleton, 1978; Spender, 1984).

Something Continued, But It Was Not Feminist

While it is now clear that political activity by women did continue throughout the period between 1920 and 1968, which is the conventional gap, many of these women did not call themselves feminist. For instance, most of the women trade unionists who fought for equal pay did not do so. Does this mean that this self-identification takes priority, so that they are lost to our feminist heritage? I am happy to appropriate such women, for example, those women civil servants who won equal pay in the 1950s, as feminists.

So am I saying that the backlash was unsuccessful, that feminism continued despite it? The answer is both yes and no. Feminism did continue, but backlash changed the way that women organized and described themselves, and the campaigns which could more easily continue.

Today, there are still women who say 'I am not a feminist but . . .' and then say and do things which we would usually identify as feminist. So feminism is not dead, even if the word is out of fashion in some quarters. In some ways it has become so commonplace that demands that were once considered radical and feminist now are not described as feminist. Who would now call someone who believes in equal pay a feminist? — yet as recently as 1975 this was not law and was controversial. Like the first-wave feminists, we should beware of underestimating both our achievements and the opposition.

But is the backlash the same? Are Faludi and Chafetz and Dworkin right to suggest that there was a common focus on pushing women back into marriage? While this theme is clearly present, I think this argument over-simplifies the situation. In particular, it underestimates the significance of attempts to allow women into the public sphere, while subordinating them there, especially in relation to employment.

Changes in the Form

I will now compare the form of the opposition in the contemporary US and UK. The current opposition to feminism is complex. I think there are some features in the contemporary opposition which are misunderstood because the notion of forward and backward for women is insufficiently theorized. And there is the question of whether Faludi has sufficiently grasped the specificity of the European configuration of gender relations in general and the new Right in particular.

Faludi suggests that the push backwards is on women to go back to the home, to be fertile, and to raise babies, to look after husbands, to marry and stay married. I agree that this is problematic, but it is not the only way in which patriarchal oppression can be intensified. There has been a regrouping of the patriarchal forces which oppose feminist successes in reducing gender inequality. The metaphor of 'backlash', and Faludi's analysis, tend to suggest simply back and forth, which is insufficient to catch the changes which are actually going on. Partly, it is a question of UK/US differences; partly, her account is just too simple. For example, the resurgence of the Right in the UK is different from that in the US.

In Britain over the 1980s we have, like the US, seen a conservative government in power. There have been some similar concerns relating to sexuality and fertility, such as attempts to restrict abortion and attempts to restrict homosexual expression via Clause 28 (see Franklin, Lury and Stacey, 1991). There have also been fundamentalist developments in some religious groupings (Sahgal and Yuval-Davis, 1992). But these developments have so far been much weaker and less successful than in the US. Pushing women back into the home has not been a major feature of governments in the UK. During this period women's participation in paid work has dramatically increased (though women's wage rates have not); the divorce rate and unmarried motherhood has soared, dramatically changing household structure, so that women live with children without men much more frequently. This is not a case of women simply being pushed back into the home. But nor is it simply progress, since the wages gap has not diminished, and female-headed households are typically very poor. This situation actually increases certain dimensions of women's autonomy, removes certain forms of control. The major attack on women, both economically and socially, has come as a consequence of pushing back the welfare state (see Lister, 1987).

Thatcherism, and now Majorism, is best seen not as representing a 'turn the clock back' type of backlash, but rather as pursuing a project of public patriarchy, rather than private. Women are not pushed back into the private, but the move into the public, which is no longer blocked as much as it used to be, is a move into other forms of subordination — such as low wages (see Walby, 1990). We need to be able to distinguish between the different forms of patriarchal systems, rather than conflate them all into a monolithic model.

We have also seen increasing divisions between women in these forms of patriarchal pressure, with an exacerbation of class and 'race' inequalities. For instance, the relatively constant wages gap hides a polarization in women's wages between those few, younger, highly educated women who are gaining entry to the professions and well-paid occupations on the one hand, and older women, with fewer skills recognized by the labour market, who take the very badly paid, insecure part-time jobs, as they re-enter the labour market after a period of full-time child and husband care. Class relations between women in the form of the differential access to well-paid, service-class occupations on the one hand and badly paid, part-time jobs on the other, have shifted. But crucial to understanding this is the change in the form of patriarchal relations: from private to public patriarchy. This was also true of turn-of-the-century feminism.

Conclusions

What are the implications for Women's Studies? The previous historical back-lashes need to be understood, not denied. Feminism was attacked, and that is one reason it lost momentum and went underground in the period between 1920 and 1968. But it was not defeated. Many accounts of the demise of turn-of-the-century feminism blame feminists for making mistakes which led to its demise — bad organization, internal division, selling out, wrong goals etc.

I think this seriously underestimates the historical significance of the backlash phenomenon, then and now. We need to understand it, and the nuances of its form, not just the 'turn the clock back' variety. In order to defeat it, feminist scholarship is crucial. The history of change in gender relations is not one of simple progress, nor one of stasis, but of a complex interrelationship between a variety of feminist and patriarchal forces.

We need to understand how patriarchal relations can be changed in form as well as in degree. The distinction between private and public patriarchy is important here. Private patriarchy is based upon household production as the main site of women's oppression, where the husband or father is the main oppressor of the woman. In public patriarchy women are not confined to the household and the mode of expropriation is more collective than individual, for instance, by most women being paid less than men. In private patriarchy the main patriarchal strategy is exclusionary, and women are not allowed into certain social arenas, such as Parliament, while in public patriarchy women are allowed in, but segregated and subordinated there. The change from private to public patriarchy was a result of both first-wave feminism and the expansion of the capitalist economy.

Faludi's book is a model of careful sifting of evidence. It is based on an accumulation of feminist scholarship which has been carried out over the last decade in the Academy. This enables us to assess the media's claims and engage in a scholarly refutation. Feminists have a base in the Academy, albeit a restricted one. It is time to come out of the margins, to assert our scholarship in the mainstream domains of academia, the media and society.

References

AARON, JANE and WALBY, SYLVIA (Eds) (1991) *Out of the Margins: Women's Studies in the Nineties*, London, Falmer Press.

BANKS, OLIVE (1981) *Faces of Feminism: A Study of Feminism as a Social Movement*, Oxford, Martin Robertson.

BARRETT, MICHELE and PHILLIPS, ANNE (Eds) (1992) *Destabilizing Theory: Contemporary Feminist Debates*, Cambridge, Polity Press.

BEGUM, NASA (1992) 'Disabled Women and the Feminist Agenda', in HINDS, HILARY, PHOENIX, ANN and STACEY, JACKIE (Eds) *Working Out: New Directions for Women's Studies*, London, Falmer Press.

BRAH, AVTAR (1991) 'Questions of Difference and International Feminism', in AARON, JANE and WALBY, SYLVIA (Eds) *Out of the Margins: Women's Studies in the Nineties*, London, Falmer Press.

BUTLER, JOSEPHINE (1896) *Personal Reminiscences of a Great Crusade*, London, Horace Marshall and Son.

CHAFETZ, JANET SALTZMAN and DWORKIN, ANTHONY GARY (1987) 'In the Face of Threat: Organised Antifeminism in Comparative Perspective', *Gender and Society*, **1**, 1 (March), pp. 33–60.

FADERMAN, LILLIAN (1981) *Surpassing the Love of Men: Romantic Friendship and Love Between Women from the Renaissance to the Present*, London, Junction Books.

FALUDI, SUSAN (1991) *Backlash: The Undeclared War Against American Women*, New York, Crown.

FALUDI, SUSAN (1992) *Backlash: The Undeclared War Against Women*, London, Chatto and Windus.

FRANKLIN, SARAH, LURY, CELIA and STACEY, JACKIE (Eds) (1991) *Off-Centre: Feminism and Cultural Studies*, London, Harper Collins.

FRASER, NANCY and NICHOLSON, LINDA (1988) 'Social Criticism Without Philosophy: An Encounter between Feminism and Postmodernism', *Theory, Culture and Society*, 5, pp. 373–94.

HARRISON, BRIAN (1978) *Separate Spheres: The Opposition to Women's Suffrage in Britain*, London, Croom Helm.

JEFFREYS, SHEILA (1985) *The Spinster and her Enemies: Feminism and Sexuality 1880–1930*, London, Pandora.

KIMMEL, MICHAEL S. (1987) 'Men's Responses to Feminism at the Turn of the Century', *Gender and Society*, **1**, 3, pp. 261–83.

LEWENHAK, SHEILA (1977) *Women and Trade Unions: An Outline History of Women in the British Trade Union Movement*, London, Ernest Benn.

LISTER, RUTH (1987) 'Future Insecure: Women and Income Maintenance under a Third Tory Term', *Feminist Review*, 27 (Autumn), pp. 7–16.

MIDDLETON, LUCY (Ed.) (1978) *Women in the British Labour Movement*, London, Croom Helm.

MILLETT, KATE (1977) *Sexual Politics*, London, Virago.

MORRELL, CAROLINE (1981) *'Black Friday' and Violence against Women in the Suffragette Movement*, London, Women's Research and Resources Centre.

SAHGAL, GITA and YUVAL-DAVIS, NIRA (Eds) (1992) *Refusing Holy Orders: Women and Fundamentalism in Britain*, London, Virago.

SOLDON, NORBERT (1978) *Women in British Trade Unions 1874–1976*, Dublin, Gill and Macmillan.

SPELLMAN, ELIZABETH (1988) *Inessential Woman: Problems of Exclusion in Feminist Thought*, Boston, Beacon Press.

SPENDER, DALE (1983) *Women of Ideas and What Men Have Done To Them*, London, Ark.

SPENDER, DALE (1984) *There's Always Been a Women's Movement This Century*, London, Routledge.

STANLEY, LIZ (Ed.) (1990) *Feminist Praxis: Research Theory and Epistemology in Feminist Sociology*, London, Routledge, pp. 113–22.

STRACHEY, RAY (1978) *The Cause: A Short History of the Women's Movement in Great Britain*, London, Virago (originally published 1928 by Bell and Sons Ltd).

WALBY, SYLVIA (1986) *Patriarchy at Work: Patriarchal and Capitalist Relations in Employment*, Cambridge, Polity.

WALBY, SYLVIA (1988) 'Gender Politics and Social Theory', *Sociology*, **22**, 2 (May), pp. 215–32.

WALBY, SYLVIA (1990) *Theorising Patriarchy*, Oxford, Blackwell.

WALBY, SYLVIA (forthcoming) *A History of Feminist Thought*, London, Sage.

WATT, SHANTU and COOK, JULIET (1991) 'Racism: Whose Liberation? Implications for Women's Studies', in AARON, JANE and WALBY, SYLVIA (Eds) *Out of the Margins: Women's Studies in the Nineties*, London, Falmer Press.

WEITZMAN, LENORE (1985) *The Divorce Revolution: The Unexpected Social and Economic Consequences for Women and Children in America*, New York, Free Press.

WILTSHIRE, ANNE (1985) *Most Dangerous Women: Feminist Peace Campaigners of the Great War*, London, Pandora.

Section III

Feminist Research and Education

Chapter 8

Researching Adolescent Girls' Perceptions of Unwanted Sexual Attention

Carrie Herbert

This paper describes the composite nature of the research methodology I used to gather data on the sexual harassment of girls in schools.[1] Probably as a direct consequence of the particular methodology, the focus of the data changed and instead of my receiving information about incidents of sexual harassment perpetrated by male teachers within a mixed school, incidents of sexual assault and other unwanted sexual attention from men outside the school were presented to me by the girls in my study. However, I shall start at the beginning and describe how I set up the original research process, followed by a description of the actual data collection period in the school, and conclude with some analysis on a revised methodology appropriate for researchers committed to a feminist-oriented approach.

Stage One: Setting Up the Research

Before I even set foot in the research site I anticipated that it was going to be a difficult topic to study, for a number of reasons. Firstly, sexual harassment is often mislabelled, people variously describing it as behaviour which is flattering, humorous, unimportant, fanciful, friendly, provoked or, indeed, just normal male behaviour. Secondly, sexual harassment was likely to be a new concept for girls of between 14 and 16, given that the year was 1986. Thirdly, talking about sexual harassment could well have proved to be embarrassing and therefore difficult for the girls, and perhaps be seen as a betrayal of their male teachers.

Because of these problems it was necessary to construct a specific methodology, which would have, on the one hand, elements of sensitive, supportive, slow, careful, and unfolding communications, whilst selectively challenging and confronting what are regarded as 'normal' interpretations. On the other hand, it was important that the method of collecting data be respectable, rigorous, valid, and acceptable to the academic community.

There were four possible sympathetic research methodologies from which I could take relevant strategies: traditional ethnography (Lacey, 1970; Ball, 1981); action research (Kemmis and McTaggart, 1982); democratic research (MacDonald and Walker, 1974); and research conducted by feminists (Mies, 1983; Oakley, 1981).

Traditional ethnography provided the academic respectability, rigour and validity necessary for the research project and to these ends I utilized participant observation techniques and diary writing.

Action research offered negotiation and collaborative decision-making as well as aiming to educate the participants.

The democratic research process, a style designed to research sensitive political issues, explored more thoroughly the process of negotiation. In particular it explored negotiation in a variety of ways: access to the site, meanings, transcripts, and written final reports. As with action research there was an element of education in helping the participants to understand the politics of their situation.

However, the research style which more clearly and comprehensively covered all the above processes, strategies and data collecting methods is that devised, implemented and used by feminists and it is this method of data collection that I found the most relevant to my research topic.

Research Conducted by Feminists

In order to develop a feminist-oriented research method, a researcher aware of feminist politics was needed, argued Mies (1983). She suggested that members of subordinate groups were in a better position to appreciate fully the everyday reality of oppression, a quality that members of the superordinate group lacked (see MacLeod and Saraga, 1988).

Working with children entailed the same sort of problems, for these could be seen as an 'exploited group' too. This difficulty was described by Okely (1978, p. 111), who argued that age and the concomitant features of limited experience and immature language command could also inhibit data collection.

Mies (1983), who had worked in Cologne with a group of battered women, drew up a list of principles for conducting research. It was these which gave me a lead. They included: raising women's consciousness; implementing an egalitarian, non-hierarchical research process; establishing an ongoing self-supported group; using other women's research and information to locate the project in a wider context of feminist and female-oriented work; encouraging participation at all levels to eradicate partiality; ensuring that the research served the interests of the oppressed, incorporating women-centred research methods for interviewing and recording; choosing research topics which were immediate and useful; developing a political awareness in the participants and for the oppressed, where possible, to carry out the research themselves; and for the researcher, if possible, to use her relative power as a scholar and take up issues which were central to the Women's Movement. These principles contained strategies that I could utilize in my project.

But I found that there were problems and concerns with research conducted by feminists which I should like to discuss briefly. First was the process of 'consciousness-raising'. Whilst this technique had been successfully used by other feminist researchers such as Farley (1978) in her research on working women and Oakley (1981) on pregnant women, I was working with a very different group of participants. I was intending to research girls with little experience either of the world or of other research projects. Was it possible or desirable to organize a consciousness-raising group for 15-year-olds involved in an imposed research topic, meeting on a weekly basis in school time, with members drawn from across a year's intake so that in all likelihood they would be mutually relative strangers, in a environment hostile to sharing honest and personal disclosures?

A second problem that I envisaged was the differences between the girls and myself. For Farley the findings of the research, whether strategic or political, had emerged from people in an exploratory mode. Although I was 'exploring' the girls' perceptions of sexual harassment, I was not exploring the area of sexual harassment *per se*, for I knew what I wanted to document. The girls did not, and were in a politically vulnerable position, while I, as the researcher, could be open to charges of manipulation, promoting propaganda and contamination.

Ultimately I felt that whilst research inspired by feminists was not exactly right either, there were modifications I could use to counter the difficulties.

In order to allow the girls the opportunity to talk about their accounts of sexual harassment by teachers, I realized that further facilities were necessary. Privacy, anonymity, time, space, individual attention, questions both asked and answered, support, with accessibility to all these at the girl's discretion, were essential. I therefore looked carefully at the way in which interviews would take place. 'Interviewing' was a classic way of gathering data, but it was also an appropriate way of providing a 'safe' and 'private' place for in-depth discussions (see also Herbert, 1989).

Briefly, I would say that it is my belief, and this research supported that belief, that reciprocity is a crucial component of interviews that concern the intimate life of the interviewee. Thus, as I was prepared to answer questions, share incidents covering a wide range of experiences in my past, discuss in a genuine way issues of sex, sexuality, boyfriends and relationships, there grew up between us a close and trusting friendship. It is true to say that I told the girls things that I hadn't discussed with anyone before, and things that I wouldn't have wanted transmitted to any others. The underlying principle to which I subscribed (Oakley, 1981, p. 49) was 'no intimacy without reciprocity'.

Stage Two: The Nine-Month Research Process

I shall describe the first six months, from January to June, only very briefly because, apart from negotiating access and setting up the research, not much happened during that period, with the exception of the girls and myself building relationships of varying strengths and intensities. I will therefore concentrate on the second part of the research process from September through to December.

January to June 1986

I came upon the school by accident, at a conference where I met the Head. He was interested in my research proposal and asked me to send him details. I met with some of his staff; we discussed various points like confidentiality, and I was in. The Head asked the governors for their approval. It was given.

The school was a large mixed-sex, mixed-race comprehensive school in the heart of London. The students were drawn from a wide geographical area and included among their ranks Cockneys, students from both sides of the River Thames and as far west as Wembley and as far east as the Docklands. There was a large Bangladeshi population as well as children from numerous other cultural and religious backgrounds. There was a nominal school uniform to which most students adhered. The school was set on three different sites.

In the first week I wrote to all the teachers involved, explaining the project in more detail, how I wanted to work, and what their role would be (non-participating). The Head of Year informed all fourth-year girls that I was in school looking for volunteers to be involved in a study of 'women's issues'.

I had forty applicants whom I interviewed over a half-hour period, making my final choice on four criteria. First, girls who were aware of 'women's issues' were to be preferred as, I assumed, they would more quickly be able to provide the data for which I was looking. Second, I wanted girls who had more men than women teachers. Third, the group as a whole should be representative of the racial diversity in the school. Fourth, the girls and I had to get on.

Fifteen girls were asked if they would like to be involved. On their acceptance I sent a letter to their form tutors and the Headteacher wrote a letter to each girl's parents asking permission for their daughter's involvement.

A week later I began small group meetings with the selected girls. On average we met once a week and, whilst the first few were group building sessions, the later ones were concerned with issues such as women's roles, stereotyping, sexual relationships and job opportunities. In the introductory session I explained the concepts of confidentiality, anonymity, transcripts, data ownership, negotiation and accessibility. I also introduced the idea of keeping a diary.

The classroom observations began immediately. These ceased within six weeks because of the intolerable sexual harassment from the boys towards the girls and myself, the modified behaviour of the male teachers and of the girls when I was in the classroom, and the totally false environment that my presence seemed to create.

The small group meetings were supported by two types of interview: 'formal' and 'informal'. The first type could be initiated by either the girls or myself. If a girl asked to talk to me about a particular problem, a time was booked and the session was recorded and transcribed and the hard copy returned to the author. If I felt I hadn't seen a particular girl for some time, I would ask for an interview.

The second type of interview was the 'informal' and unplanned type, for the girls would arrive at my door and ask to have a 'chat'. Sometimes there was already a girl there, and they would either wait, or join in the discussion in hand. The topics covered in these 'informal' interviews ranged from homework to boyfriend and girlfriend concerns and to family issues. These were informal and not specifically related to the project and many were not recorded. In retrospect, this proved to be a mistake, for as the research developed it became clear that some of these 'informal' chats, which were a crucial process in building relationships, were signalling the future disclosures which ultimately became the concern of the research. At the time, however, my focus was school-based sexual harassment, and personal problems at home were not, I thought, relevant.

These interviews were extremely important, and during them it was necessary for me to take a number of roles. Sometimes I was confidante, sometimes friend, sometimes parent figure, sometimes student like them with little power in the school, sometimes teacher, as, for example, when I led the group discussions at the beginning of the project, and sometimes political figure, challenging their beliefs, for I was not a 'neutral' researcher. Sometimes, too, I was seemingly interviewee, as the girls asked me questions.

In one of the initial interviews I was asked whether I was a feminist. When I answered 'yes', Collette said in a way that sounded conspiratorial, 'right, what do you want to know?' Approximately three weeks later when my role was that of a 'researcher', I asked her to clarify the incident for me. What had she thought at the time? Had my answer to her question affected her response? I felt it was important to reflect on past interviews with the girls in order to find out how they thought the project was going, and to make sure that we were understanding each other, or in Elliott's words, 'negotiating meaning' (1980).

Carrie:	Do you remember that first morning you walked in here and you said to me, well do you remember what you said to me?
Collette:	Are you a feminist?
Carrie:	And what did I say?

Collette: . . . Yes.
Carrie: Then what did you say?
Collette: I said 'So am I'. You see at that point I felt comfortable.
Carrie: If I had said 'no', what would your response have been?
Collette: Then why are you doing this [research]?
Carrie: If I had said, 'Well that's an interesting question but I am here to ask you questions', what would you have said?
Collette: 'Oh bloody hell, I ask her a question, what are we here for?' I would have felt 'Oh this is really it, she's looking down on me'. She's saying 'oh yes, this is a very interesting question', but she is evading it. I would have thought that straight away, because here I'm giving you a chance to form a relationship, because I am walking in and asking you a question. I'm not walking in, sitting down, and [just] saying 'yes', I'm giving you a chance.

Another important incident happened in one of the early interviews. One of the girls, Carmel, made some racist comments and told me that the men who committed rape were all black, because all black people had an anger towards white men and their way of retribution was to rape white women. At this point I had some choices. Either I ignored this racism; or I used what Oakley (1981, p. 38) called the 'quasi-psychoanalytic' tactic: 'ah, tell me more, that is interesting'; or else I confronted it and told Carmel some facts about rape and rapists. It was the third choice I made as the interview transcript demonstrates.

Carrie: Can I tell you a few facts about rape. I am not disputing that there are some black men who feel that way, but the majority of rapists are white men, some married, perfectly sane, quite normal, and the majority of people who are raped, something like 80 per cent are known either well or . . .
Carmel [interrupting]: family, that kind of thing?
Carrie [continuing]: . . . casually by the rapist. So only 20 per cent of rapes happen in the streets, in dark alleys . . .
Carmel: Listen, if I am a multi-millionaire do you think I am scared of being raped? Do you think that would be my main worry? Do you think I am going to walk down an alley, do you think I am not going to take a car?
Carrie: But you can still be raped if you are a female millionaire . . . you may get raped by your chauffeur.
Carmel [Begins talking about her childhood and how she used to take a taxi to school; suddenly says]: I never had to sit down and think, 'what will happen if I get raped?', because

> it was totally unlikely. But I will tell you that in that kind
> of condition [*sic*], to get sexually abused is very likely.
Carrie: By whom?
Carmel: By cousins and that. I think it happened to me, I am not
> sure. I think I got sexually abused as such, and I think it's
> going to affect my life.

This disclosure, I argue, was as a result of the challenge that I made to Carmel's misconceptions about the relationship between rapist and women. The link that rapists 'knew' their 'victim' in many attacks gave her the necessary information to connect and name an incident in her life. Intervention in this situation was a powerful tool to unlocking experience and memories.

The methods that I had chosen to use had been expected to generate data on sexual harassment from male teachers directed at girls. However, no data of this nature were forthcoming. I asked myself why? I was convinced from my experience as a teacher and by writers such as Mahony (1985) that this phenomenon did occur in schools, so I assumed that this school was no exception, yet I was unable to 'see' it and, further, despite the conversations we had had, both public and private, the girls were not 'seeing' it either. As the term progressed I realized that the school was more comprehending of the importance of gender issues than I had anticipated. However, I was also aware that the principles of open and overt data collection to which I had adhered had created false and unrealistic tensions in the classrooms. As the term began to draw to an end I reflected on the progress of the research. The research was sterile in terms of information on sexually harassing behaviour, but was productive in terms of my developing close personal relationships with most of the girls who were already beginning to reveal experiences which I had not anticipated.

The second period of data collection was extremely rich, whilst of a kind I neither encouraged nor desired. It happened as a result of two similar incidents which were viewed totally differently by the research group girls.

The first incident involved two students, a girl, who did not speak English very well, and a boy, neither of whom were in the research project. During a field trip the boy asked the girl if he could 'fuck' her. She, not understanding the word, had said 'yes'. When, the next day he told her to lie down in the grass, she realized what he was going to do and said 'No'. He was very angry and told her that she was a slag for saying she would in the first place and that he would tell everyone that her intentions had initially been positive. She stayed away from school for eight days and on her return she talked to one of the girls in my group who brought her to see me.

The incident was quite protracted but, in brief, the girls in the research project sided with the boy, called Maria a slag, tart and slut and made it clear to me that they believed she had deliberately set out to get Rani into trouble. No matter what I said about Maria, about women's sexual worth and status being defined by men, about there being double standards applicable for girls and boys, about sexual harassment, they remained adamant (see McRobbie, 1991, pp. 151–2). Maria was the problem, Rani had been a scapegoat.

We still hadn't really resolved this problem when the end of the term came. I was thankful it was over for six weeks. In my opinion, my research project was not going well. I had collected no data on sexual harassment of girls by male teachers and the only example of sexual harassment at all, by a boy towards a girl, not in the research, had shown that the girls really did not understand the concept of sexual harassment and still retained many of the stereotyped views about men's and women's attitudes towards sexuality.

What had begun to happen, however, was that my time was being used in a different way from that which I had originally planned. The 'Maria' incident had led to a variety of people wanting to talk about and solve this problem as well as the girls wanting to discuss their own concerns. But gradually a number of conversations developed in which the girls began to ask me some intimate questions about my life. I answered them all. At this stage the research room was constantly engaged with girls discussing a variety of topics, mostly to do with sexuality.

Autumn Term

The research programme was resumed in the second week of the autumn term with a group meeting followed by individual interviews. Two of the data collecting strategies, classroom observation and the girls' diary writing, had been abandoned, the latter owing to their unwillingness to cooperate, possibly due to their poor writing skills. I asked the girls at the first meeting what other activities would help produce data. A suggestion was made that we should go away for a few days together. They found the schedule at school inhibiting, and wanted an uninterrupted period to talk and discuss various issues. To these ends I organized a weekend in Essex.

In the meantime, two further incidents had the effect of dramatically facilitating the progress of the research. First, on 8 September, I was harassed in the local swimming pool and returned to school angry, feeling 'touched', and needing to talk about it. I told all the girls who came to see me that day. One of them was Collette, who said that a similar incident had happened to her. Her experience involved a boy two years older than her and someone she knew.[2]

The second incident, which had even more far-reaching consequences for the research project, was the attempted rape of Annmarie on 12 September, at six o'clock in the evening, as she took a short cut through an alley on her way home.

Much of the following day was spent talking with Annmarie and other girls in the group. All the girls were extremely supportive, radically different from how they had reacted with Maria.

At the end of that day another girl in the research, Alex, knocked on the office door. She told me that there were many rumours in the school as to what had happened to Annmarie, but that she had guessed. When I asked her how she had guessed she didn't answer my question, but said that Annmarie would 'never get over it'. I was surprised at the conversation, and asked why? Alex told me that she had been raped as a 10-year-old, that she hadn't spoken to anyone, that this man had been known to her (as a neighbour), and that he had attacked her. She had not told her mother or father because she had been crossing a waste piece of land near her home from which her parents had banned her. She felt it was her fault, and that her mother would be cross with her for disobeying her.

There were now five girls who had disclosed incidents of unwanted sexual attention: Carmel, Maria, Collette, Annmarie and Alex. A week later another girl, Jenny, was waiting in the library when I arrived in the morning. She told me that she had been attacked by two men in the underpass near school the previous week, and that they had forcibly held her, touched her and threatened to rape her. She had escaped by biting and kicking and had come to see me on both Thursday and Friday, but I was not in school. She had waited until Monday, and had told no-one else.

During September and October my time was spent talking with all the girls, mostly on a one-to-one basis, but sometimes in twos or threes. Sometimes I was asked to play a parent role and visit the hospital, the eye specialist, and other agencies with them. This I did. The other main activity was the group meetings, which provided a focus for the week as well as a management forum for keeping the girls up to date with various school events. By this time many of the girls were coming to see me regularly and therefore missing lessons, and problems were arising from various teachers. This issue was never adequately resolved, but flared up occasionally and was calmed down by my chatting individually with particular teachers. However, as the information the girls were giving me was confidential and sometimes traumatic for them, I did not hint that they were disclosing unwanted sexual experiences which they needed time to discuss in detail. Some were to do with the girls' experiences of being frightened by men. Zaheda had been and still was harassed by men on public transport, Chanel had been accosted by a man who asked questions and tried to take her hand and lead her away when she was a little girl, Linda had been chased by men in a car, and in addition to their own accounts they talked about other women and girls they knew who had been attacked or raped.

At the beginning of November the girls and I went to Essex. The most significant part of the weekend was the discussion on Saturday afternoon. A general conversation began about the kinds of unpleasant experiences we had all had with men. Sixteen incidents were discussed, initiated by Carmel who made public the sexual attack on her by her cousin, disclosed to me in April. The other nine girls described incidents which included men exposing themselves, masturbating in front of them, following them, chasing, propositioning, and asking for dates. One girl, Zohra, came to see me at the end of this meeting and asked if she could speak with me. She had visited me on a number of occasions in the previous six months and I knew her well and I knew her background. We had had many in-depth conversations, some of which had entailed me telling her intimate details of my own personal life, but here at Stansted Zohra told me how as a 4-year-old she had been given some money and taken by an old man up to a flat, where he had digitally raped her. The last disclosure came from Zaheda, also at Stansted, immediately after Zohra's talk with me. Zaheda told me that her brother, who was eight years older than her, had made her play with his genitals, when she was 5 or 6. Her older sister had refused, but Zaheda had not been able to.

Out of a total number of thirteen girls in the research group, seven had been sexually assaulted, and all the girls with the exception of Lucy and Ashley[3] had reported an unpleasant experience which had involved a man's, boy's or men's or boys' unwanted sexual advances.

The last few weeks of the research project, between returning from the weekend and Christmas, were spent in debriefing both the girls and myself. We had all become extremely close.

Stage Three: Conclusion

So far I have discussed and described what I intended to research, and how and why this changed. In conclusion I shall briefly sum up and make some observations about the process and the findings which may be of use to other researchers in developing an emancipatory/empowering research methodology based on feminist principles.

This research project was largely exploratory: the way forward at various points was one of closing one's eyes and jumping. At times I was in despair as to what to do next, as well as how to help particular girls at particular times. Sometimes I made the right decision, at other times I judged the situation badly.

The girls involved were clearly not a random sample. However, it must be remembered that this research did not claim to be representative or to be transferable to other groups in other settings: its aim was to study how a particular group of girls experienced, described and dealt with instances of sexual harassment from their male teachers. That this aim was not achieved was a consequence of the fact that I, as the researcher, was able to respond to the expressed needs of the participants and change my focus.

The data revealed that there were common practices which were perpetrated on young girls and then silenced and suppressed. This was mirrored in other work I have done on drawing corollaries between sexual abuse, Chinese footbinding, genital circumcision and child rape in Victorian England in the last century (Herbert, 1989). From my research it seems that sexual oppression is as prevalent today as it has been in other times and in other cultures.

I suggest that the data are unique owing directly to the methodology used. However, whilst the individual incidents which were disclosed, and the experiences both the girls and I had during the nine months' research project, cannot be repeated, it is unlikely that I stumbled across the only group of schoolgirls who have been sexually abused in such numbers. It is my contention that by using the same selection procedure, research methods and research principles, combined with political commitment and personal involvement, similar results would be obtained.

So what do the findings suggest? From data which show that eight out of thirteen girls disclosed at least one case of sexual abuse after, in some cases, years of silence, I draw two simple conclusions; the best and the worst. The 'worst' interpretation of these figures is that eight out of every thirteen girls has been sexually abused, or in other terms that 61.5 per cent of all 15-year-old girls have been sexually abused. The 'best' interpretation, however, is not much better. If these eight were the only girls in their cohort of sixty-four who were sexually abused, an incidence of approximately 12.5 per cent, this means that in every classroom of thirty-two students there could be two or three 15-year-old girls who have been sexually abused, but who have told no-one. This must warn us of the need for care when using statistics which use as their basis reported cases only. These will exclude this large and silent group of sexually abused children.

What implications does this have for education? This project provided the girls with facilities which could be reproduced within many school settings: feminist information; female-only discussions; daily support available; a private room away from the rest of the school; a close trusting relationship with an adult; time for the relationship to develop; freedom to ask questions based on reciprocity; and autonomy to determine the kind of relationship that develops. All these features enable girls to disclose incidents of sexual abuse and help them become autonomous and empowered (see also Herbert, 1992).

The findings from this research could play a significant part in the understanding of child abuse and in particular a new look at indicators used in diagnosis.

None of the research principles, processes and strategies were unique, in that all had been used before in other research projects. What is unique, however, is the way in which these particular methods, strategies and principles interacted. This methodology could be used in other studies. The research requirements it would demand are as follows:

- an overt and personal feminist commitment by the researcher to the participants and the research project;

- negotiated access to the research site with all those to be involved;

- research applicants *invited* to be involved;

- access to the researcher in the hands of the researched as far as possible;

- long periods of time to be made available for the research discussions to take place in private;

- the researcher to answer all questions asked by participants as openly and honestly as possible;

- decision-making to be shared by all concerned;

- priority to be given to participants' needs rather than data collection;

- information-giving sessions and group discussions which challenge the patriarchal world view to form a central part of the research;

- access and use of the data to be negotiated with the 'owner' of that data, i.e. the participants;

- a support network to be established both for the participants and the researcher;

- consideration be given to the ongoing 'empowerment' of and by the group once the project has finished.

Research projects which aim to uncover practices such as the sexual abuse of girls or sexual harassment may well adopt the practices described here. A researcher who is aware of the need for reciprocity, intimacy, self-disclosures, intervention, debate and democratic principles, coupled with a multi-faceted role of friend, counsellor, teacher, and confidant may be in a position to gather data from participants who think their experiences are embarrassing, humiliating, stigmatizing, unique and self-inflicted.

Patti Lather (1988, p. 7) argues that there is an enormous array of 'alternative ways of knowing' and that the focus has shifted 'from paradigms of prescription to paradigms of disclosure', and from 'are the data biased?' to 'whose interests are served in the bias?' This is what this research moved towards.

Notes

1 The research and findings described here are fully documented and are published in Herbert (1989).
2 The various attacks will be described but the details are edited out. Many of the girls' descriptions involved considerable intimacies. My decision as a researcher and feminist to withhold these details is taken on the following grounds: protection of the girls' identities; reduction of erotic material; and a belief that the details would add nothing of academic relevance to the thesis.
3 Lucy and Ashley did not attend the Stansted weekend.

References

ARDENER, S. (Ed.) (1975) *Perceiving Women*, London, Dent.

BALL, S.J. (1981) *Beachside Comprehensive: A Case-Study of Secondary Schooling*, Cambridge, Cambridge University Press.

BOWLES, G. and DUELLI KLEIN, R. (Eds) (1983) *Theories of Women's Studies*, London, Routledge and Kegan Paul.

ELLIOTT, J. (1980) 'Validating Case Studies', Paper presented at British Educational Research Conference, Cardiff, Wales, September.

FARLEY, L. (1978) *Sexual Shakedown: The Sexual Harassment of Women on the Job*, New York, Warner Books.

HERBERT, C.M.H. (1989) *Talking of Silence: The Sexual Harassment of Schoolgirls*, London, Falmer Press.

HERBERT, C.M.H. (1992) *Sexual Harassment in School: A Guide for Teachers*, London, David Fulton Publishers.

KEMMIS, S. and MCTAGGART, R. (1982) *The Action Research Planner*, Victoria, Australia, Deakin University Press.

LACEY, C. (1970) *Hightown Grammar*, Manchester, Manchester University Press.

LATHER P. (1988) 'Feminist Perspectives on Empowering Research Methodologies', *Women's Studies International Forum*, **11**, 6, pp. 569–81.

MACDONALD, B. and WALKER, R. (1974) *Safari: Innovation, Evaluation, Research and the Problem of Control: Some Interim Papers*, published jointly by Safari Project, CARE, University of East Anglia, Norwich, and Workshop Curriculum No. 1, Arbeitspapiere zu Problemen der Curriculumreform, Arbeitskreis Curriculum, Verlag Lothar Rotsch, 7401 Bebenhausen 45.

MACLEOD, M. and SARAGA, E. (1988) 'Challenging the Orthodoxy: Towards a Feminist Theory and Practice', *Feminist Review*, 28 (Spring).

MCROBBIE, A. (1991) *Feminism and Youth Culture: From 'Jackie' to 'Just Seventeen'*, Basingstoke, Macmillan.

MCROBBIE, A. and NAVA, M. (Eds) (1984) *Gender and Generation*, Basingstoke, Macmillan.

MAHONY, P. (1985) *Schools for the Boys? Coeducation Reassessed*, London, Hutchinson in association with The Explorations in Feminism Collective.

MIES, M. (1983) 'Towards a Methodology for Feminist Research,' in BOWLES, G. and DUELLI KLEIN, R. (Eds) *Theories of Women's Studies*, London, Routledge and Kegan Paul.

OAKLEY, A. (1981) 'Interviewing Women: a Contradiction in Terms', in ROBERTS, H. (Ed.) *Doing Feminist Research*, London, Routledge and Kegan Paul.

OKELY, J. (1978) 'Privileged, Schooled and Finished: Boarding Education for Girls', in ARDENER, S. (Ed.) *Defining Females: The Nature of Women in Society*, London, Croom Helm.

ROBERTS, H. (Ed.) (1981) *Doing Feminist Research*, London, Routledge and Kegan Paul.

Chapter 9

'And Gill Came Tumbling After': Gender, Emotion and a Research Dilemma

Gillian Reynolds

Jack and Jill went up the hill to fetch a pail of water,
Jack fell down and broke his crown, and Jill came tumbling after.
Up Jack got, and home did trot, as fast as he could caper,
To old Dame Dob, who patched his nob with vinegar and brown
   paper.
When Jill came in, how she did grin, to see Jack's paper plaster.
Her mother, vexed, did whip her next, for laughing at Jack's disaster.
Now Jack did laugh and Jill did cry, but her tears did soon abate,
Then Jill did say that they should play at see-saw across the gate.

This traditional version of the nursery rhyme (Opie and Opie, 1955, p. 42) begins with a joint task for man-as-boy and woman-as-girl. A mishap occurs, woman-as-girl is forgotten, woman-as-nurse tends man-as-boy's physical wounds, woman-as-mother avenges his emotional wounds, and woman-as-whore takes the initiative in the task of reconciliation.

But what did Jill do before she came home? Did she lie senseless at the foot of the hill? Did she return alone to the top of the hill to complete the task? Or did she follow Jack to Dame Dob, perhaps to be accused of not 'looking after' him?

This paper is essentially the autobiographical account of 'Gill', who juggles, simultaneously, the identities of woman-as-girl, woman-as-mother, woman-as-nurse, and woman-as-researcher. Following Sue Wilkinson (1986), I accord priority to my own experience in an examination of a methodological dilemma which has emerged during fieldwork for my doctoral thesis. The thesis itself investigates possible connections between the concepts of philanthropy and physical/sensory impairment, and some consequences in labour market practices. The multiple methods are mainly from a qualitative perspective, and include multiple interviews with a group of individuals who have found themselves classified as being 'disabled' in some way. The group comprises twenty men and ten women, all of whom are white European, aged between 20 and 65, and all living within a 30-mile radius of each other.

Bearing in mind Liz Stanley's argument that 'all knowledge is autobiographically-located in a particular social context of experiencing and knowing' (Stanley, 1990, p. 210), I begin with a brief autobiography. As a mature student, I discovered, through sociology, that the joy of learning lies in asking questions, and, together with my perceptual view of the world through a fluid synthesis of Christian, feminist, humanist and Marxian principles, this informs my research praxis. My social roles, embedded in my identities as daughter, wife, mother and grandmother, necessarily articulate with research praxis, and are significant in the subject matter of this paper.

Because my analysis is based on the interaction between one respondent and myself, it is important to have an outline biography of the respondent. This is not to pretend that my version is the only 'truthful' account of 'Jack': there are always other stories that could be told (Stainton Rogers, 1991, p. 11).

Jack has always lived in the same city, where he now has a council house on a large housing estate. Like several other male respondents in this research, he lives alone, has been divorced for some years, and has virtually no contact with his adult family. He has epilepsy, is not involved in paid employment, and is of the same age-group as me.

Having talked with Jack on two occasions in his home, my dilemma concerns whether I should cease to involve him in the research process, even though he has not, at any time, behaved in such a way as to give me *specific* cause to fear him. The three main issues which I face are:

1   my own anxiety in the interview interaction;

2   the debate concerning feminist research among men;

3   the wider social implications of a decision to continue my research contact with him.

The Methodology of the Research

In research in the field of impairment, it is important to avoid the 'alienating' methods (Oliver, 1992, p. 103) of those who perceived the impairment as *the* research problem. Mike Oliver (1990), among others, argues for a definition of disablement which focuses firmly upon social creation and construction, rather than on individual 'in-abilities'. It is therefore necessary to enable respondents to define themselves, their own identity, and their own life-situation. Jenny Morris states that

> Disabled people — men and women — have little opportunity to portray our own experiences within the general culture — or within radical political movements. Our experience is isolated, individualized; the definitions which society places on us centre on judgments of individual capacities and personalities. This lack of a voice, of the representation of our subjective reality, means that it is difficult for non-disabled feminists to incorporate our reality into their research, their theories, unless it is in terms of the way the non-disabled world sees us. (Morris, 1992, p. 161)

This ethic of enablement and empowerment also accords with the principle that, in all research, a power imbalance exists, in favour of the researcher (Stanley and Wise, 1983). Others (Smart, 1984; McKee and O'Brien, 1983) have problematized this foundational idea by suggesting that, at the time of the interview, power is weighted in favour of men.

In my research, the 'picture' of power is further complicated by the growing body of academic discourse which conceptualizes disabled people as sharing a structural experience of oppression with women, people of ethnic minority background, and gay and lesbian people. As a consequence, where the research subjects are white European disabled men, a typology is presented of people who hold contradictory social locations. As a researcher and a woman, I am also located in a contradictory way. Thus, the fundamental philosophy of my methodology (that of empowerment to define) has necessarily focused upon related, and often competing, contradictions.

Underpinning this philosophy, however, lies an assumption that we all have a reasonably rational and articulated perception of our own identity. Mostly, that is borne out empirically, but Jack seems to be different. Although, as Anne Opie (1992) says, focusing attention on difference can be a way of representing social realities more fully, a consequence of the methodological removal of disablement as *the* research problem is that other issues, such as gender, are 'freed up'. This can mean that a non-disabled researcher must face conflict within herself, which arises from previously-held assumptions of impairment as 'personal tragedy' (Oliver, 1990).

Issue 1: Interaction in the Interviews

I did not feel comfortable with Jack in the interview situation, and was puzzled when the first transcript revealed no firm foundation for my feelings in the textual language. By the time the second session was due, I suspected that the cause of my anxiety lay in my own imagination. However, my sheer relief at finishing the second interview was evident in my tape-recorded comment afterwards, that 'I found this a really scary experience', even though Jack's overt behaviour was almost more than 'proper'.

Again, the transcript revealed no immediate rational basis for my anxiety. Conceptualizing anxiety as a generalized emotional state, David Berg and Kenwyn Smith comment that it is

> not the only emotion that attends social research and it may not be the most frequently experienced, but it is arguably the most troublesome. . . . Unlike some emotional reactions to research relationships, anxiety often provides its own veil . . . that is neither transparent enough to allow easy access nor opaque enough to allow easy dismissal. (Berg and Smith, 1988, p. 215)

Berg and Smith perceive research relationships as having the capacity to produce anxiety on any of three levels for the researcher. Personal anxiety involves a perceived threat to psychological identity; professional anxiety arises in response to perceived threats to the research; group-level anxiety results from the emotional dynamics of a research team.

Having expressed such strong sentiments immediately following the second session with Jack, I began a more in-depth analysis of the transcripts, and more importantly the field notes, of both sessions. This exercise suggested various themes connected with content and language, management of emotion, and control of the interaction.

The content of the interviews frequently alluded to Jack's own acts of physical and verbal violence towards all his neighbours, which he refused, or was unable, to explain, justify, or censure. He would only say that he didn't understand, couldn't explain, didn't know. Issues of sexuality also arose, couched in the context of the cause of his epilepsy: although he used deeply ambiguous language, I understood him to mean that it was caused by too much masturbation.

My already-heightened state of anxiety discouraged me from asking for clarification of his meaning. Gender had become a priority in my perception of our interaction. I was engrossed in the management of emotion — my own lack of ease — and was perhaps looking for explanatory 'signposts' from Jack before making any comment that could be misconstrued. At the same time, I was also hampered by my own research ethics, which precluded me from establishing my own definition of Jack's behaviour. Dale Spender (1980), and Carol Smart (1984) claim that women operate as facilitators to the speech of men, not interrupting, but encouraging the continuation of their talking. Smart comments that 'on this basis I wish to argue that the job of interviewing is intrinsically *feminine* because the interviewer's job is to facilitate speech and not to interupt it' (Smart, 1984, p. 155; original emphasis). Carol Warren (1988), claiming that it is almost a truism of research that women achieve rapport more easily than men with their respondents because of their better communication skills, suggests that women may also be more reluctant to publicly acknowledge personal dilemmas in this area, because of possible consequences to future careers.

Carol Smart, on other hand, suggests that dilemmas produce a sense of frustration on the part of the feminist interviewer, because, in her reluctance (because of the research context) to express alternative views, she 'reconfirms the typical model of the male/female verbal exchange' (Smart, 1984, p. 156). In my interaction with Jack, however, I experienced the interview as oppressive precisely because I did *not* reconfirm Smart's model. Instead of facilitating Jack's speech, my most immediate point of reference became gender, and the potentially difficult situation in which I had placed myself by entering Jack's house alone. I felt 'involved in a game where only the competitor had access to the rules and that I would be punished if I lost the game' (second interview, field notes). In this analysis, in common with McKee and O'Brien, I believe I utilized a risk-reducing strategy of maintaining a 'professional manner' when the ambiguities arose (McKee and O'Brien, 1983, p. 158).

An alternative analysis could be that the content and language were Jack's attempts to control the interview process. He set the agendas obliquely, using my general enquiries to introduce topics that related to domination, and possibly waiting for me to perform my 'feminine' role of encouragement. Within this perspective, there are two sociological possibilities of 'competition' analysis. There could have been a status-driven contest for control of the interview — and certainly Jack's occasional apparent definition of my status as 'researcher = official' would lend weight to this paradigm; or there may have been a gender-driven contest for control of the interaction, in that my own behaviour could have signalled resistance to perceived domination and possible danger. Sue Scott suggests that it is often problematic to attempt to separate the issues of status and gender (Scott, 1984, p. 171).

In suggesting these analyses, I am aware of two issues. Firstly, in making implications concerning Jack's motives, I am breaking my own ethical code, and attempting to define aspects of his identity and situation. Secondly, Nancy Chodorow points out that, as researchers, we need to be especially aware of our own normative patterns of gender-consciousness. It may be that a 'hyper-gender-sensitivity' actually creates blindness to other possibilities in the analyses (Chodorow, 1989, p. 218).

This issue is problematic here, because there are other possible explanations, apart from gender and status. For example, a multitude of folk legends exist concerning causes of epilepsy, and various other pointers in Jack's accounts suggest a sense of bewilderment about the condition. In addition, the area where he lives does not seem an enviable place to be. The violence may be a rational response to an impossible life-situation. It is therefore important to recognize that an emphasis upon analysis within gender and status perspectives reflects a sociological bias towards precisely these issues.

Issue 2: Research Praxis

Mike Oliver, conceptualizing the social relations of research as 'alienating', has traced the history of research from its positivist beginnings, through the interpretive paradigm, and into the possibility of emancipatory research, in which there is a recognition that power and oppression are the social problems for disabled people. Pointing out that the emancipatory paradigm includes enabling research subjects to empower themselves, he suggests six ways in which disablism could be studied. These include descriptions of experience; a re-definition of the problem; a challenge to methodologies and ideologies of dominant research patterns; the development of emancipatory methodologies; descriptions of collective experience; and monitoring of self-run services for people with impairments (Oliver, 1992).

Although applauding the general movement towards more qualitative methods, feminists have been critical of the masculine ethics of that movement, for it largely ignored the issue of gender. More recent criticism has focused upon the masking of subjectivity, and the invisibility of emotion. Liz Stanley discusses the nature of the knowledge produced from 'grounded theory' (theory which emerges from an empirical base — Glaser and Strauss, 1967), claiming that it has little 'experiential validity'. Defining feminist epistemology as a set of ethical principles which underpin methods and analysis, she cites the relevant areas of the research process as the researcher/researched relationship, emotion as a research experience, the issue of power in the research, and the management of both 'intellectual biography' and differing realities (Stanley, 1990).

Despite the notion of the importance of differing realities, some feminist realities tend to be silenced. Stanley (1990) cites two of these as the realities of black feminists and of lesbian feminists. However, Jenny Morris points out that, as far as disabled people are concerned, feminist knowledge has remained alienated knowledge. Researchers tend not to position themselves as non-disabled people holding cultural assumptions of disablement (Morris, 1992).

Pamela Abbott and Claire Wallace (1990) describe feminist research as that which recognizes the structural oppression of women with reference to their gender. The moral imperative within humanist and feminist (or feminist-informed) research therefore demands that participants in research projects be enabled to define their own situation and/or identity. As I have demonstrated, there are problems arising from this emphasis. Firstly, it becomes evident that, although the fundamental philosophy of feminist research is that it should be 'for' women, in practice much is undertaken 'among' women. There are exceptions, of course (e.g. Laws, 1990; Scott, 1984; McKee and O'Brien, 1983; Smart, 1984).

The second problem with this epistemological position is the implicit assumption that everyone has a self-definition to offer, or that they want to offer to the researcher. Where none is offered, or the researcher is not confident of her perception, the implication is that description then takes precedence over explanation. If the issue is a straightforward 'writing-up' dilemma, this is less problematic. If, however, the dilemma arises during the fieldwork phase, it becomes interwoven with many other issues, including the life experiences of the researcher.

Morgan argues that gender enters the complete process of research, from 'the form and style of the project in its various stages from start to completion as an article or thesis' (Morgan, 1986, p. 31). I wish to argue that there are different facets of gender which come to the surface in different methodologies and different topics for research. For example, in her study of lesbian identities, Kitzinger (1986) found some accounts that she felt unable to explain, despite returning to the respondents for clarification. She locates her decision then to leave those accounts unexplained firmly within a feminist principle of emancipatory research. Thus, her decision is an essentially methodological and ethical facet of gender.

In O'Brien's (1983) research, the issue of the researcher's gender surfaces most clearly in methodology. Fortunately, the research was in its concluding moments, so she was not left in a dilemma concerning research decisions (see McKee and O'Brien, 1983). McKee and O'Brien state that 'although he [the respondent] did not initiate any physical contact, his unpredictable behaviour in the car left the interviewer very relieved to have "escaped" and at the point glad that the study was not longitudinal in nature!' (p. 158).

In common with this interviewer, I have found that it is not always a straightforward matter to steer an interview situation, especially in emancipatory research. As Sophie Laws says, a large part of feminist discourse 'has been aimed at democratizing the research process, seeing "normal" research as exploitative . . . [and] writers tend to generalize from the particular experience of a feminist researcher interviewing women' (Laws, 1990, p. 218).

In the initial stages of this research project, when I established my ethics and methodology, I believed I could use the research methods outlined in this paper. The dilemma in which I find myself reflects, I think, the 'messiness' of real research. In common with Sophie Laws, I feel that the experience

> has made me very aware of how much sociologists generally depend upon empathy with their research subjects in making their interpretations . . . [for] if social reality is indeed a matter of shared meaning, what happens when the researcher does not and cannot afford to share meaning with the researched? (Laws, 1990, p. 217)

Indeed, how do I handle this research relationship when every contact with the respondent signals 'intuitive danger'? Do I listen to my own sense of anxiety, knowing that it has been constructed from past social experience? If I continue to involve Jack in the research, and then find that my anxiety is well-founded, what kind of censure will I have to face? It is to this issue that I turn next.

Issue 3: The Consequences of Research Decisions

When considering the possible consequences, the reality of gender becomes paramount in a way which demonstrates the existence of simplistic discourse surrounding the research process. Much of this discourse identifies the process as a series of interactions between a researcher and a group of people, the implication being that the whole process is somehow divorced from other discourses and experiences. Where research has been socially located, it has usually been in the context of either funding bodies or academic institutions. I have been able to locate very little work which specifically relates gender to the wider political and social context of research (an exception is Stanley, 1990).

I believe this is an important area for discourse and analysis, for the position of women researchers is typically different from that of men researchers; not because of biology, but because of social structures and attitudes. Men may choose to undertake particularly 'risky' research — if an unpleasant or damaging consequence occurs, they receive light censure, and even begrudging admiration for taking such risks. For women researchers, the censure involves, not just the research process, but also the 'gender agenda' of social life itself.

In my discussions about this dilemma, I have already found a consensus that, as a woman, I should not continue to involve Jack in the research. It is clear that the risks appear different to my 'significant others': for me, there are three roughly equal strands to the decision — Jack, the research project, and myself. However, for others, whose 'connection' is only to me, the first two strands are of lesser importance. Nevertheless, gender also plays a part here, in the difficult issue of perceived 'contributory negligence' ascribed to women (Smith, 1989). As Pamela Abbot and Claire Wallace comment,

> the legal system marginalizes, trivializes, and belies women's victimization, and . . . blames it on the victim. Men who are beaten up are not told it was because of the way they behaved; women are. Men are not advised not to go out at night alone or not to visit certain places; women are. Women's behaviour is controlled by men and this control is reinforced not only by the media, the police, and the courts but by other women. (Abbott and Wallace, 1990, p. 183)

Earlier I pointed out that, as 'Gill', I juggle the social identities and self-identities of woman-as-girl, woman-as-mother, woman-as-nurse, and woman-as-researcher. Although these are conceptualized separately, they are, in reality, interwoven and overlapping. 'Woman' — that is, gender — is inseparable from all the others; 'researcher' is dependent upon, and mediated through, both my self-identities and the social expectations of those identities. In the context of my dilemma, there is also embedded in the identity of 'researcher', an imputed element of 'woman-as-whore', because I sometimes visit houses to talk to men who are living alone. Separate discussion of these identities is for the purpose of theoretical abstraction alone.

The social identity of woman-as-girl is located in two main areas. The first one is that of marriage, and the well-documented and well-understood

Western white middle-class ideologies surrounding the institution. The second area lies in my identity as a daughter. Mother-daughter relationships are, as Nancy Chodorow points out, a mixture of connectedness and separation. There is a sense of connectedness which often remains throughout their mutual lifespan (Chodorow, 1989). As Liz Stanley says, many of our own generation of feminists are going through the experience of caring for older people (Stanley, 1990, p. 122). Although this may not be a physical caring, cultural assumptions around 'elderly' people encourage the consideration of possible consequences of causing undue distress.

My identity as a daughter overlaps, and interweaves with, my identity as a mother of three daughters (and a son). The same principles of connectedness and separation apply to these relationship. They, in turn, are influenced, not only by my feminist/humanist principles of empowerment, but also by ideologies of motherhood, and the 'legitimacy' of family claims upon women (Wearing, 1984). The identity of woman-as-mother also occurs within the context of woman-as-researcher working among men. It is part of the 'feminine script' of motherhood to use clarity of communication, nurturance and 'rapport' (Phoenix, Woollett and Lloyd, 1991) — and these are also expected of the woman-as-researcher.

The woman-as-nurse identity is specific to this research, for when the woman-as-researcher is working in the area of impairment, she must be conscious of social perceptions of 'disability' as a medical problem, and therefore of social expectations concerning the role of researcher. In short, the role is traditionally perceived as that of a 'welfare professional' who exercises a degree of responsibility for her research subjects, because they are 'dependent', 'needy', 'childlike', or 'less able' as persons; she must 'look after' them.

In my research contact with Jack, I have experienced anxiety over my identity of woman-as-nurse. Jocelyn Cornwell has demonstrated the existence of public and private accounts of health and illness, highlighting the importance of lay definitions (Cornwell, 1984). Because this research is fundamentally committed to empowering and people's own definitions, it is necessary to be aware of the still-prevalent folk legends concerning causes of epilepsy, and fear surrounding the sometimes unanticipated behaviour of people who have the condition. Social attitudes, built upon ignorance and fear, would play their part in perceptions of my 'contributory negligence', if further contact led to a mishap. This would not help people with epilepsy, nor, by implication, other disabled people, and would not therefore constitute emancipatory research. On the other hand, I do feel responsibility for Jack as a research subject.

Conclusion

In this paper I have raised specific issues for feminist-informed research among men:

1   there is a complex problem of contradictory social locations of both the research subjects and the women researchers;

2   within the concept of emancipatory research lies an assumption that all research subjects will have the inclination and/or ability to articulate a self-definition of their social location and their actions.

In my discussion of the multiple identities of women researchers, I have tried to place the research process firmly within its wider social and political location. By doing this, I have also demonstrated some of the ways in which the 'social relations of production' in research have been conceptualized in a narrow task-oriented, male-defined way.

Perhaps because, in the absence of a clear definition from Jack, there is inevitably a choice of definitions and analyses, I find myself in a dilemma which is both methodological and ethical. Warren claims that the response of the researcher to dilemmas in which she finds herself is a consequence of balancing 'harmonious research relations in the field' with 'typically feminist politics of fieldworkers in academia' (Warren, 1988, p. 38). She quotes Gurney (1985):

We are rarely told how the researcher responded to [sexual hustling]. We also are not told how the female researcher felt about her response to the incident, whether she was satisfied that she did the correct thing under the circumstances or was uncomfortable with her own actions. . . . (Warren, 1988, p. 38)

In the context of this paper, I believe the dilemma I must resolve is more concerned with a conflict between a humanist desire to empower a respondent in an exploitative relationship, and my own socially-located fears and anxieties, rather than a balance between research relations and feminist politics. With Warren, I argue that fieldwork, like any other activity of everyday life, evokes the whole range of feelings associated with everyday life. As Sue Scott points out, 'the whole process of interviewing, and therefore the *data themselves*, are coloured by gender considerations' (Scott, 1984, p. 170; emphasis added). However, although the gender considerations are obviously of immense importance, it is not a straightforward matter to separate them from other issues, such as emotion, status and power in interviews, and — especially in research where impairment is a factor — the tendency for researchers to be perceived as some kind of 'welfare professional'.

Postscript

If I had not written this paper, maybe my anxiety would have remained veiled; an uncomfortable feeling, but one which could be set to one side by willpower, something that had a 'theoretical' existence. The act of physically forcing the words through my hands on to paper changed the way I felt. My anxiety is here, for me — and you — to gaze upon. My fear has become more real. I no longer feel able to return to Jack's home.

In response to Carol Warren's quote from Gurney (above), I do not feel at all comfortable with this decision. Although, at the conference,[1] the consensus seemed to be that I should not go back to his house, it was also pointed out that women often draw back from 'tricky' situations, and that this may help to perpetuate stereotypes of us as 'weak' people. I understand this, and — up to a point — agree. It may be that some dilemmas simply do not have any 'comfortable' options, and that we can only resolve them by choosing the one that is less uncomfortable. Would my decision have been different if I had not articulated and analyzed my own anxiety? The answer remains unknowable.

Note

I should like to express my thanks to friends, and to women at the conference, for their advice, and helpful comments on the earlier version of this paper. I have endeavoured to incorporate their points into this version.

1 The 1992 Women's Studies Network (UK) annual conference at Preston.

References

ABBOTT, PAMELA and WALLACE, CLAIRE (1990) *An Introduction to Sociology: Feminist Perspectives*, London, Routledge.

BELL, COLIN and ROBERTS, HELEN (1984) *Social Researching: Politics, Problems, Practice*, London, Routledge and Kegan Paul.

BERG, DAVID and SMITH, KENWYN (1988) *The Self in Social Inquiry*, London, Sage.

BURGESS, ROBERT G. (1986) *Key Variables in Social Investigation*, London, Routledge and Kegan Paul.

CHODOROW, NANCY (1989) *Feminism and Psychoanalytic Theory*, Cambridge, Polity.

CORNWELL, JOCELYN (1984) *Hard-Earned Lives*, London, Tavistock.

GAMARNIKOW, EVA, MORGAN, DAVID, PURVIS, JUNE and TAYLORSON, DAPHNE (Eds) (1983) *The Public and the Private*, London, Heinemann.

GLASER, BARNEY and STRAUSS, ANSELM LEONARD (1967) *The Discovery of Grounded Theory*, Chicago, Aldine Publishing.

GURNEY, J.N. (1985) 'Not One of the Guys: The Female Researcher in a Male-Dominated Setting', *Qualitative Sociology*, **8**, pp. 42–62.

KITZINGER, CELIA (1986) 'Introducing and Developing Q as a Feminist Methodology: A Study of Accounts of Lesbianism', in WILKINSON, SUE (Ed.) *Feminist Social Psychology*, Milton Keynes, Open University Press.

LAWS, SOPHIE (1990) *Issues of Blood: The Politics of Menstruation*, Basingstoke, Macmillan.

MCKEE, LORNA and O'BRIEN, MARGARET (1983) 'Interviewing Men: "Taking Gender Seriously"', in GAMARNIKOW, EVA, MORGAN, DAVID, PURVIS, JUNE and TAYLORSON, DAPHNE (Eds) *The Public and the Private*, London, Heinemann.

MORGAN, D. (1986) 'Gender', in BURGESS, ROBERT G. (Ed.) *Key Variables in Social Investigation*, London, Routledge and Kegan Paul.

MORRIS, JENNY (1992) 'Personal and Political: A Feminist Perspective on Researching Physical Disability,' *Disability, Handicap and Society*, **7**, 2, pp. 157–66.

OLIVER, MIKE (1990) *The Politics of Disablement*, Basingstoke, Macmillan.

OLIVER, MIKE (1992) 'Changing the Social Relations of Research Production?', *Disability, Handicap and Society*, **7**, 2, pp. 101–14.

OPIE, ANNE (1992) 'Qualitative Research, Appropriation of the Other', *Feminist Review*, **40** (Spring), pp. 52–69.

OPIE, IONA and OPIE, PETER (1955) *The Oxford Nursery Rhyme Book*, Oxford, Clarendon.

PHOENIX, ANN, WOOLLETT, ANNE and LLOYD, EVA (1991) *Motherhood: Meanings, Practices and Ideologies*, London, Sage.

ROGERS, WENDY STAINTON (1991) *Explaining Health and Illness*, Hemel Hempstead, Harvester Wheatsheaf.

SCOTT, SUE (1984) 'The Personable and the Powerful: Gender and Status in Sociological Research', in BELL, COLIN and ROBERTS, HELEN (Eds) *Social Researching: Politics, Problems, Practice*, London, Routledge and Kegan Paul.

SMART, CAROL (1984) *The Ties That Bind*, London, Routledge and Kegan Paul.

SMITH, JOAN (1989) *Mysogynies*, London, Faber and Faber.

SPENDER, DALE (1980) *Man-Made Language*, London, Routledge and Kegan Paul.

STANLEY, LIZ (Ed.) (1990) *Feminist Praxis: Research Theory and Epistemology in Feminist Sociology*, pp. 113–22, London, Routledge and Kegan Paul.

STANLEY, LIZ and WISE, SUE (1983) *Breaking Out: Feminist Consciousness and Feminist Research*, London, Routledge and Kegan Paul.

WARREN, CAROL (1988) *Gender Issues in Field Research*, London, Sage.

WEARING, BETSY (1984) *The Ideology of Motherhood*, Sydney and Hemel Hempstead, George Allen and Unwin.

WILKINSON, SUE (Ed.) (1986) *Feminist Social Psychology*, Milton Keynes, Open University Press.

Chapter 10

Women's Studies as Empowerment of 'Non-Traditional' Learners in Community and Youth Work Training: A Case Study

Louise Morley

Introduction

This paper is a case study of the role Women's Studies plays in professional training for community and youth work. It examines how the exploration of difference and diversity in students and in the subject matter can be facilitated to enable women to work collectively and collaboratively, and how feminist theory can inform liberatory pedagogical practice and group process.

The Course

The Women's Studies course on which I teach is a module of a professional training course leading to the award of a diploma/BA (Hons) degree in Community and Youth Studies. This qualifies students to work in youth centres, detached youth projects, community organizations and a variety of related settings. The course comprises university-based taught modules and supervised fieldwork. The taught component includes modules on sociology, black studies, social psychology, management, equal opportunities, social policy, interpersonal and groupwork skills, principles and practice of youth work.

In providing formal training for community and youth work, the course aims to develop reflective practitioners, and as such, is informed by theories of personal, organizational and societal change. Lather (1991, p. 13) suggests that 'reflective practice is privileged as the site where we can learn how to turn critical thought into emancipatory action'. The applied focus of the community and youth work course necessitates the ability to translate theory into practice and to theorize practical experience.

As post-experience vocational training with entry criteria which value experience and equality of opportunity, the course attracts an annual intake of twenty-five to thirty-five black and white, male and female students from a wide geographical area. Many students define themselves as working-class. In so far as educational backgrounds and racial and class composition differs from the traditional student profile within UK universities, these students come under the category of 'non-traditional learners'. This term is widely used now in higher education in the UK. The concept itself has normative connotations and is culturally specific. It contains a risk of marginalizing women, black and working-class students as a remedial group by defining them as 'other' to the 'traditional' or dominant group. Furthermore, the term implies lack rather than difference.

Difference, diversity and anti-oppression work are key concepts in both training and professional practice. The Women's Studies module provides an opportunity for women to theorize power, to develop an analysis of the social construction of gender and to explore their experiences and professional practice in a group work setting.

The concept of empowerment has become institutionalized in the profession and the Statement of Purpose (Report of Second Ministerial Conference, 1990) states that youth work should offer young people opportunities which are 'educative'; 'designed to promote equality of opportunity'; 'participative' and 'empowering'. As a tutor I am particularly interested in the role that both the content and pedagogical processes in Women's Studies can play in the empowerment of a professional group which is officially charged with the empowerment of others.

Patti Lather (1991, p. 3) challenges the fashionable use of the term empowerment in relation to 'individual self-assertion, upward mobility and the psychological experience of feeling powerful'. Rather, she uses the term to mean 'analysing ideas about the causes of powerlessness, recognising systematic oppressive forces and acting both individually and collectively to change the conditions of our lives' (Lather, 1991, p. 4).

Collective action and collaborative working relationships form part of the value base and learning outcomes for initial training. Empowerment work in Women's Studies cannot simply focus on the self but must include the ability to understand the structures of inequality, power and powerlessness (Nemiroff, 1989).

Gender is perceived as one category of difference and courses and workshops on black studies, race, class, disability, sexuality and social class are an integral part of the course. Given the context of the work, Women's Studies needs to work for multiple sets of liberatory policies and resist additive approaches to oppression (Collins, 1990, p. 222).

The Organizational Context

The community and youth work course is based within the Department of Community Studies which incorporates a range of post-experience, professional training courses. The department was formed as a result of the merger between a college of higher education and a university in 1989. The relocation of the community and youth work course to a university revealed many policy issues which arise as a consequence of improved access opportunities and new models of provision in higher education.

The legitimacy gap which often exists between Women's Studies and other disciplines has also arisen between Community Studies and other more traditional university departments. For example, the community and youth course has entry criteria which prioritize professional experience over educational achievements. In terms of the curriculum, anti-oppression work underpins the acquisition of professional skills and vice versa.

As change agents, community and youth workers work with individuals, groups and organizations to develop personal potential, organizational structures and policies. Thus Women's Studies is taught as an intervention as well as an academic discipline. Change is effected by a clear feminist or woman-centred approach to the range of professional roles, e.g. counselling, advice, advocacy, group facilitation. As a consequence of such situated theory, students are motivated and emotionally engaged in their learning as they attempt to integrate theory, practice and life experience.

The critical and analytical skills which students develop in relation to practice are also applied to the organizational context of their training. The under-representation of women in academic posts in conjunction with the increased casualization of teaching (Aziz, 1990; Hansard, 1990), and the lack of policies and strategies for equality in British universities mean that the organizational context of Women's Studies is often in itself disempowering. In addition, many of the students on the community and youth work course are trainees employed by local education authorities. As such they are witnessing changes in social policy and widespread cuts in public expenditure which have a direct impact on service provision for women in the community, such as the abolition of some local government units on equal opportunities, women and race.

If Women's Studies is counter-hegemonic and designed to create and sustain opposition to the present maldistribution of power and resources (Lather, 1984), the challenge therefore exists for it to empower women to work towards change whilst simultaneously understanding and resisting the limitations, structures and processes of disempowerment.

Student Diversity

It would be erroneous to suggest that students enter the course as powerless victims, but, for many women students, consciousness of identity based on membership of oppressed groups frequently interacts with the role universities have traditionally played in maintaining strands of domination and perpetuating social inequalities. Paradox and contradiction can therefore arise as women enter the academy to be trained and empowered on a course which is viewed with suspicion by the institution. Hence, democratic pedagogical processes take place within a restrictive institutional context (Ramazanoglu, 1987; Lowe and Lowe Benston, 1991; Bricker-Jenkins and Hooyman, 1987).

The Women's Studies course I teach takes place in a women-only group. The male students work separately with male tutors. The substantial number of re-entry women students means that there are varying levels of participation in the Women's Movement and of identification with woman-centredness. For some, Women's Studies represents the first experience of working in a women-only setting. For others, many of whom have worked in women's community and youth projects, girls' projects, Women's Aid or rape crisis counselling, the subject is an extension of their wider commitment to feminist intervention.

Within the group, women define themselves in terms of interests and identity based on social class, disability, sexuality, race and ethnicity, age, or role. It is rare for white women to define themselves in terms of race, or heterosexual women in terms of their sexuality. Commonalities among women are invariably rooted in social class and commitment to professional activism. Ellsworth (1989, p. 321) believes that it is important to recognize that 'a multiplicity of knowledges are present in the classroom as a result of the way difference has been used to structure social relations inside and outside the classroom'. She also maintains that these knowledges are 'contradictory, partial, and irreducible'.

Divisions and conflict in groups in the seven years I have been teaching the course occur most frequently around race and sexuality. Some women come from local authorities and communities where there is an absence of dialogue or critical perspectives on these issues. For these women exposure to new ideas can activate strong feelings.

Within Women's Studies on this course there is the opportunity to divide into black and white groups for some work. The division is not always unproblematic as it poses questions of definition. This is particularly relevant to women with ambiguous racial and ethnic identity: ambiguous in the sense that their self-definition might not always correspond to how other women perceive them.

Membership of the black group is open to women of African, Asian and Caribbean descent. But in the past, there have been other women on the course who have identified as politically black, for example, Turkish women. Attempts to join the black group were met with rejection and many black women resented that their 'empowerment' time was being taken up with discussion of terms of membership. Irish, Jewish and Yugoslav women have also raised objections to their inclusion in the white group. Whilst they made no attempt to join the black group, they felt that they had suffered from Britain's colonial past as victims of racism, anti-semitism, imperialist feminism and xenophobia. One solution was to create opportunities for these women to lead sessions on anti-semitism or anti-Irish oppression for the whole group and allow debates about identity and difference to provide rich material for consciousness-raising.

Evaluating the Effectiveness of Women's Studies

Judging from participant evaluation and personal feedback, the majority of women on the course express enthusiasm about the empowering effect Women's Studies has had on their lives and on their relationships with other women. For example, women frequently observe how their ability to construct and sustain feminist arguments in mixed and single-sex settings is enhanced, both as a result of increased knowledge and a sense of value as women. The development of process skills to facilitate conflict and confrontation and the ability to negotiate from an empowered position are also noted. Many women express their delight in the subject in terms of quasi religious conversion. Janice Raymond (1985, p. 53) identifies the 'profound religious dimension' to Women's Studies and recognizes that many of us 'see women's knowledge as having revelatory power'.

Disappointment is often posed in terms of perceived areas of omission, i.e. avoidance of certain issues, or conflict arising from differences. Comments appear to refer more to the level of group engagement with the subject, rather than to the frequency of discussions. These qualitative/quantitative observations raise questions about performance indicators for the evaluation of effectiveness in Women's Studies. If the student voice is used to inform more effective teaching strategies, attention needs to be paid to the 'social construction of feelings and their manipulation by the dominant culture' (Weiler, 1991, p. 463). Ellsworth (1989, p. 305) also reminds us that voices of students and professors are 'partial and partisan'. This view appears to contradict the notion that feelings are a source of truth and problematizes the role that Women's Studies plays in validating the epistemological value of both feeling and experience.

bell hooks (1989, p. 53) discusses the complexity of evaluation in Women's Studies.

> I began to see that courses that work to shift paradigms, to change consciousness, cannot necessarily be experienced immediately as fun or positive or safe and this was not a worthwhile criteria to use in evaluation.

If women find that they are beginning to think about themselves in disquieting new ways, there is a risk of dissonance between actions, self-image, lifestyle and beliefs. Hence student evaluation frequently contains a combination of information and statements of hurt, delight, resistance and confusion.

I have observed how student evaluation differs from one year to another. By the end of the course disappointment and statements of powerlessness are less frequently expressed. Women appear to move away from attacking, blaming and holding others responsible for meeting their needs. There is a marked increase in the ability to appreciate themselves and other women. They focus more on opportunities rather than obstacles for influencing change. The question arises as to whether this style of evaluation constitutes empowerment, with women in possession of enhanced interpersonal and intellectual skills, and therefore less likely to 'lash out' and 'antagonise' (Schniedewind, 1987, p. 18), or whether it is an example of the more cynical view of the incorporation of members of oppressed groups in dominant organizations. The 'defiant speech' and 'talking back' (hooks, 1986/7, pp. 123–8) from communities of resistance gives way to more socially acceptable forms of self-expression.

Donna Haraway (1990, p. 197) discusses Chela Sandoval's (1984) concept of 'oppositional consciousness'. Haraway defines this as the skills for reading webs of power by those refused stable membership in the social categories of race, sex or class. This 'oppositional consciousness' is applied by students to their evaluation of pedagogical practices and tutor styles and attitudes. There is a low tolerance for people Collins (1990, p. 208) describes as 'educated fools'. Discrepancies between theory and behaviour are rapidly perceived and tutors' failure to model good practice results in loss of confidence, confrontation and student cynicism.

This 'oppositional consciousness' informs many 'non-traditional' students when they feel/sense they are being patronized, manipulated or undermined. The empowerment work allows them to express this in ways which do not reinforce victimhood and are less harmful to themselves. For example, the ability to separate self from others represents a major piece of personal development. As women become more empowered they are better able to realize when their distress is activated by someone else's treatment of them. They are then more likely to give feedback without storming, attacking or blaming others. For example, in response to an unsatisfactory session with a visiting lecturer, certain women felt that she had 'oppressed' and 'patronized' them. Other women described the experience in different terms and felt that she lacked a class analysis in relation to gender, and was obviously more experienced in traditional methods of teaching. Instead of feeling attacked, endangered and victimized by the visiting lecturer's actions and seeing her as omnipotent, her role and authority were evaluated in the light of her skills and knowledge.

The Empowerment Process

As Women's Studies incorporates a matrix of commonalities and differences there is the potential for this 'oppositional consciousness' to find expression in group interactions. Roles of oppressed and oppressor shift as women discover points of contact and discontinuity with other women in the group. Brimstone (1991, p. 125) writes:

there is no straightforward, easily identifiable opposition between centre and margins, oppressor and oppressed, for within the terms of this binary classification system the splittings are so infinite and so unstable that what we invariably end up arguing about is the relative degree of participation each of us has in one or the other position at any given time.

These simultaneous and contradictory positions of oppression and dominance raise interesting challenges for the organization of separate space for different oppressions within feminism. Cameron McCarthy (1988) names the struggles among people oppressed differently by different groups as the 'nonsynchrony of oppression'. The delegitimization of some women's experiences and the privileging of others have been an important part of black feminist debate (Lorde, 1981, 1984; Amos and Parmar, 1984; Brooks-Higginbotham, 1989; Collins, 1990; Mohanty, 1988). Exclusionary practices in Women's Studies (Baca Zinn *et al.*, 1986) have reinforced racism and have often placed the burden on black women to draw attention to power differentials based on race. So, while having direct experience of a form of oppression may confer 'epistemic privilege' (Narayan, 1988), it can also represent additional responsibility.

As many 'non-traditional' learners view white women as the custodians of Women's Studies, an essential part of the empowerment process is the composition of the staff team. In this particular case, Women's Studies is taught by black and white women with the possibility of work in separate groups. Contradictions arise when a single individual can experience oppression in one sphere while being privileged or oppressive in another. For many white women, having their oppressor role pointed out to them whilst they are in the early stages of analyzing their role as oppressed provides considerable discomfort and confusion (Green, 1987; Morley, 1992). Separation into black and white groups is experienced in terms of rejection and loss. Some white women question how they are going to learn about race in the absence of black women. They are unable to see the racism in the idea that black women exist as resources for white women and are not entitled to space free from the inhibiting presence of white women to explore issues of interest to them as black women. Childers and hooks (1990, p. 71) make a similar observation:

As long as white women within feminism still ask black women to teach them about race, we are still being put in a servant/served relationship.

The pedagogical task is to enable this perspective to be 'unlearned' and to confront some of the rigidities of information and attitude which allow racism to flourish. For an anti-racist perspective to be the norm in Women's Studies (Watt and Cook, 1991) resistance has to be minimized. Collins (1990, p. 229) points out that

> Although most individuals have little difficulty identifying their own victimisation . . . they typically fail to see how their thoughts and actions uphold someone else's subordination.

Experience and understanding of one form of oppression does not necessarily sensitize one to other forms. Without wishing to reinforce white privilege, I have had to find pedagogical interventions which enable white women to develop an anti-racist consciousness and strategies without activating the negative feelings many of them already have about themselves. One strategy is to encourage women to analyze situations of oppression they have experienced. This frequently involves locating and strengthening the hurt part of the self that receives misinformation about self and others. But cathartic personal work needs to be accompanied by action for change. Acknowledgement of racism is only effective if it leads to transformation (hooks, 1991, p. 35).

Unlike many other disciplines, Women's Studies does not aim to educate and inform 'on top' of the individual's sense of self, but seeks to locate the self at the centre of the learning process. Hardy Aiken *et al.* (1987, p. 263) observed that their Women's Studies seminars functioned simultaneously on

> at least two levels: an intellectual, consciously rational discourse set in tension with dynamics approaching those of an encounter group.

Women's Studies cannot always be safe and comfortable as one woman's comfort represents another's discomfort. But the challenge exists as to how difference and diversity can be explored without reinforcing and re-enacting the hurt women have experienced via their particular forms of oppression. For example, how can the reality of others be analyzed without tokenizing and exposing 'others' in the group to unaware attitudes, language and fears?

In addition, many of the women have had negative experiences of the education system in the past and are very conscious of the potential for hurt and humiliation in educational settings. This often translates itself into fear of saying the wrong thing and showing ignorance of issues, or using inappropriate language in group discussions. In the early stages of the group process, it is not uncommon for women to struggle to achieve a balance concerning 'the visibility that speech gives without giving up the safety of silence' (Ellsworth, 1989, p. 313). As misinformation via language plays such a prominent role in the establishment and maintenance of power, it is difficult to avoid the restimulation of profound feelings of victimization when members of oppressed groups hear themselves referred to in terms associated with their prolonged subordination (Morley, 1991).

The valuing of experience has always been a key feature of empowerment work with women (Hanmer, 1991). Claims about experience as a source of women's knowledge can create assumptions about commonalities in women's lives (Weiler, 1991). The challenge also exists for Women's Studies to extend women's experiences to include understanding difference, as well as contradict some of the harmful effects of negative experiences based on oppression and discrimination.

It is not uncommon for women on the course I teach to express confusion about the apparently mixed messages they believe are being transmitted in Women's Studies. On the one hand they are being told that their experiences as women are central and valid and on the other hand the message is that experience is partial, exclusionary or privileged. For example, a white working-class woman recently produced an essay on women's oppression written entirely in the first person from her own perspective. Her justification was that her experiences had always been excluded from academic study in the past and that it was an intensely political act to make herself the subject of her enquiry. This raised questions about the interpretation of the label 'woman' as 'white woman', and by making herself the subject of work on women's oppression, she had purported to speak on behalf of black women, lesbians, women with disabilities too. The challenge was how to validate and celebrate her experience, but also to acknowledge that it was only a partial view and had also been constituted by exclusionary practices. The student's initial understanding of this feedback was rooted in the belief that she had broken the patriarchal academic rule of thought and study by grounding her knowledge in her own emotional, social and psychic experiences of oppression.

To ignore difference and diversity between women in Women's Studies in the interests of a false sense of sisterhood would be inappropriate. But to explore difference without pedagogical attention to intrapersonal and inter-personal dynamics can be disempowering. Kathleen Barry (1989, p. 572) also observes that

> Whenever differences are emphasized without first recognizing collectivity, commonality, and unity among women, gender power is depoliticized.

This dynamic was visible some years ago, when some women in the group suggested that heterosexism should be the first topic for study. When the session took place, tension levels soon rose as some women related to the subject as a 'special need', i.e. what information did they need to have about lesbians and gays in order to provide a non-discriminatory professional service. They were unable to see how heterosexuality as an institution and as ideology upholds female oppression. This refusal to examine their own implication in the information blocked the development of dialogue and resulted in lesbians in the group feeling objectified and pathologized by heterosexual women. Things were left unsaid or encoded on the basis of what Ellsworth (1989, p. 313) describes as 'a highly complex negotiation of the politics of knowing and being known'. Frustration and anger were expressed in the group, and women accused each other of attacking, oppressive behaviour. When the processes of democratization and participation appeared to 'fail', some women wanted to re-centre the authority and hold me responsible for finding the solution.

The psychoanalytical terms of transference and counter-transference have established connections with feminist pedagogy (Culley and Portuges, 1985, p. 15). Counter-transference had to take place without depoliticizing the subject matter. But it appeared that women were engaging with the subject from their hurt. Internalized oppression was operating to ensure that anger and rage were being vented on each other (Morley, 1992). This dynamic challenges the teacher of Women's Studies to consider how empowerment can take place without an overemphasis on directive pedagogical methods. I needed to provide a challenge to the heterosexism in the group without it being seen as authority-led and thereby activating more unhelpful feelings. But more importantly, I needed to share my thinking about group process and interrupt the destructive blaming games which were being enacted. Certain women felt that the 'I'm OK, you're not OK' game was being played, and this activated strong feelings of powerlessness in the face of attacks and disapproval. Some women were experiencing the interaction in terms of politically correct thinking and yet 'another coercive discourse added to their lives' (Lather, 1991, p. 143). Women were concealing their hurt and vulnerability by revealing their anger and thus appearing to react from a dominant position. Part of the empowerment process involves creating opportunities for a wider range of feelings to be expressed and heard. An important stage was also to question the sources of the diverging responses (Lewis, 1989). The differences exposed in the exploration of the larger social/political issue allowed a clearer focus on power and process within the group, and the relationship between macro- and micro-systems of prejudice, misinformation and domination.

In my experience, when conflict arises out of difference, women in the 'oppressor' role often resent the intrusion and disruption caused by women drawing attention to power differentials. Women in the 'oppressed' role resent the fact that some women can make a choice whether or not to concern themselves with issues that other women are not in a position to forget (Childers and hooks, 1990, p. 75).

Conclusion

'Non-traditional' learners are not prepared to be disempowered by didactic forms of teaching. A participative approach to Women's Studies does not create strong feelings, but enables them to be expressed more overtly. Part of empowerment is to take emotions seriously and find creative ways of working with them, rather than seeing them as hindrances in the pursuit of academic knowledge. The women I teach are in a strong position to disseminate feminist ideas in the wider community. It is important that they engage with their professional role from an empowered position, seeking influence and intervention, rather than domination, control and manipulation. Knowledge of formal power relations and how power is structured and enacted should enable women to work across differences in alliances which may vary from time to time, place to place. Empowerment allows women to interact with structures, groups and individuals with a strengthened sense of their own effectiveness and the ability to identify external conditions and internalized patterns that foster powerlessness.

References

AMOS, VALERIE and PARMAR, PRATIBHA (1984) 'Challenging Imperial Feminism', *Feminist Review*, 17 (July), 3–19.

AZIZ, ADRIENNE (1990) 'Women in UK Universities: The Road to Casualisation?', in STIVER LEE, SUZANNE and O'LEARY, VIRGINIA (Eds) *Storming the Tower*, London, Kogan Page, pp. 33–46.

BACA ZINN, MAXINE, WEBER CANNON, LYNN, HIGGINBOTHAM, ELIZABETH and THORNTON DILL, BONNIE (1986) 'The Costs of Exclusionary Practices in Women's Studies', *Signs*, **11**, 2, (Winter), pp. 290–303.

BARRY, KATHLEEN (1989) 'Biography and the Search for Women's Subjectivity', *Women's Studies International Forum*, **12**, 6, pp. 561–77.

BRICKER-JENKINS, MARY and HOOYMAN, NANCY (1987) 'Feminist Pedagogy in Education for Social Change', *Feminist Teacher*, **2**, Bloomington, Indiana University, pp. 36–42.

BRIMSTONE, LYNDIE (1991) 'Out of the Margins and Into the Soup; Some Thoughts on Incorporation,' in AARON, JANE and WALBY, SYLVIA (Eds) *Out of the Margins: Women's Studies in the Nineties*, London, Falmer Press, pp. 119–30.

BROOKS-HIGGINBOTHAM, EVELYN (1989) 'Race in Women's History', in WEED, ELIZABETH (Ed.) *Coming to Terms: Feminism, Theory, Politics*, London and New York, Routledge, pp. 122–33.

CHILDERS, MARY and HOOKS, BELL (1990) 'A Conversation about Race and Class', in HIRSCH, MARIANNE and KELLER, EVELYN FOX (Eds) *Conflicts in Feminism*, New York and London, Routledge.

COLLINS, PATRICIA HILL (1990) *Black Feminist Thought*, Boston and London, Unwin Hyman.

CULLEY, MARGO and PORTUGES, CATHERINE (Eds) (1985) *Gendered Subjects: The Dynamics of Feminist Teaching*, London and New York, Routledge and Kegan Paul.

ELLSWORTH, ELIZABETH (1989) 'Why Doesn't This Feel Empowering? Working Through the Repressive Myths of Critical Pedagogy', *Harvard Educational Review*, **59**, 3, pp. 297–324.

GREEN, MARGARET (1987) 'Women in the Oppressor Role', in ERNST, SHEILA and MAGUIRE, MARIE (Eds) *Living with the Sphinx*, London, Women's Press, pp. 179–213.

HANMER, JALNA (1991) 'On Course: Women's Studies — A Transitional Programme', in AARON, JANE and WALBY, SYLVIA (Eds) *Out of the Margins: Women's Studies in the Nineties*, London, Falmer Press, pp. 105–14.

HANSARD SOCIETY COMMISSION (1990) *Women at the Top*, Hansard Society for Parliamentary Government.

HARAWAY, DONNA (1990) 'A Manifesto for Cyborgs: Science, Technology and Socialist Feminism in the 1980s, in NICHOLSON, LINDA (Ed.) *Feminism/Postmodernism*, New York and London, Routledge, pp. 190–233.

HARDY AIKEN, SUSAN, ANDERSON, KAREN, DINNERSTEIN, MYRA, LENSINK, JUDY and MACCORQUODALE, PATRICIA (1987) 'Trying Transformations: Curriculum Integration and the Problem of Resistance', *Signs*, **12**, 2, pp. 255–75.

HOOKS, BELL (1986/7) 'Talking back', *Discourse*, **8**, Fall/Winter, pp. 123–8.

HOOKS, BELL (1989) 'Toward a Revolutionary Feminist Pedagogy in HOOKS, BELL *Talking Back: Thinking Feminist — Thinking Black*, London, Sheba, pp. 49–54.

HOOKS, BELL (1991) 'Sisterhood: Political Solidarity Between Women', in GUNEW, SNEJA, *A Reader in Feminist Knowledge*, London and New York, Routledge, pp. 27–41.

LATHER, PATTI (1984) 'Critical Theory, Curricular Transformation and Feminist Mainstreaming', *Journal of Education*, **166**, 1, pp. 49–62.

LATHER, PATTI (1991) *Getting Smart: Feminist Research and Pedagogy With/in the Postmodern*, New York, Routledge.

LEWIS, MAGDA (1989) 'The Challenge of Feminist Pedagogy', *Queen's Quarterly*, 96/1 (Spring), pp. 117–30.

LORDE, AUDRE (1981) 'The Master's Tools will Never Dismantle the Master's House', in MORAGA, CHERRIE and ANZALDUA, GLORIA (Eds) *This Bridge Called My Back*, New York, Kitchen Table, Women of Colour Press, pp. 98–101.

LORDE, AUDRE (1984) 'Age, Race, Class and Sex: Women Redefining Difference', in *Sister Outsider*, Trumansberg, New York, The Crossing Press, pp. 114–23.

LOWE, MARIAN and LOWE BENSTON, MARGARET (1991) 'The Uneasy Alliance of Feminism and Academia', in GUNEW, SNEJA (Ed.) *A Reader in Feminist Knowledge*, London and New York, Routledge, pp. 48–60.

McCARTHY, CAMERON (1988) 'Rethinking Liberal and Radical Perspectives on Racial Inequality in Schooling: Making the Case for Nonsynchrony', *Harvard Educational Review*, 58, pp. 265–80.

MOHANTY, CHANDRA (1988) 'Under Western Eyes: Feminist Scholarship and Colonial Discourses', *Feminist Review*, 30 (Autumn), pp. 61–88.

MORLEY, LOUISE (1991) 'Towards a Pedagogy for Empowerment in Community and Youth Work Training', *Youth and Policy*, 35, pp. 14–19.

MORLEY, LOUISE (1992) 'Women's Studies, Difference and Internalised Oppression', *Women's Studies International Forum*, **15**, 4 (July).

NARAYAN, UMA (1988) 'Working Together across Difference: Some Considerations on Emotions and Political Practice', *Hypatia*, **3**, 2 (Summer), pp. 31–47.

NEMIROFF, GRETA HOFFMAN (1989) 'Beyond Talking Heads: Towards an Empowering Pedagogy of Women's Studies', *Atlantis*, **15**, 1, pp. 1–15.

RAMAZANOGLU, CAROLINE (1987) 'Sex and Violence in Academic Life or You Can Keep a Good Woman Down', in HANMER, JALNA and MAYNARD, MARY (Eds) *Women, Violence and Social Control*, Basingstoke, Macmillan, pp. 61–74.

RAYMOND, JANICE (1985) 'Women's Studies: A Knowledge of One's Own', in CULLEY, MARGO and PORTUGES, CATHERINE (Eds) *Gendered Subjects: The Dynamics of Feminist Teaching*, London and New York, Routledge and Kegan Paul.

REPORT OF THE SECOND MINISTERIAL CONFERENCE (1990) *Towards a Core Curriculum — The Next Step*, Leicester, UK National Youth Agency.

SANDOVAL, CHELA (1984) *Dis-Illusionment and the Poetry of the Future: The Making of Oppositional Consciousness*, PhD qualifying essay, University of California, Santa Cruz.

SCHNIEDEWIND, NANCY (1987) 'Teaching Feminist Process', *Women's Studies Quarterly*, **XV**, 3 & 4, Fall/Winter, pp. 15–31.

WATT, SHANTU and COOK, JULIET (1991) 'Racism: Whose Liberation? Implications for Women's Studies', in AARON, JANE and WALBY, SYLVIA (Eds) *Out of The Margins: Women's Studies in the Nineties*, London, Falmer Press, pp. 131–42.

WEILER, KATHLEEN (1991) 'Freire and a Feminist Pedagogy of Difference', *Harvard Educational Review*, **6**, 4, pp. 449–74.

Chapter 11

Disability as a Focus for Innovation in Women's Studies and Access Strategies in Higher Education

Julie Matthews and Lynne Thompson

In January, 1990, the Foundation Studies Programme at (the then) Lancashire Polytechnic was offered to mature students in the Preston and surrounding areas. This new, 'second-generation' access programme contained several experimental and radical approaches within its remit of Polytechnic 'mass access' student-provision for the 1990s. A key approach lay in the Programme's emphasis on student-centred and student-managed provision, which is characterized by its mentor scheme. This enables ex-Programme students to act as role models, teachers and confidence-builders to each new intake of over 170 students annually, which was a principal reason for the Programme winning the 1991 British Gas Partnership Award for widening access to higher education.

We had little idea in 1990 which client groups would respond to the marketing and targeting strategies employed in recruiting our first cohort, or what issues would emerge as a consequence. But we were determined to implement a 'more means different' approach to access, rather than the 'more of the same' strategies usually employed in higher education, which then result in the recruitment of white, middle-class and often male students. We wished to promote a somewhat subversive aim, which was to demonstrate good practice with regard to the teaching and learning of adults, and to permeate this good practice into higher education.

However, such an approach has its pitfalls. We often promise more than can be delivered to mature students, especially those with disabilities, or minority ethnic groups. As will be seen below, access strategies are not always women-friendly either. It is assumed that access practitioners know what is best for mature students since practitioners are perceived to be pioneers in a relatively unknown territory, often outside mainstream academic (and male-dominated) activity, but who possess a certain expertise. Yet, as this chapter will show, it is students who, once empowered and encouraged to take control of their own learning, and that of others, are the real practitioners and innovators in higher education. Access, at its best, is merely a facilitative process for such activities to take place, and by which higher education institutions can initiate real change. Women's Studies has provided a most useful and necessary continuum by which students who, hitherto unrepresented in higher education, can both challenge and contribute to a woman-centred and dynamic curriculum.

The first Foundation Studies Programme applicant was Julie Matthews, a disabled woman whose autobiographical account of her experiences as an access and undergraduate student informs this chapter. We will expound further upon the Foundation Studies Programme insofar as it serves to highlight issues she raises, which illustrate the need for them to be addressed by a feminist and disability-based programme for action in higher education. After being offered a place on the Foundation Studies Programme, Julie Matthews had reservations as to whether or not she should actually attend.

Julie's Autobiographical Account

My excuse was that for several years of my life I had been under the control of 'others' including the medical profession, and my husband, from whom I had recently separated. I had difficulty in walking, and was therefore unused to public transport. I was afraid of going out on my own. Was I intelligent enough? And, most importantly, I was afraid of failure.

My disability, perhaps self-pity and lack of self-esteem, impaired my judgment. However, the negative way that I had been made to feel about myself is inherently linked to the refusal to accept that 'I am different'.

Women who are confined to the home due to family commitments experience similar fears. For example, a 'good' mother does not leave a child in order to fulfil her own needs and ambitions. Unconsciously, then, it is true to state that 'dependency causes vulnerability'. As women, most of us were afraid, and

> Fear is one of the most basic human emotions which motivates us all the time. Often, it lies dormantly in our subconscious. It is too hard to live openly with our fear so we put it to one side, only allowing it out at dark moments. All the real terror of it then floods our system and its discomfort can be so acute that we may even be disabled by it. Simply, fear is a response to a believed threat. (Pearson, 1991, p. 35)

Foundation Studies made me realize that most women have suppressed their own needs and ambitions. For example, the obligations that we have internalized, and that are appropriated to a woman living in a patriarchal society, have shaped and defined our whole existence. Susie Orbach and Louise Eichenbaum note that women are over-preoccupied with the reactions of others and tend to experience anger as uncomfortable and dangerous because it is an assertion of self-needs over what they regard as the natural primacy of others. They judge themselves as lacking if they don't meet this standard, and come to identify the satisfaction of their needs through meeting the needs of others. (Franks, 1990, p. 89)

As women, learning to shift the focus of attention away from others, it is then that we begin to break this self-destructing habit, which increasingly becomes unacceptable. In effect, we become empowered, which many of us at this initial stage had failed to realize. For the first time in our lives we had taken control, although uncovering and disclosing our anxieties is never easy, primarily because inner conflicts pertaining to our new-found self often lead to isolation from former friends and family. Beginning to realize the importance of self-value and rediscovering facets of our personality that had lain dormant for years are all part of the process. We were taking responsibility, and deciding positively about our future, even if that was simply turning up again the next week. We have to undermine the ability of those who rule, and who assume control and power which are not rightly theirs. Vida Pearson rightly asks:

Who can indicate that they have no disabilities? If, as women, we have been taught to rely on a man for income or protection, status or wisdom, then we have stopped our own abilities in these areas. (Pearson, 1991, p. 205)

In order to continue and complete the Programme, I had to reject my differences, but accept that I had difficulties, as follows:

- I was unable to use the library because I was unable to use public transport.

- The seating proved to be uncomfortable.

- Some of my chosen classes were on the third floor, which was not accessible by lift.

- The first session was held in the lecture theatre. This meant that I had to walk down stairs with the aid of a stick to obtain a front seat in order to keep my leg straight. This process only took two minutes, but to me it felt like a lifetime. Added to that, I felt that all eyes were on me.

In the group sessions, we were encouraged to talk about ourselves. I did not wish to discuss my life, my disability or separation. In other words, I was so wrapped up in myself, and my own feelings of discrimination pertaining to disability, previous life experiences had been temporarily forgotten. At times my fears were so sharp! What did I have to offer? I felt that I was an oddity. Talking to other people, however, helped to alleviate this, and helped me confront my own obsessions and hang-ups. What did not occur to me at this stage was that many of my problems could have been easily resolved, if I had not kept them to myself, but had discussed them with various members of staff, or, alternatively, and perhaps more importantly, with my mentors. The need to communicate with women, confide in them about our difficulties and anxieties, is vital to our self-development and cannot be overemphasized. I for one would not have sustained the course without such support.

This deep sense of unease had to be addressed. An integral and important part of this painstaking process was to identify and acknowledge my own prejudices. I had to overcome my own anger and feelings of inadequacy, and come to terms with able-bodied people's behaviour towards me. Pam Evans, herself a wheelchair-user, has pointed out that the idea of normality is inherently tied up with ideas about what is right, what is desirable, and what belongs:

> Normal implies that which is average within any social structure. Those who do not conform to what is average in terms of appearance, function, behaviour or belief are no longer 'normal'. The degree to which they fail to conform indicates the scale on which they will be mistrusted, feared and finally rejected. . . . They do not 'belong' because they no longer represent the collective values of the status quo. They challenge the way in which their society is certain it is right and admirable to be. (Morris, 1992a, p. 16)

Successfully completing the Foundation Studies Programme enabled me to continue my studies as an undergraduate. To have access to so many facilities that most able-bodied people take for granted is itself empowering. To be able to act as a role model, a mentor, and a teacher, encouraging and supporting other women, would have been inconceivable twelve months earlier.

In short, I was taking responsibility, as a facilitator for the learning and progress of other students, and making decisions about my own future. I had achieved a sense of dignity and self-worth, and although I had, and continue to have, fears and reservations pertaining to issues of disability, Foundation Studies has taught me to concentrate upon my abilities as opposed to my disabilities.

Perhaps because of previous and personal experiences in Health, it seemed quite natural that I would choose a path of study incorporating Health. At this stage I was determined to major in Physiology and minor in Health Studies; Women's Studies was my third option. This was an option I believed was an easy one, and of little significance and importance. I evidently wasn't aware at this time to what extent consciousness-raising is a key component of the Women's Studies curriculum. What changed my mind?

The Women's Studies Curriculum

The Women's Studies curriculum provides women with the opportunity to examine women's lives. It aims to highlight specific aspects of women's experiences, for example social and cultural attitudes. Ultimately, a pragmatic approach is taken, to raise our consciousness and awareness of the position of women at all social levels. Specific reference is made to women's oppression, and their resistance to it. Students are encouraged to share their experiences, and student-led workshops are an important part of the course. This enables students to build on the learning strategies of the Foundation Studies Programme, and create an alternative method of learning to that of other disciplines.

Women's Studies is multidisciplinary and interdisciplinary, it is not static. Women's Studies did not judge me by society's narrow-minded views pertaining to disability. Acknowledging diversity and difference is an integral and important feature of Women's Studies. Women's Studies therefore provided me with a platform to address and share my own knowledge and experience of disability, and to demonstrate that disabled women have largely been ignored by feminism, and that disabled women do have a voice. Charlotte Bunch states:

> In looking at diversity among women, we see one of the weaknesses of the feminist concept that the personal is political. It is valid that each woman begins from her personal experiences and it is important to see how these are political. But we must also recognize that our personal experiences are shaped by the culture with all its prejudices. We cannot therefore depend on our perceptions alone as the basis for political analysis and action — much less for coalition. Feminists must stretch beyond, challenging the limits of our own personal experiences by learning from the diversity of women's lives. (Bunch, 1988, quoted in Morris, 1992a, p. 8)

Why are disabled women's issues omitted from the Women's Studies curriculum, when other issues of difference are addressed, such as racism and lesbianism? Ultimately, it is up to disabled women to speak out.

As a disabled woman myself, I needed to acknowledge my disability and 'come out', euphemistically speaking. The effect of this was a double-edged sword. On the one hand, students became aware that all women are disabled, simply by being women, and on the other hand, it enabled me to recognize why I had pretended to be normal. As Lesley Child has observed:

> We often feel that we have to deny any difficulties that we have, to deny our disability itself, in order to assert that our lives have value. (Morris, 1992b, p. 6)

Taking the initiative and incorporating disability issues into the Women's Studies curriculum, informing staff and students of the multiple oppression incurred by disabled women, takes courage and persistence. Examining the oppression of disabled women involves challenging the very definitions of feminist discourse. For years I had been a passive spectator rather than an active participant. I was inherently concerned with 'getting it right', and felt, and to some extent still do feel, that I was not as well informed on issues of disability as I would have liked to have been. Nevertheless, the realization that there is no one voice or authority which can express a universal truth, based on the life experiences of all women, effectively helps you to overcome many of your doubts and uncertainties. To draw a parallel, one could say it is like reading a book. Each one of us may interpret it differently, yet there is no right or wrong interpretation. What is important is not so much how we interpret it, but more that we become aware of new issues, and raise our consciousness. Therefore, putting disability on the agenda must be seen in a positive light, as an action that brings change and empowerment to all women. Breaking down the barriers of fear and guilt is sometimes painful. In some ways, it is like starting a journey that you think will never end; but when you begin the sense of relief is rewarding.

Issues Affecting Disabled Women

Disabled women have the same human aspirations as other human beings, and it is not so much the disability which disempowers us, as the disablement created by society. There is an enormous need to explore the subordination that exists amongst disabled women, in order for us to form positive self-definitions. Examining the ideas and actions of excluded groups is crucial if we are to raise essential issues affecting disabled women. For example:

Sexuality: The Right to Choose

In England, present legislation pertaining to abortion is discriminatory towards disabled people. From a disabled woman's perspective, the justification of an abortion purely on the basis of preventing disability not only denies the woman the right to choose, but also is construed in eugenic terms, rather than from a woman-centred perspective. It is common for a disabled woman to have to defend her right to reproduce because we live in a society that is hostile to disability.

Myths Surrounding Disabled People

Disabled women may have internalized oppression in the knowledge that being disabled, as opposed to able-bodied, influences the way disabled women are seen and judged. We may be frightened to speak out. This is hardly surprising, when literature predominantly focuses on the negative aspects of disability, the helplessness and the sense of inferiority. Often in their portrayal of disabled people, charities, for example, reinforce the self-fulfilling prophecy believed by many, that a disabled person's life is of no value. As Elspeth Morrison, who has been involved in disability art for some years, asks:

> If we have no representation of ourselves other than those images used in charities' advertising, cripple witches in children's books, brave and tragic media stuff, theatre and film's metaphorical use of disability as a social inadequacy, social decay, if there is no expression of life as we live it, how do we begin to validate ourselves and learn about each other? (Morris, 1992b, p. 16)

The Sexual Division of Labour

Monotony, fragmentation and isolation are, for many women, an inherent feature of their lives. Traditional attitudes which reflect men's working lives and not women's remain an inherent component in contemporary society. However, a disabled woman is twice as unlikely to receive a positive response from an employer when applying for work, as all disabled people are considered to be economically unproductive. A report by Eileen Fry in 1986 found that

> A non-disabled person is 1.6 times more likely to receive a positive response from an employer than a disabled person with the same level of qualifications and experience. (Birkett and Worman, 1988, pp. 11–12)

If a disabled person is successful in finding employment, it is usually low-paid, low-status work, often combined with poor working conditions and little security. Although legislation has been passed, such as the 1944 Disabled Persons (Employment) Act, which gave disabled persons the right to work, with the introduction of a quota system, such legislation has been largely ineffective. Social security benefits are often a disabled person's only form of income, and the social security system discriminates against women. The main disability benefit in Britain is Invalidity Benefit, which is dependent on the individual having paid sufficient National Insurance contributions. Given the employment history of women, many disabled women are not eligible for Invalidity Benefit, because they have not fulfilled the contributory conditions. The alternative benefit available to them is Severe Disablement Benefit, which is set at only 60 per cent of the level of Invalidity Benefit. The Department of Health and Social Security reported in 1988 that the majority of people who received Invalidity Benefit were men, and the majority of people who received Severe Disablement Benefit were women (Lonsdale, 1988).

Disabled people, however, are increasingly forming organizations, and collectively demanding the right to be treated as equal citizens, with equal rights. 'Existing women's groups could make valuable contributions merely by expanding their area of concern' (Boylan, 1991, p. 91). The deconstruction of race, class, disability, and sexuality gives us genuine insight into the representation of differences. Investigating women's experience thus reveals much about the universal processes of domination. Familiar themes of oppression can look quite different, depending on the consciousness one brings to them. We begin to connect with other women, and understand their anger and pain, and begin to value them, and in doing so we begin to value ourselves.

Disability Issues in Women's Studies

Once disability has been addressed, it can forge its own identity and culture, and challenge the very power structure which has marginalized disabled women. Although we do not envisage an overnight revolution which could change the consciousness of individuals, including the authors in this statement, disabled women must be included in all core courses. It is our contention that if disability is not universally addressed in Women's Studies, then the opportunity for exploring the full range of our commonalities and differences will be lost, and then, to all intents and purposes, women will continue to be segregated from each other.

We appreciate that there is not a conscious decision to exclude disabled women, but if we are to produce authentic knowledge, then we must begin by sharing our experiences. To take into account the experiences of all women, accept that all women have a voice, so in effect to deny there is a privileged or authoritative group is necessary, if we are to identify and analyze subordination, and promote change:

> Disabled people, as a group, are made up of Black people, women, gay men and lesbians as well as of white people, men, and heterosexuals. Sexism, racism, and heterosexism affect us all, and the struggle against them must be a part of any disability politics. (Morris, 1991, p. 180)

By aggregating and articulating individual expressions of consciousness, a collective group consciousness becomes possible. In this case, a disabled feminist consciousness should embrace the views and thoughts of disabled women. Disabled women are increasingly forming groups and alliances in an attempt to support each other. In *In from the Cold*, a magazine produced by the Liberation Network of People with Disabilities, Micheline Mason wrote that 'There is an essential common core to all liberation movements: the right to be both different and equal' (Morris, 1992a, pp. 188–9).

A rearticulated feminist consciousness would empower disabled women.

It is therefore crucial to involve all women, in particular disabled women, Black women and lesbian women. The concept of deviance has, at some time or other, been attached to us all, simply because we do not conform to the dominant social norms at any given time in history. Effectively stigmatized, we are then denied certain privileges and personal autonomy. Therefore, in order to gain empowerment, we must each acknowledge our oppression, and so connect to each other. Joining together for social and political liberation, we begin to undermine the impact of discrimination. Women must identify with each other, and find strength in our differences!

> If we confront our fears and prejudices and work together as communities of people who experience discrimination, we will take our rightful place in society. We are out, proud, brothers, sisters, lovers, parents. (Gillespie-Sells and Ruebain, 1992, p. 20)

In a society that has devalued women, it is necessary that disabled women speak out. This will empower and liberate all women. As Rosemary Tong comments:

> Feminist thought, then, is that although it has a beginning, it has no end, and because it has no predetermined end, feminist thought permits each woman to think her own thoughts. Apparently, not the truth, but the truths are setting women free. (Tong, 1989, p. 138)

Women as Facilitators for the Learning of Others

Issues concerning powerlessness, a sense of inferiority, lack of self-esteem, fear, self-disclosure, or challenging what is perceived to be normal, are relevant to all women. Joining an access course can be the beginning of a voyage of self-discovery whereby feelings of dependency can begin to be jettisoned. It is pleasing to note that over two-thirds of students on the Foundation Studies Programme are now women, and new access routes at local colleges are now available via franchised variations of the Programme. There is, however, no room for complacency here, since, although there may be strength in numbers, women need to become aware of this, once on course. After three years of operation, there seems little doubt that women mentors are a vital part of this process. The scheme is a valuable exercise in personal development, whilst raising the consciousness of women students. This, in turn, provides women with essential support, whilst achieving a higher retention rate of students on the Programme overall.

There is qualitative evidence to support this claim. In order to obtain the Programme award, students are expected to comment upon their experiences weekly, via a 'critical evaluation log', with particular reference to Programme delivery and the mentor scheme. These logs provide evidence of the contribution of mentors, their quality and relevance. Mentors themselves are expected to evaluate their own contributions, and monitor the scheme as a whole, since some gain academic credit for their endeavours, which provides valuable feedback as follows:

> I have known cases which, but for the presence and sympathetic support of female mentors, would have resulted in women leaving the Programme. This has been because women are subjected to pressure within their own families and that means they should forgo their studies. (Mentor Report, 1991)

Ambition, therefore, is not so much absent in women, but likely to be suppressed. A woman-centred mentor scheme can counter this, and other perceptions of higher education.

Mature students often have a preconceived idea of people in authority (lecturers and other professionals), who often appear to be alienating, but mentors who have successfully completed the Programme, and are themselves undergraduates, make it easier for new students to express their anxieties. This is important during the first six weeks of the Programme, where mentors take responsibility for the teaching and learning strategies employed, or when they mutually present discipline-based sessions with members of staff, and are available for consultation and advice thereafter.

The experiences of these students can be compared with those of off-campus and franchised women students, whose courses are not yet established enough to benefit from their own mentor scheme. For example, one college cohort of twenty-six women students in an area of high unemployment lost two-thirds of its members, due, in many cases, to personal and family-based problems. This included the wholesale destruction of one woman's books, papers and coursework by her partner. Since so many women describe the reasons for leaving study programmes as being personal, it may well be that this is a euphemism for harassment from partners or parents, but it may equally be a result of women subsuming their own needs to those of others, thus reinforcing patterns of dependancy and vulnerability.

A recent Access publication further demonstrates the problems women face when returning to study. Christine Jarvis has found that one-third of women students surveyed on a specific access course had 'experienced domestic violence, during their year on the course, and that partnerships frequently break down' (Jarvis, 1992, p. 12) and has called for opportunities within the curriculum for women to study on their own. Since the Foundation Studies Programme is offered to students on a part-time basis, it is even more important that women students require support and assistance from other women.

The example of women taking responsibility for their own and others' learning as teachers and mentors is, therefore, a valuable vehicle for personal development and an increasing awareness of self. It encourages women to begin to discover the commonalities and diversities of their experiences, and to make connections between what is, and what can be achieved by the example of others. To go from being an access student to being a teacher of other mature students in as little as eighteen months provides increased self-esteem, confidence and communicative ability for women whose day-to-day study is permeated by the values of a male-dominated learning environment.

Just as issues pertaining to women's disability inform the Women's Studies curriculum, they also create an alliance between access and feminist philosophy. Even though women-centred and disability-based consciousness-raising within an institution can be assisted by the appointment of officers whose role it is to promote such issues, we feel that these strategies can be counter-productive, since they can be seen as a 'top down' response to issues which are no longer (officially) perceived to exist. However innovative access courses appear to be, they are designed to accustom students to conform to existing power structures and hierarchies which exist in higher education. In many respects, a mentor scheme, however woman-centred, colludes with this process. It is high time, therefore, that women unite in order to create a feminist approach which challenges the methods, delivery and assumptions which underpin the higher education curriculum. As Liz Stanley and Sue Wise write, feminism is a way of living our lives:

> It occurs as and when women, individually and together, hesitantly and rampantly, joyously and with deep sorrow, come to see our lives differently and to reject externally imposed frames of reference for understanding these lives, instead beginning the slow process of constructing our own ways of seeing them, understanding them, and living them. For us, the insistence on the deeply political nature of everyday life, and on seeing political change as personal change is, quite simply, feminism. (Stanley and Wise, 1983, p. 192)

References

BALL, C. (1990) 'More Means Different: Widening Access into Higher Education', in *A Report for the Royal Society for the Encouragement of Arts, Manufacture and Commerce*, London, RSA.

BIRKETT, K. and WORMAN, D. (1988) *Getting On With Disabilities: An Employers Guide*, London, Institute of Personnel Management.

BOYLAN, E. (1991) *Women and Disability*, London, Zed Books.

BUNCH, C. (1988) 'Making Common Cause: Diversity and Coalitions', in McEWAN, C. and O'SULLIVAN, S. (Eds) *Out the Other Side*, London, Virago.

CAMPLING, J. (1979) *Better Lives for Disabled People*, London, Virago.

FINGER, A. (1991) *Past Due*, London, Women's Press.

FRANKS, H. (1990) *Mummy Doesn't Live Here Any More*, London, Doubleday.

FRY, EILEEN (1986) *An Equal Chance for Disabled People?*, London, Spastics Society.

GILLESPIE-SELLS, K. and RUEBAIN, D. (1992) *Double the Trouble, Twice the Fun*, London, Channel Four Television.

HOPKINS, L. (1991) *I'm Alive*, Liverpool, Changing Places Publications.

JARVIS, C. (1992) 'Keeping Them Down: Women and Access Provision', *Access News*, 13, Polytechnic of North London.

KARACH, A. (1992) 'The Politics of Dislocation: Some Mature Women's Experience in Higher Education', *Women's Studies International Forum*, **15**, 2.

LONSDALE, S. (1988) *Women and Disability*, Basingstoke, Macmillan Education.

MENTOR REPORT (1991) Foundation Studies Programme, University of Central Lancashire.

MORRIS, J. (1991) *Pride against Prejudice: Transforming Attitudes to Disability*, London, Women's Press.

MORRIS, J. (1992a) *Disabled Lives: Many Voices, One Message*, London, BBC Education Developments and Information.

MORRIS, J. (1992b) *Alone Together*, London, Women's Press.

NEWTON, S. and LILLEY, A. (1990) 'Mentorship: Supporting the Adult Learner. An Investigation of the Working of a Mentorship Scheme', *Journal of Further and Higher Education*, **14**, 3, pp. 71–82.

PEARSON, V. (1991) *Women and Power: Gaining Back Control*, Sheffield, Pavic Publications.

STANLEY, L. and WISE, S. (1983) *Breaking Out: Feminist Consciousness and Feminist Research*, Routledge and Kegan.

TONG, R. (1989) *Feminist Thought*, Unwin, Hyman.

Feminists: In or Out of the Academy?

Chapter 12

Academia and the Feminist Movement in Latin America

Virginia Vargas

I would like to offer a personal reflection on the complex relationship between the feminist movement and feminists working in academia. I will draw on my experiences and articulate some of my multiple identities:[1] as a founder, activist and organizer in the Peruvian feminist movement, intermittent professor, and as a founder/employee in a feminist non-governmental organization, the Flora Tristán Centre in Peru.[2] I will begin with a brief overview of the women's movement in Latin America and focus primarily on the relationships and tensions between the movement and academia, the ways in which the movement has contributed to a better understanding between these two and its reflections on how to put this into practice. I will discuss the experiences of the feminist meetings in Latin America and the Caribbean that have been taking place since 1981 in different countries. More than any other space, these meetings represent the advances, difficulties and problems in the formation of movements and the production of knowledge. At the most recent meetings, women from academia have participated with force and enthusiasm, contributing in this way to closing the gap that had been widening since the initial stages of the feminist process in the region.

The Context of the Latin American Women's Movement

Latin America is a multi-cultural, multi-ethnic continent of enormous contrasts and tremendous inequality. An incomplete and subordinate process of modernization has had an ambivalent effect, increasing the marginalization of wide social, regional and cultural sectors on the one hand, while at the same time facilitating the integration and a broadening of the horizons of these same sectors, giving rise in the past few decades to a chorus of voices coming from the latter who have been traditionally marginalized from the process of political transformation. As a result of this process, one of the most notable characteristics of Latin America is the rich diversity of cultures, peoples, regions and social sectors — all of which have different demands, struggles and movements — juxtaposed alongside a system of profound inequality in terms of access to resources and the means of production.

The women's movement has not been immune from this reality and has tended to reflect both characteristics. It is an enormously pluralistic movement formed by three basic strands: the feminist movement itself; those women whose life and commitment is found within the institutional, formal sphere of political parties, unions, federations, universities, etc.; and women who, from their roles as mothers, wives and daughters, continue to advance and become aware of their existence as part of a subordinate gender. The movement is not a homogeneous process, but is a plurality of processes that demonstrate the diverse and contradictory realities of women.

In each of these three strands, gender relations and their priorities depend on the identities and interests of women, and according to the contacts women make at different moments in their lives. The social, ethnic, cultural and geographic plurality of the continent and the women's movement form part of each strand, influencing their development and the role that the different social actors take on. Finally, each strand has its own means and forms of action, expression and generation of knowledge. At the same time, each one of them has limited access to resources and 'legitimate' ways of generating knowledge.

The Feminist Movement and Academia: A Creative or Paralysing Tension?

My personal story perhaps is typical of the lives of many other feminists of my generation, not only in Peru but in all of Latin America. My work as a professor began in 1970 at the University of Chile in Santiago. It was a creative period of left-wing militancy which undoubtedly influenced our academic work. The military coup led by General Augusto Pinochet brought an end to this work and to the commitment of building utopia. When I returned to Peru I spent several years working at the university and in public administration. My commitment to the Left continued to develop and along with other women of my generation we became more demanding in our proposals for political transformation. Although the first feminist groups existed, only in the second half of the 1970s did the movement come together in what is now known as the Peruvian feminist movement.

Although I left academia several years earlier for reasons beyond my control, it was, paradoxically, academia that brought me closer to feminism. In 1978, the first seminar on women and development was organized at the Catholic University. The seminar was the product of a similar event that had been organized a year earlier at the Institute for Social Studies (ISS) in Holland. Kate Young, of Sussex University, was in charge of the academic side, Wicky Meynen, of the ISS, was in charge in Holland, and I was responsible for the programme in Lima. We lived through three months of intense contact with feminist ideas which attracted us both out of fear and fascination, and which were absolutely new to us. Struggling against our own preconceived ideas, we began an enriching process of questioning old paradigms of knowledge and action, and slowly we began to develop the spaces to discuss what had not been discussed before.

It was an enormously enriching and subversive experience that stirred a restlessness that we were already beginning to feel, but for which we did not possess an explanation or a way to express it. European and Peruvian women together began a process of exchange and interchange that continues today. The impact of the workshop was such that of the thirty-five women who participated, 95 per cent went on to work with women or on issues related to women. From Flora Tristán new organizations were born and the experience served as a catalyst for the founding of feminist movements in other countries throughout the region.

A large number of Flora Tristán's founders came from academia which would explain why one of our first intentions was to undertake feminist research. Nevertheless, the demands and the pleasure we got from organizing and building a movement were even stronger than our academic leanings at the time. We decided that we did not want to be a group of volunteers who dedicated their spare time to reflecting on and struggling for women's rights, but to look for ways to carry out this work full-time. The Flora Tristán Collective became the Flora Tristán Centre. We left behind our jobs, the universities, and the political parties and dedicated ourselves with little money but lots of audacity — to opening a space for political action and interaction in a society based on a feminist perspective.

Moving from academia to a 'grass-roots' movement was the first source of tensions between the women academics and the feminists. Those of us who opted for the movement were faced with a loss of credibility. My partner at the time clearly expressed what was happening in this process. In what he considered to be my best interests, he asked me how it was possible that a woman as intelligent as me, with so many possibilities for a successful university career, could leave behind everything to waste my time on something as ridiculous as liberation.

Some of us took the risk of losing credibility, while others decided to remain at their universities. Both options were legitimate, but we did not see them this way at the time, which was the beginning of the gap between the two groups. There was little time, however, for us to think about any problems, because we had embarked on a new, complicated and enriching experience. It was also a time of insecurity. For example, at that time I had already published a number of articles and a book about peasant movements, but my fear of reflecting on and writing about my new feminist experiences was great. I also experienced an enormous sense of guilt. I felt as though I never had enough time to read, systematize and analyze all the material that existed, especially when it was time for me to start writing. There was also a sense of guilt caused by my desire to finish reading a new book on feminism or finish writing an article, when I should have been participating in a meeting of the feminist movement. For an activist coming out of an academic setting these tensions are always present. What is important is that these contradictions are no longer as paralyzing as they were in the beginning and, in some ways, they may lead to an even richer experience of reflecting on the complexities of women. Once the initial insecurity and guilt was overcome, we began a wonderful experiencing of individual and collective knowledge that fed on itself. In a certain sense, the 'ownership' of the production of new ideas began to recede and the focus was no longer on articles and books, but on the creation of a basic common feeling that brought us together. The reflection/ clarification/interchange of ideas and concepts through feminist theory workshops replaced what was lacking in gender studies at the universities.

It was a collective experience that allowed me to recover my sense of security and gain a new audacity to continue writing and reflecting. It was also a time in which we laid the foundations for what is the feminist movement in Peru today and what we consider to be contributions to the creation of feminist theory in Latin America.

The tensions between the movement and academia, never well defined or particularly aggressive, but still uncomfortable and paralyzing, continued to grow partly because we never talked about them and treated them as if they did not exist. The suspicions of some of us made the level of communication difficult and created mutual distrust. This feeling was increased by an attitude that considered the work of some as more valid, truthful and scientific than that of others. Some of us in the movement and in academic life confronted common fears, but we did so in an antagonistic way. In the movement we feared that what was being produced in the universities had no foundation in reality, did not consider the dynamics of the feminist movement, and did not look at the subjective or the symbolic. The women working in academia feared that what was being produced in the movement was not scientific, and was too ideological and radical. On both sides we were afraid of our own ghosts and we were both right. Both in the feminist movement and in academia, when the bridges of communication collapsed we ran the risk of creating partial knowledge that was idealized, aseptic, without scientific foundations or theoretical qualities and lacking in the richness of different experiences — in brief, unable to confront pluralistic and complementary visions. As a result, neither side had the strength to offer a feminist proposal in or out of academia. The tensions, nonetheless, revealed a more profound and complex process: the difficulty in breaking down traditional paradigms and accepting the possibility of multiple focuses and 'truths'.

In this process, however, in Peru as well as in other Latin American countries, the feminist movement advanced in questioning old paradigms and other beliefs that were still strong in the political and cultural climate of the 1970s. Within this context, we developed new paradigms of social criticism, confronting traditional subject disciplines and demonstrating that their universal 'truths' were only partial in character.

But the development of new ways of thinking and the subversive quality of the feminist proposal did not manage to vanquish all of the ghosts of the old paradigms. From the beginning of the movement to create new ways of thinking, there existed polarized, imposed and mixed visions that at times were enriching and at other times limiting. At one end, there was an amplitude of vision, the subversive and probing examination of authoritarian logic, the recognition of the richness found in differences, and the move to politicize daily life. On the other, there existed causal explanations, exclusive logic, reductionism, myths and partial experiences that were portrayed as universal.

In summary, the questioning and rupture of old certainties also generated a compensatory practice that ran the risk of being reductionist and exclusive.

Feminist Meetings

These visions have been developed and expressed at the different feminist meetings held in Latin America between 1981 and 1990. The feminist meetings have become a barometer for measuring the growth of the movement. I shall concentrate on the significance of each meeting in terms of theoretical advances and the subjective climate of feminist opinion. My focus will be on the last two meetings because I believe that they best demonstrate the past and present tensions within the feminist movement.

In 1981, the 'First Encounter' of Latin American and Caribbean feminists was held in Bogota, Colombia. The meeting was a hallmark for the movement in the region, offering

> a first opening of Latin American feminism to the world . . . Bogota marked the era of the recuperation of spaces for women. . . . It marked the moment for an unorganized assault on order . . . Bogota was the first vivid experiment in this enormous sense of women being together. It was the first time all expectations were shattered. (Kirkwood, 1986, p. 214)

The Bogota encounter had at least two important features: we experienced the recognition of 'sisterhood', the explosion of self-affirmation of knowledge and space for women and, in relation to this new awareness, we developed a sense of a 'complete and immediate' revolution (Kirkwood, 1986, p. 215).

The second Feminist Encounter, which was held in Lima, Peru, in 1983 and attended by 650 women, was a time for reformulating questions and looking for answers.

> In Lima, the demand for answers and for the formulation of new, complex questions engendered new feminist political strategies. We suffered from exasperated impatience to know it all, to solve even the questions that cannot be answered. (Kirkwood, 1986, p. 215)

This was the meeting at which it seemed absolutely necessary to demonstrate — through the presence and persistence of patriarchy — feminism's capacity to provide analyses of women and society, to contribute to the theoretical status of the movement. Twenty simultaneous workshops run by Latin American and Caribbean feminists analyzed patriarchy. A rich discussion emerged and revealed the global concept of the period: the segmentation of women's reality into specific themes that only made sense in comparison to patriarchal categories.

In the third meeting, which took place in Bertioga, Brazil, in 1985, about 1,000 women participated. It was at this meeting that some of the women resisted the structured form of the organization, the perception that women's subjectivity was a fundamental element in their lives, and recognized the necessity for stimulating the equal participation of all women.[3] It was an effort 'to ensure that each woman would participate equally without hierarchies of any kind. No woman was accorded a greater or lesser status because of her feminist militancy or experience in political parties or because she was a specialist' (meeting document).

Independent of the advances at these meetings that permitted the consolidation of the feminist movement in Latin America, a new richness and variety of networks and proposals for development, the meetings also gave rise to a new body of ideology and theories to interpret women's reality and the world. This ideological consistency, however, began to take on the qualities of 'an absolute', in which we felt that by opening up to a more plural and complex movement we would lose our base. This tendency had an impact on the theoretical and political practices of the movement.

On a political level, this led the movement to lose touch with the different specifics of the various strands within the women's movement, assuming that the universality of women's suffering was the key to inter-class and transcultural unity.

On a theoretical level, this process was expressed through an attempt to look for a category that offered us a global explanation. At the forefront was patriarchy, considered as a solitary fact; and then gender, which was not analyzed in all of its complexity and in relation to other social conditions, but as a category to explain the subordination of women as an empirical notion in relation to inequality, producing an all-inclusive vision not only for women but for social conflict. The difference began to take on the characteristics of a universal, moving the feminist proposal dangerously close to reductionism.

We arrived at the fourth feminist conference in Taxco, Mexico, in 1987 with an almost intuitive determination to distance ourselves from our past practices. It is here that Latin American feminists confronted a dark and defensive politics that many felt was keeping us from advancing to a more democratic process. Mexico was also the scene of the first confrontation — both jolting and enriching — over the issue of diversity. The tension between homogeneity and diversity appeared not so much in the issues presented as in the strategies different groups wanted to pursue.

In the climate of the fourth encounter, participants reflected on the 'myths' which crystallized the tensions between the political ideas and the social practices of the feminist movement. It became clear that the feminist utopia was in crisis. In the face of this, the movement generated its own mechanisms of compensation. Instead of recognizing the contradictions that we were living, we constructed myths about what we were as a movement. These myths — many of which still exist — did not constitute a utopia but rather a new vanguardism that excluded difference. The myths carried with them a counter-proposal to patriarchal power that claimed a feminine capacity that could not be overtaken by contradictions, an essentialism that some authors have called 'womanism' (Lamas, 1990). These myths included a vision of the future in which homogeneity, and not difference, would ensure equality and power.[4] The myths detected at the time were:

- feminists are not interested in power;
- feminists do politics in a different way;
- all feminists are equal;
- there is a natural unity in just being women;
- any small group is representative of the movement;
- women's spaces in themselves guarantee positive processes;
- because I as a woman feel something, it is valid;
- the personal is automatically political;
- consensus is democracy.

It is easy to state that none of these myths are true: we have innate contradictions; we adopt traditional patterns of behaviour when we get involved in politics; consensus can serve to hide authoritarian practice when it tries to quiet differences. Not all women are equal and unity among women is not a given, rather it is something that has to be constructed based on our differences. Feminism does not mean constructing a political system of women for women, but must also be something in which men can participate. Our personal sentiments can also be arbitrary when only considered within their individual dimension. The personal can be political only when it combines action with awareness.

The document about myths had a tremendous impact on the feminist movement. It became 'a tool to work within the movement, breaking the barriers of romanticism and candy-coating' (Tornaria, 1991). But above all, it demonstrated to Latin American feminism the need to revise its social practices.

In 1990, three years after the closing session in Taxco, we arrived in San Bernardo, Argentina. The fifth Feminist Encounter, which brought together 3,000 women, was held in a Latin America where democratic values were beginning to take hold. The spirit of the meeting was influenced by the crisis within the authoritarian governments of the region, the collapse of socialism in Eastern Europe and, to a lesser degree, the crisis within the Left in Latin

America. The general disenchantment, influenced by the deepening economic crisis and by a loss of confidence in political institutions, reinforced the discontent with analyses based solely on class struggle and confrontation. The conference gave more room to democratic and pluralistic ideas.

In this climate, the feminist movement was able to spread and to contribute to the changes. It could extend itself into new spaces and reach new women who brought different life experiences, different subjectivities and different realities to feminist debates. This meant that some myths were revised, reformulated, confronted, although it was not possible to overcome a utopian vision based solely on a universal feminism.

The problems around the movement's lack of respect for diversity surfaced once again in Argentina, but this time with much more force. The expansion of the feminist movement in Latin America during this time consolidated the process we had begun in Mexico in 1987: the participants at the fifth meeting were not only militant feminists whose work centred on the issues involving gender. At the same time, these new participants demanded a space within the feminist movement. They criticized the old leadership and their organization. This new plurality defined the conference, but also contributed more to fragmentation than to respect for differences.

A workshop, 'Feminism in the 1990s: Challenges and Proposals', was organized to deal with some of the tensions resulting from the conference. The workshops tried to untie some of the knots in the movement: diversity, democracy, leadership, construction of knowledge,[5] financing, and our relationship to state and society.

The meeting was not as ideological as in the past. There were no great new theories proposed to define specific strategies to confront concrete problems. We incorporated new days into the Latin American feminist calendar: a day in which we would struggle for pro-choice rights, another to analyze the treatment of women within the media. New networks were constructed that reflected our changing reality: Latin American and Caribbean feminist historians, feminists in political parties, environmentalists, academics. All of the women at the conference, despite their enormous diversity, were interested in being there, wanting to take part and in being recognized as part of the movement. They were looking to take part in society from different angles and on different issues, from different cultures and differing realities. They wanted to be valid spokeswomen for feminism within their respective societies and groupings.

The debate on diversity within the feminist movement is marked by an ambivalence in the transition from one stage to the next. As a result, diversity has become the crux of the process by which we must complete unfinished tasks and formulate ideas for future organizations that will include all women. This will not be easy, but on our success rests the possibility of constructing a more democratic and egalitarian society in Latin America.

I would like to end with a personal testimony that I believe reflects the enormous and rich possibilities the women's movements in Peru and throughout Latin America have for producing knowledge. Instead of writing about academia or a strand within the feminist movement, I want to quote what I wrote about Maria Elena Moyano, a grass-roots feminist leader in Peru who was killed on February 15, 1992 by the Shining Path faction (Sendero Luminoso).

> On January 16, 1992, I presented my latest book and I asked Maria Elena if she would take part in the panel. Her comments were generous, warm and full of anecdotes about our relationship. Several days earlier, while she was reading the manuscript, she told me that she liked it very much, that she agreed with many things and disagreed with others. She said it would be important if we could bring our agreements and differences about constructing the movement to light. Right then we decided to write a book together that would unite our two visions: I am a middle-class feminist and Maria Elena was a working class feminist. What would we say about the dynamics of the movement, about the relationship between feminist non-governmental organizations and grass-roots women's groups, our relationships with the government, with the political parties? Of course, we also knew that we would include a chapter on our personal experience, about sexuality, relationships with our partners, our children, our ways of reconciling our leadership roles with those of being a mother. In summary, the many things that make up our daily lives but are never considered as part of our public lives. We had already designed the cover: a face with two profiles, hers and mine.
>
> This book will never be written, at least not as we had planned. I will write it in her name, dedicated to her, inspired by her, with pain and anger, but also with love. I will write it.

Notes

1 I have lived these multiple identities for the past three years. For six months of each year I teach on the Women's Programme of the Institute for Social Studies in The Hague, Holland; and for the other six months I work for the Research Programme of the Flora Tristán Centre. In both activities I try to maintain an active role in the feminist movement.

2 The Flora Tristán Centre in Lima, Peru, was founded a decade ago in memory of Flora Tristán, a French feminist and socialist radical reformer (1803–44), who had a Peruvian father. The Centre has as its main objective the encouragement and promotion of activities to strengthen the organization of Peruvian women, particularly in the field of discrimination. It carries out research into social policy and state planning on behalf of women at national, regional and local levels, and supports and coordinates a variety of activities between women and women's organizations.

3 At this meeting, the participants called the founders of the movement 'fossils', in an attempt to both recognize their historic participation and marginalize them.

4 These myths were expressed in 'From Love to Necessity', a document produced by eleven women during the Mexico conference.

5 Part of the reflection on this issue maintained: 'We need to produce knowledge in relation to the transformations and new economic and political challenges on the continent, as well as the symbolic-cultural models that take longer to transform. We need to produce knowledge from our personal and social practices, which implies transforming experiences into theory. We need to produce knowledge from a reflection on methodology, looking for ways to read the realities that touch the movement. We need to incorporate new specializations and abilities into the movement, that makes our actions more efficient in the political and social world. We need to ensure fluidity in relation to knowledge, generating new forms of relations between practice and theory that are not based on hierarchies or differential values.'

References

KIRKWOOD, JULIETA (1986) *Ser Politica en Chile. Las Feministas y los Partidos Politicos*, Santiago, Chile, Ed. Flacso.

LAMAS, MARTA (1990) Editorial, in *Revista Debate Feminista*, año I, vol. 2, Mexico.

TORNARIA, CARMEN (1991) 'Los gozos y las sombras de un Encuentro fraterno', in *Mujer/Fempress*, II, Santiago, Chile.

VARGAS, VIRGINIA (1992a) 'The Feminist Movement in Latin America: Between Hope and Disenchantment', in *Development and Change*, **23**, 3, London, Sage.

VARGAS, VIRGINIA (1992b) *Como Cambiar el Mundo sin Perdernos*, Lima, Peru, Ed. Flora Tristán.

Chapter 13

Inside and 'Out' or Outside Academia: Lesbians Working in Scotland

Jennifer Marchbank, Chris Corrin and Sheila Brodie

Introduction

When Chris Corrin tried to establish a new Honours option in 'Feminist Thought and Political Theory', her Head of Department wrote to her, suggesting that it might be that she was 'too politically committed to teach a course in feminist theory in a completely neutral manner, such as those on Fascism[!] and Liberalism', and if this were the case then she should disqualify herself. It seemed to Chris that, since she came 'out' at work, many of her colleagues (all the other twelve members of academic staff are male) had worked hard to find 'bias' in her work. Sheila Brodie and Jennifer Marchbank found that they too could draw on such experiences. Chris felt that the atmosphere of working as a lesbian in academia seemed different in Scotland than in England and this seemed a prime question which required investigation.

As three lesbians working in education, we recognized at the outset similarities and differences in our situations, but particularly important was that of being 'inside' or 'outside' formal academia. By 'formal' we meant university-level, mixed education. For Sheila, her choice to remain within adult education was a very definite and positive one for her. Having the opportunity to work largely with women in the community was very much a plus. Both Jen and Chris had various reasons why they felt it important to remain within the Academy, in terms of challenging misogyny and heterosexual norms, in addition to placing feminist ideas before audiences — of both colleagues and students — who would not otherwise be faced with such arguments. For Chris, formal academia could only be tolerated as a 'temporary' measure, and for Jen, working part-time as a youth worker made her situation more tolerable.

Women's Studies Network Scottish Group

Nowhere in any of the Scottish institutions of education is there an under-graduate programme of Women's Studies, nor is there a choice of postgraduate courses.[1] Although several institutions offer occasional course options which tackle gender issues, there is a dearth of courses covering sexuality and violence against women.[2] Given this situation, many Scottish WSN members do not actually teach or study Women's Studies. The Scottish Group of the WSN attempts to ameliorate this through meetings and seminars to stimulate feminist discussions and support.

There is a distinctive hierarchy to Scottish educational institutions, operating to the detriment of Women's Studies. The Scottish educational culture still incorporates the notion of the 'lad o' pairts',[3] that is, one can utilize the supposedly accessible Scottish educational system to escape the restrictions of one's birth through academic excellence. This validates subject divisions and legitimizes concepts of academic competition. It is not difficult to perceive that Women's Studies, with its cooperative character, working in non-traditional, supportive and interdisciplinary fashions, is marginalized within this structure.

However, not only are women's views of the world derided within the Scottish academy, but the external society is also fairly indifferent to women's concerns.

Scottish Cultural Context

Before addressing the experiences we all face as lesbians in Scottish education, an awareness of West Central Scotland in terms of its predominant culture, expectations, and behaviour, is required as background. The common perception is of a male, working-class culture, reinforced and reflected by the dominance of the Labour Party in Scottish politics. This does not produce an atmosphere of radicalism towards women, rather most of our social, political and educational institutions contain an ethos of patriarchal conservatism.

The educational system upholds the 'virtues' of the patriarchal system. Few women teachers become Heads, despite over-representation in the lower grades. At university level, women professors are equally rare and not anticipated — a recent article in a Glasgow newspaper referred to an eminent woman professor as 'he' throughout.

The public face of this culture is exemplified by the elected representatives both locally and at Westminster. They tend to be Labour, male and conservative in outlook — there is more emphasis on maintaining the established (Labour) order than on challenging society's structures. Recent left-wing challenges[4] to this status quo do not serve women any better.

This patriarchal conservatism is supported by the influence of the churches. Both the Catholic and Protestant churches retain a considerable degree of authority and some quite fundamentalist views. These views cover the role of women within the family, the structure and values of the family unit, homosexuality, contraception, and abortion. In West Central Scotland the influence of these churches is particularly strong given the concentration of Catholic and Orange communities.

These factors, and others, combine to restrict our opportunities as women, feminists and lesbians, to teach and research the issues in which we are interested, and to live our lives as we choose. These conservative and traditional attitudes have also discouraged discussion of issues of sexuality, both within academic and community-based education. This was demonstrated by Strathclyde Region's attempted implementation of Section 28[5] by, for example, banning youth workers from discussing issues of sexuality with their young clients, or refusing a college's Lesbian and Gay Society permission to use rooms for meetings or even to display posters.[6]

We feel that the experience of being lesbian in Scotland is very different from that in more tolerant areas of England. Lesbianism is far more marginalized in Scotland, allowing homophobic sentiments to be more frequently expressed, with less threat of challenges and less chance of punitive action being taken. We have been informed that as feminists (read lesbians) we are too politically committed to teach feminist theory, and we have to accept serious consideration being given to students in our departments who complain about feminist issues being raised in lectures. We also have to suffer the inherent homophobia within our institutions — revealed when an equal opportunities statement by one establishment excluded discrimination on the grounds of sexuality, and yet had an accompanying statement on sexual harassment which included same-sex approaches.

We are aware that sexism and heterosexism are endemic not only in Scottish society but across academia, and that the Academy 'is not often a place where radical feminism is welcomed or supported' (Stanko, 1991). Nonetheless, based on our own experiences of working in other areas of Britain, we feel that the liberal veneer of toleration which exists elsewhere is thinner in Scotland.

Ourselves

Common Ground

Working through our common and different experiences helped us to locate some of our motivations towards academic work and our reactions to the varying oppressions we have encountered. Our common ground is that we are all lesbian; all opposed to organized patriarchal religions. We all have degrees and postgraduate qualifications, and a history of activism. For all of us, work, both paid and unpaid, equals political activism. We are all 'white' ((charles), 1992).

Those of our readers who are lesbian will realize how many differences there are amongst us, yet how, in isolation or situations of being distinct minorities, our lesbianism becomes so important. For each of us, being lesbian is a very major part of our lives, our identities, our 'situations'. Yet within the supposedly 'liberal' atmospheres of our respective workplaces, we each have to be careful in our 'telling'. Each of us has chosen to 'come out' in various ways and stages. In her first year Chris came out only to sympathetic colleagues and to students — later telling all her colleagues, including clerical staff on whom she relied for female contact. For both Jen and Sheila it was important that their immediate bosses in community-based education knew, and then they chose their 'allies' as necessary. Such reticence did not restrict Jen within the formal education mode where she allowed some to know and others to work it out.

Our opposition to organized patriarchal religions stems partly from individual experiences — Sheila's Jewish background, and Chris and Jen's 'Christian' ones — and partly from the broader social forces which we witness at work. Women are often viewed within organized religions as the original sinners (Eve's apple), and are also posed as the silent sufferers. Images of madonna and whores abound. These images translate into social realities, for example, the dreadful consequences of the patriarchal nature of organized religion, in terms of women's lack of control over our bodies and fertility, of women being oppressed by male ideas of 'good' and 'bad'. The idea of suffering in the here and now for something 'better' later runs counter to the feminist recognition of women's power to change our lives. Organized patriarchal religions do not empower women, and with their primal prejudices they certainly do not empower lesbians.

Our degrees bracket us all as 'academic', yet it is unclear whether or not our own histories of activism led us towards the subject matter of politics. We each feel more centred within a politically active environment, where we can act to change women's situations for the better. Perhaps our wider definitions of what 'politics' entails puts us onto a different 'wavelength' from our patriarchal colleagues, who think only of government and parties. Feminist political analysis includes the politics of housework alongside foreign policy studies. Our political activism within our communities is a vital ingredient in our academic activism — our paid and unpaid work constitutes political activism. While working with a group of lesbians one evening a month, and discussing the isolation that many of us feel in society, the difficulties for lesbian mothers, and the problems of socializing when older or with children; while with survivors of male violence; or while teaching forty 19-year-old students — we know our work to be political.

As to us all being 'white', conceptions of 'whiteness' are only beginning to be problematized. For Sheila, others' perceptions of Jewishness often battle with 'whiteness', and with her son, who has darker skin, racists don't stop to ask questions. Yet we are all apparently white, and as such are not treated in an openly (or subtly) oppressive manner by racists. It is virtually impossible for us to imagine the levels of prejudice and power-tripping which white, heterosexual (and often very sexually-repressed) academic men could indulge in with black, lesbian colleagues. One common aspect of our 'whiteness' is that we have each chosen to be actively anti-racist, which is a process we live through. Challenging some people's racism, especially within a 'liberal' academic context, is often seen as tantamount to challenging their virility. Pervasive patriarchal structures combine in powerful terms over racism and homophobia, and often seem a much too powerful cocktail for some individual white heterosexual patriarchs.

Different Experiences

As outlined above, we obviously do have a certain number of things in common — but there are also many differences among us. On a personal level there is the fact that two of us have been married and one of us has children. Our ages are different also — one of us is in her twenties, one in her thirties and one in her forties. Other differences require greater explanation.

Looking at our cultural backgrounds in detail it is clear that there are many differences despite the fact that we are all British-born and white. One of us was born and raised on the Isle of Man in a semi-rural area and in a working-class family. Another was born and brought up in a rural, working-class area in south-west Scotland. Both these women have nominally Christian backgrounds. The third was born in the north-east of England, of Jewish parents (both born in this country), and was brought up in Scotland in an urban working-class environment.

Our working-class parents (skilled or unskilled) differed in their attitudes towards education. Chris's parents did not appear to feel that education beyond school-leaving age was very important, and no positive encouragement was given to her to go on to higher education — even when she became a mature student. Both Jen and Sheila went to university straight from school, as education was more valued. However, there was no awareness of education for education's sake or for personal development, within either of their families.

Within Judaism there has always been a certain emphasis on learning. For Sheila, with a Jewish immigrant background, this was intensified by the view that an education and a profession are signs of success — signifying that you have 'made it' in this country, having moved from immigrant worker to professional. For Jen, as a member of a patriarchal extended family, education was the route out of the career expected of her by the extended family of 'nice wee job' and marriage to a Young Farmer. Fortunately, her parents also valued her education, expecting her to achieve — whereas this was not viewed as important for her equally scholarly brother.

We differ in other ways too. Our jobs are different: one of us is a full-time university lecturer, one in adult education, one a postgraduate student working part-time in both higher education and community education. We have differing definitions of feminisms, resulting from our personal experiences, our personal histories, and our work.

Feminisms and Activisms

Chris

As we have emphasized, for each of us our feminisms and activisms are intertwined. For me feminism means praxis, the meeting of theory and practice. The phrase — 'Don't agonize — organize' — still has value for me. Although I recognize the need to see patriarchal relations at work and to explain such relations to others, I am happiest organizing leaflets or getting a banner ready for something! In my work within Glasgow Lesbian Line my feminism guides many of my responses to situations. Again, the split between theory and practice disappears when we do 'brainstorming' exercises about women's isolation in society and apply these to lesbians. Being part of a group which is constantly recognizing our oppression and working to overcome it is empowering. Dealing with prejudice forms part of a process, and within this process we have choice as to when, how far and if we wish to act. For young women coming to terms with being lesbian in an aggressively homophobic atmosphere, this recognition of choosing between options of how to deal with others' ignorance is often a lifeline.

Within the academic context of my work with women's groups in Central and Eastern Europe, choosing when to 'claim' my feminism, let alone my lesbianism, has often been difficult. With feminism being such a 'dirty' word through negative propaganda, it was often problematic if I was introduced as a feminist. For some women this meant that I was not serious, and certainly could not be carrying out any unbiased 'scientific' research. Yet in personal terms my feminist commitment to empowering women often won through against learned prejudice, as women recognized my feminism as something practical. Then we were able to talk about the power of feminist theoretical work to challenge 'accepted' or, at least, unproblematized academic prejudices. Certainly in recent years, with changing relations in many countries of East-Central Europe, women in academic settings and in grass-roots groups are engaging in feminist dialogues at many different levels.

In the Scottish context, my challenging of myths and ignorance about women's abilities and oppression has had mixed reactions. When I showed a video about pornography and violence against women to a group of students, most were shocked by the connections that had been made and stimulated to discuss their feelings about the video. However, four somewhat arrogant young men felt 'disgusted' that they had been made to watch such a video as part of a Politics course, because (of course) it was not 'proper politics'. Both they and I knew that had they complained to my Head of Department he would have wholeheartedly agreed with them.

More positively, when two of my gay male students on the European Politics course came to me wishing to present gay rights in Europe as part of the Human Rights section, we chose to jointly present a seminar to the whole group. Not only did the other students take this seminar 'seriously', but genuine interest was shown in the different situations across Europe, and some were amazed at the comparative level of prejudice and legal oppressions apparent.

Jen

Like Chris, I am happier 'doing' feminism rather than theorizing. My personal history reveals far more lobbying, marching and leaflet-writing than discussion groups developing feminist theory. My activism also involves placing myself in non-feminist situations to be the feminist voice — entering bureaucratic processes to use the 'boys'' tools to our benefit. There is a great danger in this sort of activity — I might get sucked in and assimilated. I retain my feminist sense of perspective by action, be it demonstrating for a woman's right to choose or nagging my MP (and anyone else's) to support childcare, but most of all through living my life as a lesbian in a sexist and heterosexist culture.

The activism that currently dominates my time is working with a group of adolescent girls under the umbrella of local government youth work. Obviously, I am extremely careful not to be seen to be 'promoting' homosexuality, but I still stand out from many of my counterparts (in neighbouring areas) in that I don't condemn it, make derogatory jokes, nor use homosexual terms as insults. Through raising issues — alcohol, drugs, careers, disability, music, sex — to encourage the girls to think about their own expectations, I introduce feminist concepts to an audience which thinks that feminism is as passé (for aren't they equal to the boys?) as the Bay City Rollers. Assisting these girls in the development of their abilities to analyze and question the world in which they live, and to actively choose how to live their lives, is to me the ultimate feminist action.

Choosing to work with teenage girls was a political decision — taken in the context of a recognition of the second-class treatment girls usually receive from youth clubs. The form of girls' work that I do is also a political decision — others may offer disco dancing and make-up, but these do not appear on our agenda unless it is to question why they are seen as being of interest to girls. Of course, some of the girls I work with are interested in these activities, but they all agree and understand that the girls' group is 'different'. It is a place where they set the agenda, make the rules and smoke innumerable cigarettes! We discuss boys, families, peer group influences, lesbianism, teenage pregnancy, school expectations — all of which could pass for lecture material on socialization — the girls receive and use feminist theories to discuss their lives without acknowledging the source.

Working in homophobic and sexist arenas is exhausting and often one is tempted not to devote depleted energies to outside interests, or to adding feminist dimensions to our current employment. However, without my involvement in campaigning, supporting and awareness-raising activities, I would not feel able to carry on isolated in the malestream.

Sheila

Feminism to me has a number of different, interrelated aspects — both theoretical and practical. It is a continually developing critique of society, which draws out its patriarchal, male-oriented basis. This analysis reveals where power and authority lie, and how they are maintained, for example through the insistence upon the value of the family, the educational system and the state.

Feminism means working with other women to challenge the patriarchy and to encourage change in society, by, for example, making women aware of choices regarding contraception, abortion, education, sexuality, childcare, relationships and work. It means also, through awareness of my own oppression as a woman and a lesbian, fighting other oppressions such as racism, while remaining aware of the variety of experiences (all of them important and valuable) that different women have and undergo.

I work with women on these issues, and support women who have been affected by the way power is distributed in society, and as a result of how that power finds outlets in violence against women and children (through Rape Crisis). Feminism means centring my life around women and the issues that concern us. Equally important is ensuring that lesbian issues and rights are kept to the fore among discussions in feminist circles.

Out: A Continuing Process

In Britain, with legal restrictions such as Section 28, the decision to be 'out' as a lesbian is political as well as personal. In our work, we have all decided to be 'out' to some extent — often utilizing different stages for different situations. As student populations constantly change, the process of 'coming out' not only is continual, but continually demands that we make decisions.

It could be expected that an awareness of, and more sound attitudes towards, the range of human sexualities should exist amongst practitioners of higher education and community education — that 'coming out' would be unnecessary. However, despite the range of workplaces which our collective experience covers, such an awareness is rare: rather, we find that assumptions of heterosexuality pervade. Not only is a lesbian identity not anticipated in educational employees, nor part of community consciousness, it is also not included in the agenda of academic discourse (except perhaps as a study of sexual deviance). Being open about our lesbianism can force sexuality issues onto courses, but at a personal and professional cost which may be losing our jobs if we work with children, or simply being denied access to community groups due to the groups' homophobia.

One danger of being 'out' is the risk of being perceived as 'professional lesbians' — that others will see everything we do as 'tainted' by our sexuality. Our professional interests are seen as 'too political', we are viewed as crank feminists by some and as too radical by those who would claim to be our sisters. We are often accused of being on our hobby-horses when we raise issues of women's socialization and oppression, or question the validity of working to raise men's consciousness. All of these attitudes are legitimated by the fact that we are known to be lesbians, and therefore we automatically challenge the accepted norms of society and the academic fora which they support just by our presence.

Nonetheless, whether we are 'out' or not, we take our lesbianism into every area of our work, just as we take in our personal politics, our personal histories, and every other aspect of ourselves. This does not prevent us from being rigorous and professional but perhaps we are more aware of our own standpoints, as feminists, as women, and as lesbians, than are some of our colleagues.

Workshop Participants' Comments

In discussion we found that there are many similarities in being lesbians throughout British education, but also some distinct differences. Most of the workshop participants at the WSN (UK) conference in 1992 had experienced degrees of isolation, though, as one woman highlighted, being closeted did not prevent these experiences — for we are isolated if hidden and isolated when 'out'. Tolerance and acceptance levels appear to differ between Scotland and other areas of Britain — the Welsh situation, we were informed, is accepting within its academic institutions, in direct contrast to a lack of recognition and approval within the Welsh culture.

Women working and studying in English institutions seemed to have encountered a lesser degree of intolerance and ridicule than those of us in Scotland — or to live amongst a more accepting community. Women who had lived in other parts of the world (Ireland and Latin America) described the openness which they currently enjoyed in England. Nonetheless, many women felt that to be 'out' actually hampered our ability to do our job, for we would not be allowed to work — not necessarily, or always, by being sacked, but by being refused respect concerning our views and our persons.

It was suggested that institutions can be prepared for the idea that lesbians exist through the organization of feminist activities. This incrementalist approach was accepted as valid by the participants, though whose responsibility it is to do this was debated — is it our job as lesbians, or is it the responsibility of non-homophobic heterosexual feminists? One view was that all women are at different stages of the same journey of examining sexual relations and preferences — somewhat akin to Adrienne Rich's (1983) lesbian continuum — and that, given this, the responsibility lay with all feminists. A different perspective is that the possibility exists to adjust the established agenda of educational practices to include lesbians and our philosophies. But do we dare? Perhaps the personal risks are too great in the current social and economic climate?

The main conclusion which arose from this discussion was that working as lesbians in education is not simple. Patriarchal assumptions and ignorance regarding women's sexualities pervade our workplaces wherever we are — but are stronger in some geographical areas, including Scotland, than in others. Survival aids, such as a supportive network within and external to our workplaces, are vital, but they too are regionally influenced.

Conclusion

Each time we discussed these issues we realized that we cannot generalize. We are all lesbian, but we are all different lesbians. We all have academic quali-fications and work in education, but within very different situations. Each of us has slightly different aspects of our feminism which we choose to prioritize, and we deal with the various aspects of prejudice that we experience in dif-ferent ways. Yet we all believe that in attempting to theorize about homophobia within education generally, and about the situation of lesbians in particular, women like ourselves need to come together to discuss our different experiences within similar patriarchal structures, and to recognize our common ground.

Although oppressed as lesbians, we recognize that our positions as 'white' qualified women working within education can be, at times, powerful — in challenging some of the patriarchal heterosexual myths, as role models of sorts for some women students, and as mentors or at least listeners in terms of welfare needs of students. For those of us in the formal sphere of higher education we certainly get more than our share of students wishing to talk with us about their 'work'. Such talks can range across any issue, from lack of support or downright obstruction from their male supervisors or tutors to problems of poverty, poor housing, working at paid work as well as academic work, or personal matters concerning pregnancy, sexuality and general isola-tion. Difficulties can arise in such situations, in that the time needed to help students sort our their difficulties seriously impinges on our time for preparing, teaching and administering courses — let alone doing research. Whether we attempt to educate our colleagues to be more aware of students' needs, or press our bureaucracies to employ more counsellors, it all takes time and energy — with no guarantees of success.

We all feel that all students must receive a feminist input, that they must be exposed to the different ways in which people view the world. To opt out of education would be to neglect our responsibilities in this area — so too would remaining in education and not challenging and educating our colleagues as well as our students. Part of our challenging is in the production of feminist and lesbian research.

Adrienne Rich (1979) has written that the male-focused academy can be used as a base for feminist research but there is the danger of becoming detached from our foundations in feminism. Women's Studies cannot be divorced from women's movements, but how many of us can theorize all day, yet neglect to carry our banners any more? There is a real concern that Women's Studies and Feminist Theory will become no more than a career path within academia — a recent Glasgow conference presented the women in the audience with advanced theoretical papers, but a very substandard creche. Hopefully, this will remain an isolated example, and theorists and academics will not spend too much time with word-games and not enough relating back to real experiences of women. To mean anything to women's movements, we must always remember where we come from as feminists, and not where we could go in the malestream.

We each recognize the strength we gain from the wider women's movements, and that our struggles do, in turn, feed back into wider concerns. Sometimes our students will decide to start a feminist reading group, or activate the lesbian side of the Lesbian and Gay Soc, or start tackling male members of staff about the lack of a gender consciousness in their courses. Whichever way our activism works through the student body, it is at least raising questions (and sometimes complaints) about the important issues that have long gone unnoticed — or been consciously buried. Being able to introduce aspects of Women's Studies courses into our differing fields of education has provided frameworks for initiating discussions and challenging perceived 'wisdoms'. It is an uphill battle at times though, and we know many colleagues dream of opening that bookshop or women's café. The one thing that we are all aware of battling against is being 'sucked into the system', in terms of relaxing our vigilance to question, attack and discredit outmoded and prejudicial notions. To stay in academia, be it formal or community, for the money and the holidays, would not be a soft option for any of us. It would at best be a sign of defeat, but more importantly it would be living hell. It is no option to stay 'inside' and not challenge but there is always the option to go back outside and work for some sort of 'right-on' lesbian group — if only!

Notes

1 Strathclyde University offers a two-year MLitt in Women's Studies — the only one in Scotland.
2 Dundee University stands alone in offering complete classes in Women and Violence.
3 The 'lad o' pairts', the legend says, is a boy from humble beginnings who, through a combination of his intellectual talents and the availability of educational

opportunities, succeeds in being educated into a higher social class. Note that the legend does refer to boys.

4 The recent development of Scottish Militant as a separate political party challenges and threatens the Labour Party dominance in certain areas. However, women continue to be marginalized, as our issues are claimed as working-class concerns rather than women's concerns.

5 Section 28 — a legal restriction which seeks to prevent the use of public funds to 'promote homosexuality'. Although this has not yet been legally tested, the fact of its existence and the media coverage which accompanied it reveal deep resentment towards public services being provided for lesbians and gay men, and the easy acceptance of the denial of our rights by the majority of the public.

6 This occurred within one of the Region's own colleges.

References

(CHARLES), H. (1992) 'Whiteness — The Relevance of Politically Colouring the "Non"' in HINDS, H., PHOENIX, A. and STACEY, J. *Working Out: New Directions for Women's Studies*, Falmer Press.

RICH, A. (1979) 'Towards a Women Centered University' in RICH, A. *On Lies, Secrets and Silence*, Virago.

RICH, A. (1983) 'Compulsory Heterosexuality and Lesbian Existence,' in ABEL, E. and ABEL, E.K. (Eds) *The Signs Reader: Women, Gender and Scholarship*, Chicago, University of Chicago Press.

STANKO, B. (1991) 'Angst and Academia', in *Trouble and Strife*, No. 22, Winter, pp. 19–21.

Chapter 14

Queer Subjects: Lesbians, Heterosexual Women and the Academy

Tamsin Wilton

For all women their involvement in Women's Studies as an academic discipline can be problematized by conflict between the subjectivity validated by the Women's Movement and the objectivity demanded by the academy, a contradictory positioning which can be distressing. Our lived experience of oppression is the raw material of our academic study, and this can be at the same time powerful and painful, empowering and incapacitating. In the face of this complex intermingling of intellectual rigour and emotion it is to our shared experience, the 'sisterhood' of pre-postfeminist days, that we look for support and validation.[1] After all, we may remind ourselves, the personal is political. It is at precisely this point that the inadequacy of a romantic belief in the commonality of womankind becomes clear; when we look for shared experience we are confronted by what it has become fashionable to call 'difference'. In this paper I want to move beyond recognition of differences among women, the liberal pluralist position which feminism seems to have become stuck in, towards a political strategy which enables us to develop something more radical and strategically useful than the vertiginously proliferating identity politics of postmodern chic. The position of 'difference' which I have chosen to focus on is lesbianism.[2]

I write this from complex personal experience. In the last three years I have been a lesbian teacher, trainer, writer and postgraduate student, working in different contexts where the number of lesbians has ranged from a high point of 4 out of 6 people to a low point of 1 out of 72 people. Although I choose never to hide my sexuality, the degree to which I am proactively self-identified as a lesbian varies quite considerably. In short, I am a veritable Swiss Army knife of sexuality, with a useful identity for every eventuality! For all these circumstances require me to present myself and my sexuality in a considered and professional way for a variety of audiences in a variety of contexts, rather like an academic call girl. When I say that I take my work home with me, I mean that I never stop either being a lesbian or dealing with how other people react to my lesbianism. In a peculiar way my identity, my sense of self and my work become a hermeneutic circle in which the world and I collude to author myself. Sometimes this is joyful and enriching experience (the ultimate answer to alienating labour), at other times it is nightmarish.

To a certain extent, this circularity is also something intrinsic to Women's Studies wherein we are all simultaneously both subject and object. But my focus here is the specificity of the lesbian experience within Women's Studies, and I want to acknowledge that this piece springs as much from personal experience as from feminist theory. It is not 'detached'.

Lesbians and Women: Kith and Kin?

It is ten years since Adrienne Rich stated that she wrote *Compulsory Heterosexuality and Lesbian Existence* because she 'wanted, at the very least, for feminists to find it less possible to read, write or teach from a perspective of unexamined heterocentricity' (Rich, 1982, p. 24). This is not an unreasonable objective, but it is one which remains far from realized. Lesbianism has an important place historically, culturally, theoretically and politically within feminism and yet continues to be marginalized or entirely absent from Women's Studies (Cruikshank, 1982; Brimstone, 1991; Wilton, 1992). In addition the position of lesbians in relation to Women's Studies courses is a difficult one. Whereas in one sense all women's lives are the object of study on such courses, for lesbians Women's Studies may (and usually does) offer the experience of being marginalized, excluded, labelled as 'different' or studied as 'other'. The process of deconstructing sexual identity, involving as it does a set of ruptures of common-sense understandings of what it means to be and/or to study 'women', is of course problematic for lesbians and non-lesbians alike. It is, however, crucial to recognize the relative power which accrues to non-lesbian women (and I mean by this both self-identified bisexuals and heterosexuals) by reason of heterosexual hegemony. Just as Black women and white women must approach the issue of racism or the work of women of colour from positions which are set in opposition by the dynamic of racism, so lesbians and non-lesbian women are faced with the need to negotiate homophobia and heterosexism from conflictual positions. This is not a scholarship of equals! The liberal strategy of including 'difference' within Women's Studies means that lesbians share with other minority women the experience of being exposed to a kind of scholarly voyeurism, an experience which can only be disempowering and distressing. Where does such voyeurism originate? What does it suggest about the failure of Women's Studies to meet the needs of lesbian students and to integrate lesbianism into feminist theory?

Historically, the relationship between lesbian and non-lesbian feminists has been a difficult one, leading to the first of many angry challenges to the notion of universal sisterhood. A rupture occurred in the Women's Movement, both in the USA and later in Britain, that was to leave deep scars and a profound sense of mistrust on both sides. Indeed some commentators have gone so far as to suggest that it was this 'gay/straight split' as it came to be known (Tuttle, 1986) which was responsible for the break-up of the Women's Liberation Movement in Britain.[3]

In Britain in 1979 the Leeds Revolutionary Feminists published *Political Lesbianism: The Case Against Heterosexuality*, stating that the only acceptable sexual identity for feminists was that of political lesbian, a creature they defined as 'a woman-identified woman who does not fuck men' (Leeds Revolutionary Feminists, 1981). The response, from some lesbians as well as from heterosexual feminists, was outrage (Onlywomen Press, 1981). The fervour of the reaction was remarkable. The Leeds Revolutionary Feminists were, after all, not in any position to *dictate* to anyone. They were not high court judges or Members of Parliament. They were a small group of lesbians, among the most disempowered minorities in British society. Yet the overwhelming impression that remains of this bitter conflict is of the astonishing depth of defensiveness, rage and anxiety which their paper clearly provoked in many women reading it, a degree of feeling which was quite out of proportion to the stimulus and which, I believe, continues to incapacitate feminism today in its response to lesbianism.

Why was the reaction so extreme? The letters written in answer to the Leeds paper reveal a painful defensiveness which suggests that non-lesbian women were angry not because they thought the paper was wrong, but because they suspected it was right, and that left them in an intolerable situation. The bare logic of the Leeds paper was, and still is, unassailable. The pain comes from being forced to confront what must be the logical conclusion of all but the most unregenerately liberal of feminisms, that women who are not lesbian live within and, willy-nilly, profit from the oppressive structure of heterosexuality, that paradigm of the hegemonic patriarchal institution.

We live in a society wherein the deployment of social and political power is constructed around an absolute binary demarcation of gender, Additionally, (hetero)sex is totemized not only as the principal conduit for the embodiment of that power differential, but simultaneously as the (only) accepted and acceptable arena for the expression of individual needs and desires for intimacy, physical contact, nurturing, dependency, aggression, playfulness and companionship. Lesbian relationships do not, of course, exist in some extra-societal vacuum free from contamination by male supremacy, but they do side-step the most poignant and privatized dilemma of heterosexual feminism, looking to the oppressor for the satisfaction of so many personal needs and desires.

It is both the pain and the privatized nature of this conflict which I believe is at the root of the failure of Women's Studies to engage with lesbianism and to meet the needs of lesbians. The tendency of non-lesbian feminists[4] to step back from the need to address the apparently oxymoronic status of heterosexual

Tamsin Wilton

feminism has all too often resulted in the isolation of lesbian feminists, an isolation undoubtedly enabled by the enduring respectability of homophobia. Thus Angela Neustatter (1989) writes: 'I have disliked intensely the . . . abuse of heterosexual women by the political lesbian lobby, however much I can understand, intellectually, the arguments'. It is unlikely that she would feel able to write about Black women's anti-racist initiatives in this offensive way (however much she might wish to), because there is a general public agreement among the white middle-class that racism is wrong. However hypocritical such a stance may be, however great the unwillingness to tackle the social realities of racism, the *idea* of racism is publicly challenged in many ways, from anti-discriminatory Acts of Parliament to Rock against Racism.[5] The idea of homophobia, on the other hand, is given legislative support through various Acts of Parliament and is promoted with vigour in the press (Armitage *et al.*, 1987; Watney, 1987). It is against this powerful and deep-rooted homophobia that the failure of Women's Studies[6] to incorporate lesbianism must be seen.

Sexual Problems for Feminism

The seductive notion of universal sisterhood, which seemed so empowering in the sixties and seventies, has been revealed as a liberal sham by the struggles of women silenced by and excluded from the Women's Liberation Movement. Women of colour, older women, Jewish women, disabled women, working-class women and lesbians have all had to fight to be heard within feminism and have all vigorously criticized feminist politics and scholarship for perpetuating their marginalization. The response to this seems to have been for feminism to fragment into a proliferation of feminisms. Guilty recognition of the oppressive nature of what might with some irony be termed 'mainstream' feminism has not yet resulted in any radical changes to the theory or practice of feminism. Discrete lip service is paid to the principle of representing 'different' women, but this coexists with a refusal to take on board the realities of marginalization. Lynne Segal suggests, for example, that we should 'pay more attention to the needs of Black women at a practical and descriptive level' (Segal, 1987, p. 64). Felly Nkweto Simmonds, by questioning who is the assumed audience here, who exactly is it who needs to 'pay more attention to the needs of Black women', neatly exposes the reactionary nature of this standard response to the demands of marginalized women (Simmonds, 1992). By constructing 'difference' as a set of discrete organizational categories, the hard and necessary work of transforming our own oppressive beliefs and practices is pre-empted. It is also, of course, to situate 'different' women as precisely different *from* the presumptive 'normal' agent of Women's Studies, white, middle-class, heterosexual, able-bodied gentile women. The struggle of 'different' women for recognition of their rightful agency and authentic subjecthood is thus co-opted and refused/defused by a straightforward reaffirmation of the hegemonic norm.

Adherence to the liberal notion of 'difference' leads us to police what happens in the Women's Studies classroom in a very limiting way. For example, we may assume that the Black students/teachers on our courses should be the ones to talk about the work of Alice Walker or Carolivia Herron, while the out lesbian students/teachers will all be burning to offer us their interpretations of Adrienne Rich or Jeanette Winterson. (Presumably, if Audre Lorde appears on the syllabus, there will have to be a fight for ownership!)

There is, however, more to the continuing failure of Women's Studies to take account of lesbianism and lesbians than a refusal to interrogate and relinquish 'difference'. The particular 'problem' of lesbianism is that recognition of lesbian possibility obliges non-lesbian women to recognize not only their own anti-lesbian feelings but also their own positioning as the sexual partners of men. Until non-lesbian feminists begin deconstructing the heterosexual imperative,[7] and developing a radical heterosexual feminist politics, lesbianism will continue to face denial, ghettoization[8] and rejection within Women's Studies, and this denial is costing feminism dear.

This ghettoization ironically parallels the position of feminism itself within the academy. Increasingly feminism happens in a discrete set of intellectual and pedagogic spaces: in Women's Studies courses, in feminist journals and books, at Women's Studies conferences, through feminist publishing houses or the Women's Studies lists of mainstream publishers (all of which are under siege). We are, I believe, absolutely right to keep men out of Women's Studies, and to reject co-option into the depoliticization implied by 'Gender Studies'. Yet there are very real dangers in accepting the limited freedom of the academic ghetto. Outside the spaces where feminist thinking happens, the rest of the world appears curiously untouched. The dangers of this are obvious to anyone reading, for example, *Equal Opportunities: A Feminist Fallacy*, the latest publication from the Institute of Economic Affairs (Quest, 1992). This slim volume claims, with unconscious irony, to be setting out in a 'quiet scholarly manner' to contest the 'wholesale rejection of rational debate' represented by feminism (Green, 1992, p. iv). In fact its scholarship is intellectually redundant, couched in terms left over from the seventies and relying on a kind of romanticized biological determinism that I for one thought had died a suitably embarrassed death. By refusing to take feminism seriously and to engage with current feminist thought, the authors have simply fallen into a theoretical time warp; they are the Dad's Army of the patriarchy.

It seems obvious to me that unless/until feminism engages with current lesbian feminist thought, it risks a similar fate. An unquestioningly heterosexist feminism is intellectually and politically moribund. It is a failed feminism. Women's Studies can achieve little without a rigorous critique of sexual difference, gender, sexual desire, sexual identity and the heterosexual imperative. Such a rigorous critique has developed most succinctly within lesbian feminism.

News from Nowhere: Male Power through Lesbian Eyes

Sarah Franklin and Jackie Stacey suggest that 'the marginality of lesbianism in this society may provide a vantage point from which to *denaturalise* assumptions about sexuality' (Franklin and Stacey, 1986; emphasis in original). I would suggest that it is not marginality *per se* which makes the lesbian perspective so crucial to feminism, but rather its specific positioning *outside heterosexuality*. Heterosexuality functions as the bedrock of male supremacy, not merely on the symbolic level by which, as some radical separatists would have it, penile penetration is an act of male colonization of women's bodies[9] (Leeds Revolutionary Feminists, 1981, p. 6), but because, as Gill Dunne recognizes, 'The "naturalness" of heterosexuality conceals the arbitrary nature of gender-specific experiences and patterns of living' (Dunne, 1992, p. 86). By ignoring lesbian possibility, much feminist writing fails to challenge the naturalness of heterosexuality, throwing out, with the bathwater of lesbianism, a very important feminist baby, namely the recognition of the arbitrary nature of gender. The exposure of that arbitrariness is one of the founding principles of radical feminism (not to mention poststructuralist feminism) and failure to engage with the construction of gender on an ideological level is one of the important limitations of both liberal and socialist feminisms, so the refusal of a lesbian-inclusive perspective exercises profound restrictions on feminist thought and politics. An example from the field of social policy makes this point clear. Christine Griffin, writing about the major gender divides that exist in 'leisure', comments that

> Women are an integral part of men's leisure, as 'escorts' whether paid or unpaid, or in relation to the myriad ways in which women must present and construct themselves for men, both materially and psychologically. (Griffin, 1981, in Deem, 1986, p. 122)

This assertion, while doubtless true for most (if not all) heterosexual/bisexual women, is certainly not true of most (if not all) lesbians. But because she effectively conceals the point that it is *heterosexual* women whose lives and identities are so shaped by their relation to men, Griffin pre-empts the possibility of identifying the social mechanism responsible for this deplorable state of affairs. This is surely critical! If feminists are to disrupt and transform the process she describes, we have to understand that it is not something intrinsic to women, materially or psychologically, which causes them to be 'an integral part of men's leisure', but a characteristic of the social practice of heterosexuality, a product of the heterosexual imperative. Recognition of lesbian existence brings this into sharp focus. As a lesbian reader, this damaging omission positively screams off the page at me, yet I never cease to marvel at the look of wonder which spreads across the face of heterosexual colleagues when it is pointed out to them. Non-lesbian readers cannot rely on there always being a lesbian interpreter around, and unless all women develop what might be called 'lesbian antennae', Women's Studies will go on running aground on the shoals of the heterosexual imperative.

An awareness of lesbian existence provides a powerful tool for feminist scholarship, yet it is one which non-lesbian feminists, with a few honourable exceptions, refuse to wield.[10] Historically the social control of women's sexuality has included either punishment of lesbians or the denial of the possibility of lesbianism. The social construction of lesbianism at any point in history, or within any specific culture, is a powerful litmus test of the position of women at that time and place. Yet all too often feminist texts which claim to discuss the history, cultural politics or sociology of 'sexuality' turn out upon inspection to be undertaking no such thing (see, for example, Smart, 1992; Kuhn, 1988; Abbott and Wallace, 1990; Webb, 1985). 'Sexuality', I have discovered, is just as likely to mean 'heterosexuality' to a feminist writer as to Barbara Cartland.

It is, too, surely important to Women's Studies that lesbianism is one of the strategies by which women have historically resisted male power, and as such has, along with other aspects of women's struggle, been silenced and erased from the record by the historians of the patriarchy (Rich, 1981; Faderman, 1985). Differing ideas throughout history about what it means to be a woman engaged in a sexual relationship with another woman offer us a powerful insight into the socially constructed nature of sexuality and the deployment of the sexual in the service of male supremacy (Faderman, 1992).

The existence of lesbians in itself offers a potent challenge to the phallocentrism of cultural constructs of female sexuality. It challenges biological, psychological, religious, medical and juridical discourse concerning the 'naturalness' of women's passivity, dependence and subordination, and represents the one symbolic construct of 'woman' which exists outside and beyond the definitional referent of 'man'.[11] Male anxiety about lesbianism deserves feminist scrutiny; Roger Scruton, for example, has this to say about lesbians:

> There is not the same emphasis in the sexual organs and on the moment of sexual excitement; instead there is an extremely poignant, often helpless, sense of being at another's mercy. The lesbian knows that she desires someone who will not typically make those advances that are characteristic of a man, even if she wants to; nor can she make these advances herself without compromising the gender-identity which (she wishes to believe) is integral to her own attractiveness. She can only wait, and wish, and pray to the gods with . . . troubled fervour. (Scruton, 1986)

He is claiming, of course, that *all* women share a sexuality which is essentially different from and dependent on male sexuality, passive, non-genital and 'helpless'. This picture of lesbian desire as a despairing condition (for which of course his penis is the only real remedy) reveals just how deep are the anxieties aroused in him by lesbianism, anxieties which should alert us as feminists to the significance of sexuality in the maintenance of male supremacy and to the importance of lesbian possibility for an oppositional feminist construction of sexuality.

The fact of lesbian stigma, usually more brutally expressed than in Scruton's vapid lyricism, and its use to reinforce heterosexuality and gender-appropriate behaviour among all women exposes the importance to male power of unrestricted sexual access to women and calls into question the extent to which notions of 'consent' or 'choice' are in any way meaningful for *all* women. It exposes the specifically sexualized mechanisms of the social control of women by men.[12] Futhermore, by co-opting stigma into a transgressive reverse discourse of deviant desire, lesbians embody and celebrate a unique possibility for female sexual agency. On another level lesbians, as women who organize our lives independently of men, demonstrate by our very existence the inadequacy of a straightforwardly materialist analysis of women's oppression, an analysis which is itself profoundly shaped by unexamined heterosexism.

Lesbianism is of central significance to feminism and to Women's Studies. The failure to incorporate lesbian issues and a lesbian perspective seriously weakens our ability to critique, deconstruct and disrupt male power. Indeed, the denial of lesbianism within feminist discourse acts powerfully to reflect and reproduce the ideological hegemony of the hetero-patriarchy — which is not to say that incorporating lesbianism into Women's Studies is easy. There are certainly institutional constraints on any such incorporation within the formal structures of further and higher education. Resources are unlikely to be forthcoming (Brimstone, 1991), and lesbianism is still widely regarded as deviant and academically suspect (Hanmer, 1991). But lack of resources and lack of academic credibility has never stopped us before, or there would *be* no Women's Studies!

From my viewpoint, I see too many feminists eagerly colluding with the patriarchs of the mainstream/malestream Academy to perpetuate the invisibility and non-viability of lesbian studies. There are many who would agree with Christine Griffin that 'you can't get away with calling something lesbian studies' (Wetherell and Griffin, 1992, p. 153). This simply reinforces, by characterizing lesbian studies as something to 'get away with', the inalienable right of men to decide who speaks, whose story is told, within the Academy. Indeed, contemporary feminist scholarship embraces a denial of lesbian possibility hardly less total than it was when Rich wrote *Compulsory Heterosexuality and Lesbian Existence* a decade ago, as a quick search for 'the L word' in the index of many feminist books reveals. It is depressing to find in Patricia Hill Collins's (1990) brilliant book *Black Feminist Thought* no mention of the existence of Black lesbians, an incomprehensible omission given the importance to Women's Studies of Black lesbian writers, but it is positively shocking to realize that the authors of *Feminist Practice in Women's Health Care* (Webb, 1986) are only concerned with *heterosexual* women's health. Such texts construct a 'feminism' which is at best incomplete, at worst actively misogynistic in its refusal to countenance women's autonomous sexual desire, activity and identity.

What about the Lesbians?

If Women's Studies has suffered from its failure to incorporate lesbianism (and I use 'incorporate' here to mean take into the body of feminist knowledge), it is lesbians who have suffered most directly from that failure. In my experience, the unresolved conflict intrinsic to heterosexual feminism has painful consequences for lesbians working in Women's Studies. If we bring up lesbian issues in the classroom, we are accused of guilt-tripping non-lesbian feminists or of being obsessed with sexuality, but waiting hopefully for someone else to mention lesbianism is a bit like waiting for the next Labour government. We become accustomed to being demonized as the 'thought police' of a radical feminism constructed as authoritarian and dogmatic. Our experience is invalidated with breathtaking totality by non-lesbian women who comfortably insist that we are all women-loving/women-identified women on the lesbian continuum, and who you choose to have sex with is inconsequential. We have to listen, gob-smacked, to heterosexually active women identifying themselves as 'lesbian feminists' on the basis that they have close women friends, or telling us that having sex with women is male-identified and hence politically incorrect. And if we presume to set aside safe lesbian space to help us deal with all this, we are accused of excluding and oppressing non-lesbians and of being divisive![13]

Where the Buck Stops

Women's Studies has a clear responsibility, ethical, theoretical, political, pastoral and pedagogic, to lesbians, as it does to women of colour, working-class women, Jewish women, disabled women and older women. The currently fashionable notion of 'difference' functions in direct collusion with and acts to perpetuate a set of oppressive discourses radically inimical to feminism. There is also a very real need to consider, in the light of the heterosexism of Women's Studies, what the ultimate goal of feminism is, because unless it is to abolish men there can be no moving forward without deconstructionist and strategic interventions in heterosexuality. Such interventions are not possible unless/until feminism can achieve the radical paradigmatic shift necessitated by recognition of lesbian possibility.

Strategies for incorporating lesbianism into Women's Studies are straightforward. Feminists must fight for lesbian space as relentlessly as we have for women's space; not as a charitable act towards an oppressed minority, but as an intrinsic part of the struggle against male supremacy. The cop-out notion of 'difference' must be replaced by active engagement with the various oppressions of minority women and by a transformation of oppressive practices within feminism, and feminism must re-examine and reaffirm a commitment to women's sexual autonomy.

Above all, and inclusive of all the above, is the development among all feminists of what I have called 'lesbian antennae', an incorporation of lesbian possibility into the way we interpret the world. Feminism is changing; we are, however haltingly, beginning to recognize and challenge oppressive practices such as racism and classism. I would like to think that we won't have to wait another ten years before 'feminists find it less possible to read, write, or teach from a perspective of unexamined heterocentricity' (Rich, 1982).

Notes

I would like to thank Norma Daykin for helpful comments on a first draft, and for talking through some of these ideas with me. Huge thanks are due too to Patsy Staddon, Jackie Baron and Carole Truman, who made it possible for women at the Women's Studies Network conference to hear and discuss this paper even though I had to drop out through illness. Who says sisterhood is dead?

1 This is, of course, probably the most powerful argument for keeping men out of Women's Studies. Studying your own oppression is deeply painful, and the emotional and intellectual implications of doing it under the nose of your oppressor are too powerfully collusive with male power/voyeurism to be acceptable.
2 As a lesbian chosing to focus on lesbianism in this paper, I am all too aware of the irony of launching headlong into precisely the kind of painful interpenetration of subjectivity and objectivity previously identified!
3 For a vitriolic and self-righteously lesbian-blaming account of this rift in British feminism, see Angela Neustatter's chapter 'Sexuality and Schism' in her history of the British WLM, *Hyenas in Petticoats*.
4 This tendency is, of course, prevalent among some lesbians as well, especially lesbian separatists. However, it is within lesbian and gay theory that some of the most subtle and sophisticated critiques of heterosexuality have developed. See, for example, essays in Fuss (1991) and Epstein and Straub (1991). Readers interested in recent steps to address the problem of heterosexuality from a feminist perspective are referred to Kitzinger, Wilkinson and Perkins (1992).
5 I would comment at this point that lesbians and gay men, both of colour and white, marched through the streets of London on June 27th 1992. Europride, under the banner 'Lesbians and Gays Against Racism and Fascism'. Similar support from the Black community in the fight against homophobia is at this point hard to imagine. This is not to propose a hierarchy of oppressions, nor is it to deny that racism exists in the lesbian and gay 'community', but simply to illustrate the broad base of homophobia and its respectability across many communities.
6 I am writing here about British Women's Studies. There is some evidence to suggest that lesbians have been less marginalized in the USA and some European countries where the tradition of homophobia is less entrenched than in Britain. The difference is not great (see, for example, Cruikshank, 1982), but I am only able to speak about the British experience here, and generalizations should be avoided!
7 I use the term 'heterosexual imperative' in preference to Rich's 'compulsory

heterosexuality' because I do not find the notion of 'compulsion' helpful in prompting heterosexuals to critique the institutional nature of heterosexuality. It is all too easy to declare that nobody compels anybody to be heterosexually active, whereas it is perhaps easier to recognize the more general control exercised by an imperative.

8 Sarah Franklin and Jackie Stacey (1986) suggest, in a useful insight, that lesbianism is ghettoized within Women's Studies by being 'dealt with' under the heading of radical feminism rather than being fully and productively integrated.

9 Of course, this symbolic level *is* of central significance in the maintenance of male supremacy. For a discussion of the role of penetration in the expression of and reproduction of men's social and political power, see Wilton (1992).

10 There are few such exceptions, one being Cynthia Cockburn, whose supportive awareness of lesbian existence makes her work on young women's experience of training schemes, *Two Track Training*, genuinely inclusive.

11 Here I am, of course, in tactical disagreement with Monique Wittig, whose assertion that 'lesbians are not women' (Wittig and Zeig, 1980, p. 438) is based on the premise that 'women' are, and may only be, defined in relation to 'men', on whose terms (literally) they exist. My own belief is that insisting that 'women' include 'lesbians' acts to disrupt and subvert the patriarchal discursive constitution of 'women' and to situate lesbian power where it belongs, namely with women (rather than with gay men or within the political limbo of 'genderfuck' currently in vogue).

12 Radical feminism has been ridiculed recently by anti-censorship feminists for supposedly reducing male power to sex (see, for example, essays in Segal and McIntosh, 1992). Clearly it would be absurd to suggest that there is nothing more to male supremacy than rape and sexual violence, but it is equally clear to me that the patriarchal construction of sexuality — both men's and women's — is absolutely fundamental to women's oppression on both a symbolic and a material level. While it is certainly true that women are subjugated by men materially (and that most of the world's women live in poverty), any attempt to understand *why* that state of affairs has come about must engage with the struggle for control of women's bodies/sexuality/reproductive potential.

13 In case any of this seems far-fetched, all of these comments and responses have been directed at me by students and colleagues during 1991 and 1992.

References

ABBOTT, PAMELA and WALLACE, CLAIRE (1990) *An Introduction to Sociology: Feminist Perspectives*, London, Routledge.

ARMITAGE, GARY, DICKEY, JULIENNE and SHARPLES, SUE (1987) *Out of the Gutter: A Survey of the Treatment of Homosexuality by the Press*, London, Campaign for Press and Broadcasting Freedom.

BLACKMAN, INGE and PERRY, KATHRYN (1990) 'Skirting the Issue: Lesbian Fashion for the 1990s', *Feminist Review*, 34, Spring.

BRIMSTONE, LYNDIE (1991) 'Out of the Margins and into the Soup: Some Thoughts on Incorporation', in AARON, JANE and WALBY, SYLVIA (Eds) *Out of the Margins: Women's Studies in the Nineties*, London, Falmer Press.

C.L.I.T. COLLECTIVE (1974) 'C.L.I.T. Statement No. 2' in HOAGLAND, SARAH LUCIA and PENELOPE, JULIA (Eds) (1988) *For Lesbians Only: A Separatist Anthology*, London, Onlywomen.

COCKBURN, CYNTHIA (1987) *Two Track Training: Sex Inequalities and the YTS*, London, Macmillan.

Tamsin Wilton

COLLINS, PATRICIA HILL (1990) *Black Feminist Thought*, Boston and London, Unwin Hyman.

CRUIKSHANK, MARGARET (1982) *Lesbian Studies: Present and Future*, New York, The Feminist Press.

DEEM, ROSEMARY (1986) *All Work and No Play: The Sociology of Women and Leisure*, Milton Keynes, Open University Press.

DUNNE, GILL (1992) 'Difference at Work: Perceptions of Work from a Non-Heterosexual Perspective', in HINDS, HILARY, PHOENIX, ANN and STACEY, JACKIE (Eds) *Working Out: New Directions for Women's Studies*, London, Falmer Press.

EPSTEIN, JULIA and STRAUB, KRISTINA (Eds) (1991) *Body Guards: The Cultural Politics of Gender Ambiguity*, London, Routledge.

FADERMAN, LILLIAN (1985) *Surpassing the Love of Men*, London, Virago.

FADERMAN, LILLIAN (1992) *Odd Girls and Twilight Lovers: A History of Lesbian Life in Twentieth-Century America*, London, Penguin.

FRANKLIN, SARAH and STACEY, JACKIE (1986) *Lesbian Perspectives on Women's Studies*, University of Kent at Canterbury Women's Studies Occasional Papers No. 11.

FUSS, DIANA (Ed.) (1991) *Inside/Out: Lesbian Theories, Gay Theories*, London, Routledge.

GREEN, DAVID (1992) 'Foreword', in QUEST, CAROLINE (Ed.) *Equal Opportunities: A Feminist Fallacy*, London, Institute of Economic Affairs.

GRIFFIN, CHRISTINE (1981) 'Young Women and Leisure', in TOMLINSON, A. (Ed.) *Leisure and Social Control*, Brighton Polytechnic, School of Human Movement.

HANMER, JALNA (1991) 'On Course: Women's Studies — a Transitional Programme', in AARON, JANE and WALBY, SYLVIA (Eds) *Out of the Margins: Women's Studies in the Nineties*, London, Falmer Press.

HAUG, FRIGGA (Ed.) (1987) *Female Sexualization: A Collective Work of Memory*, London, Verso.

KITZINGER, CELIA, WILKINSON, SUE and PERKINS, RACHEL (Eds) (1992) *Special Issue of 'Feminism and Psychology' on Heterosexuality*, **2**, 3, London, Sage.

KUHN, ANNETTE (1988) *Cinema, Censorship and Sexuality 1909–1925*, London, Routledge.

LEEDS REVOLUTIONARY FEMINISTS (1981) 'Political Lesbianism: The Case Against Heterosexuality', in ONLYWOMEN PRESS *Love Your Enemy? The Debate Between Heterosexual Feminism and Political Lesbianism*.

LEES, SUE (1991) 'Feminist Politics and Women's Studies: Struggle, Not Incorporation', in AARON, JANE and WALBY, SYLVIA (Eds) *Out of the Margins: Women's Studies in the Nineties*, London, Falmer Press.

LOWE, MARIAN and LOWE BENSTON, MARGARET (1984) 'The Uneasy Alliance of Feminism and Academia', in GUNEW, SNEJA (Ed.) (1991) *A Reader in Feminist Knowledge*, London, Routledge.

NEUSTATTER, ANGELA (1989) *Hyenas in Petticoats: A Look at Twenty Years of Feminism*, London, Harrap.

ONLYWOMEN PRESS (1981) *Love Your Enemy? The Debate Between Heterosexual Feminism and Political Lesbianism*, London (no editor credited).

QUEST, CAROLINE (Ed.) (1992) *Equal Opportunities: A Feminist Fallacy*, London, Institute of Economic Affairs.

RADICALESBIANS (1970) 'The Woman-Identified Woman', in HOAGLAND, SARAH LUCIA and PENELOPE, JULIA (Eds) *For Lesbians Only: A Separatist Anthology*, London, Onlywomen Press.

RICH, ADRIENNE (1981) 'Compulsory Heterosexuality and Lesbian Existence', in RICH, ADRIENNE (1987) *Blood, Bread and Poetry: Selected Prose 1979–1985*, London, Virago.

RICH, ADRIENNE (1982) *New Introduction* to Rich (1981).

SCRUTON, ROGER (1986) *Sexual Desire*, London, Weidenfeld and Nicolson.

SEGAL, LYNNE (1987) *Is the Future Female? Troubled Thoughts on Contemporary Feminism*, London, Virago.

SEGAL, LYNNE and MCINTOSH, MARY (Eds) (1992) *Sex Exposed: Sexuality and the Pornography Debate*, London, Virago.

SHERIDAN, SUSAN (1991) 'From Margin to Mainstream: Situating Women's Studies', in GUNEW, SNEJA (Ed.) *A Reader in Feminist Knowledge*, London, Routledge.

SIMMONDS, FELLY NKWETO (1992) 'Difference, Power and Knowledge: Black Women in Academia', in HINDS, HILARY, PHOENIX, ANN and STACEY, JACKIE (Eds) *Working Out: New Directions for Women's Studies*, London, Falmer Press.

SMART, CAROL (Ed.) (1992) *Regulating Womanhood: Historical Essays on Marriage, Motherhood and Sexuality*, London, Routledge.

TUTTLE, LISA (1986) *Encyclopaedia of Feminism*, London, Arrow.

WATNEY, SIMON (1987) *Policing Desire: Pornography, AIDS and the Media*, London, Methuen.

WEBB, CHRISTINE (1985) *Sexuality, Nursing and Health*, Chichester, John Wiley and Son.

WEBB, CHRISTINE (Ed.) (1986) *Feminist Practice in Women's Health Care*, Chichester, John Wiley and Son.

WETHERELL, MARGARET and GRIFFIN, CHRISTINE (Eds) (1992) 'Feminist Psychology and the Study of Men and Masculinity: Open Forum. Part II: Politics and Practices', *Feminism and Psychology*, 2, 2, London, Sage.

WILTON, TAMSIN (1992) 'Desire and the Politics of Representation: Issues for Lesbians and Heterosexual Women', in HINDS, HILARY, PHOENIX, ANN and STACEY, JACKIE (Eds) *Working Out: New Directions for Women's Studies*, London, Falmer Press.

WITTIG, MONIQUE (1992) 'The Straight Mind', in *The Straight Mind and Other Essays*, Hemel Hempstead, Harvester Wheatsheaf.

WITTIG, MONIQUE and ZEIG, SANDRA (1980) *Lesbian Peoples: Material for a Dictionary*, London, Virago.

Chapter 15

'Room of Our Own':
An Alternative to Academic Isolation

Ruth Holliday, Gayle Letherby, Lezli Mann,
Karen Ramsay and Gillian Reynolds

The Truism of Academic Isolation

a woman must have money and a room of her own if she is to
write . . .

Thus, Virginia Woolf (1977, p. 7) identifies the minimum material requirements for the production of literature. This chapter aims to explore the relevance of this statement to the PhD research process with specific reference to
the experiences of five female postgraduates.

John Hockey comments that 'A number of studies highlight the potential
isolation of postgraduate researchers' (Hockey, 1991, p. 324), and that relationships are of fundamental importance in enabling postgraduates to stay in
control of the 'inevitable disorientation' (p. 323) in PhD work. He conceptualizes potential isolation as being on two levels — social and academic.

Social isolation is manifested in loneliness, disorientation, and depression.
Academic isolation, often indistinguishable from social isolation, is seen as
detrimental to the PhD process, because the ability to think creatively occurs
as a response, and not in a vacuum. Renouf (1989) claims that scholarship is
a group activity, and that the process of intellectual isolation inhibits the
process of learning through experience. He claims that it can lead instead to
crises of confidence, motivation, distraction and insecurity. Hockey suggests
that formal research training programmes and communal activity days to
develop support networking represent attempts to generate collegiality.

This chapter suggests that there may be an alternative, and possibly more
effective, way of avoiding the 'feelings of helplessness, inadequacy, . . . inability to cope, intellectual stagnation and confusion' (Renouf, 1989) associated
with the isolation, and so counter-productive to the learning process. Whereas
Hockey, and others (e.g. Elton and Pope, 1989, p. 325), suggest typically
male-defined, task-oriented solutions, which depend upon institutional structure, we are concerned to develop person-oriented ideas, perhaps more suited

to the 'motivation', 'independence' and 'self-confidence' perceived as prerequisites for successful postgraduate students (Hockey, 1991, p. 329).

Hockey points out that the doctoral student brings into the PhD process a set of expectations and assumptions concerning the nature of that process. This is confirmed by all of us:

> I expected it to be a fairly isolating and lonely period of my life. 'Good authority' assured me that this was the way it was. Having always enjoyed the company of others . . . the prospect of complete aloneness for three years was not too appealing. (Gayle)

> I expected it . . . to be a lonely isolating time . . . I had always worked best at home, and expected to use the office for storing my work and for meeting people. I generally expected to find that the other women would already have a life here which would not include a newcomer. (Karen)

> I envisaged three years at home, with perhaps a weekly 'library-run' to the University[1] . . . I would be enjoying my own company, keeping control over my day-to-day life. (Gillian)

The 'normal' pattern of the PhD process is isolating and lonely, and this was experienced by Ruth and Lezli, who started their work a year before Gayle, Karen and Gillian.

> The euphoria at being told I could undertake . . . a PhD was tempered by warnings of future isolation, potential poverty . . . and horror stories of incompletion rates. . . . Having spent a year working on my PhD before I joined the room, I had already experienced the isolation I had been warned about, and further isolation I had not been warned about. (Lezli)

> When I arrived . . . I was brought by my Director of Studies to a 'derelict' building . . . and told to report back when I had something to say. . . . After a week I found the courage to leave my office. . . . After a month I discovered that I was entitled to use 'official' stationery. . . . After three months I discovered . . . [a short cut] to the department. (Ruth)

Expectations and experience thus confirm the existence of a 'normal' pattern, suggesting that, without the physical and emotional space of a 'room of our own', our lives might have followed and validated that pattern for several years to come.

Epistemology and Methodology

In drawing on our experiences this piece is largely autobiographical/biographical. As bell hooks (1989, p. 158) argues, writing one's autobiography 'is a way to find again that aspect of self and experience that may no longer be an actual part of one's life but is a living memory shaping and informing the present'. As we hope will become clear we feel that autobiographical writing woven with analysis and theory is the best way to explore how our experience has been different from the traditional 'expected' PhD experience as a period of both personal and academic isolation.

Feminist work is concerned with making women's lives visible, whether through primary empirical research or through studying secondary sources. This piece is part of that tradition. We recognize the importance of what Liz Stanley (1990, p. 209) calls our 'intellectual biography' by providing '*account-able* knowledge, in which the reader would have access to details of the contextually-located reasoning processes which give rise to the "findings", the outcomes'. Furthermore we would argue that our intellectual and personal biographies have been in some way altered by our group membership and that this is relevant not just to the writing of this paper but to any collective and individual work we do in the future.

The methods we used to write this collective paper were as follows: we began by talking, and decided to write personal stories of our perceptions of the history and experience of our relationships. More talking and writing of other sections — individually, in pairs and as a group — followed; then more talking and much editing of all that we had written. 'Talking' has often been the most difficult part, whereas normally we find this an easy aspect of our relationships. Thus, in this instance, talking is more difficult than being. Editing has also been difficult. For the sake of brevity this piece often contains the edited highlights of what we think is important. This is particularly relevant to our stories which were originally four to five times longer.

Personal Accounts

This section is specifically autobiographical. The brief introduction to each of us is followed by extracts from our subjective accounts. The accounts are thematic, as suggested by the subtitles.

Summaries

Lezli completed her Sociology degree after an engineering background and is now undertaking a part-time PhD. This explores how young people use fashion as a medium for creating and expressing identity, reflecting interests in culture, ideology, images and appearances.

After twenty years of parenting, Gillian returned to education for self-fulfil-ment. Having completed a BA (Hons) degree at Staffordshire Polytechnic, she gained a scholarship in 1990 for a doctoral thesis on physical and sensory impairment, philanthropy and the labour market.

Karen completed her first degree, a BA (Hons) in Organization Studies, when she was 29. She moved from Bradford to Staffordshire when she began her PhD in 1990. Her project is a study of organization cultures in higher educa-tion institutions. Her academic interests include sexuality and emotion in organizations.

In 1989 Ruth arrived at the institution to do a PhD on operations management in small manufacturing firms. She had just completed a degree in Electronics and Management Science at Keele University after doing a diploma in elec-trical and electronic engineering.

Gayle's return to higher education at Staffordshire Polytechnic was preceded by several different work experiences over a period of eight years. She ob-tained her degree in 1990. Her PhD project is concerned to explore experi-ences (predominantly women's) of involuntary childlessness and infertility. As a childless woman herself, her interest is personal as well as academic.

Karen: 'Starting Out'

My earliest memories of the Polytechnic are of a long, dark corridor which seemed almost uninhabited and a small departmental office which struck me as out of bounds to students because of the photocopying machines. At that time I thought of myself as a student, more responsible and grown-up than yesterday, but still a student. The room at Winton House, although isolated from the central point of the department, was bright and there I found others who, like me, were not quite sure whether they were students, staff or some other breed!

I was not sure what I was entitled to as a postgraduate in the department and was very excited when Gillian told me that we would have our own phone. This seemed terribly grand to me. I could give out my extension number to people. Not only did I have a room (and therefore an address), a phone number, a desk and a pigeonhole for mail, I also had, greatest of all, a bunch of keys. Forget 'penis envy'; I experienced 'key envy'! Keys are very symbolic, they symbolize access to space, to resources and ultimately to power. With a bunch of keys (one for the room, two for the desk, one for the filing cabinet, one for the photocopying room and the house key) I was somebody. I had arrived! I laugh at myself now. People are the real keys to resources, to space, to power. But then, having a bunch of keys gave me an enormous amount of comfort. They told me that I was allowed to be there and that I was supposed to be there.

By the end of the first term we had begun to revise our definition of 'isolation'. While we were geographically isolated from the department, there was no way that we could conceive of ourselves as isolated individuals, emotionally, socially or academically. At this time we began to be noticed by members of the department. We had a presence which derived partly from our shared status (there was a critical mass of postgraduate students for the first time) and partly from a shared identity. This shared identity was rooted, I believe, in the character of the room, its separateness from the rest of the department and the space it provided for us to form relationships which were bounded both by our shared experiences and our shared physical space.

The separation of the room from the rest of the department and the relative smallness of our space interacted with my need for belongingness as a postgraduate new to the polytechnic. This created a situation where I was in close proximity with people whom I might not have met under other circumstances and I had to learn a new form of connectedness which was based on acceptance of difference, rather than on similarity. The move in the relationship from friendliness to friendship was gradual and almost unnoticed at times. It developed out of long discussions, talks which shifted from text to experience, from theory to description, from intense concentration to help-less giggles. All the time, we were exploring ourselves and each other and at any moment we could move from personal revelation to theoretical analysis and back to experience without changing the tempo or personal connection. This was possible because we had the physical space and privacy of the room.

Lezli: 'Moving In'

I accepted the invitation to join the room hesitantly. What if we didn't get on? At last, I had a base to work from and also learned that I had access to stationery and photocopying. Suddenly I existed and although this was some-thing I had yearned for it made me question whether we can only be seen to exist through others. Another perceived drawback was the location of the room on a cheerless site, separate from our department, although this physical isolation became a distinct advantage and a means of creating personal space.

My fears proved to be unfounded. The room is small but with space to manoeuvre. Personal boundaries are represented by desks and a filing cabinet and 'public' boundaries by communal shelving, kettle etc. As our friendships developed these physical boundaries shifted in form and dimension. Origin-ally, each of us had 'our own' coffee cup; now they are used without any sense of ownership. Similarly, we are free to peruse the books on each other's shelves and collect each other's mail from the department office.

Initially I was wary of talking openly. Gradually I began looking forward to our coffee breaks, when two or more of us would go to the common room for ten minutes and come back an hour or so later. Rather than being a distraction from our work, these breaks invariably generated critical analyses of both common-sense and abstract ideas. Here at last was sociology in practice and oh, what joy to discover that I did after all have the ability to theorize and philosophize as many 'everyday events' became the subject of much debate.

Now we all have unique relationships with each individual and different relationships with the various combinations of group members. The boundaries of these relationships are fluid and are based, not necessarily on shared experience, but on shared trust and acknowledgment of the room as a safe space in which we can work out feelings of unhappiness, frustration etc. Of course, we cannot always be in tune with each other's feelings but we have learned that it is OK to be happy when someone else is sad and vice versa.

The boundaries of this safe space can be threatened by periods spent away. In particular, studying part-time results in only short periods of time in the room, rushing to complete outstanding tasks leaving little time for giving or receiving support. This is compounded by feelings of envy as others progress with their research while I fall behind, leading to feelings of isolation and fears of not being as academic as everyone else. This was reflected in the difficulty I experienced in writing this paper.

The most valuable experience gained from being part of this group is discovering that our differences are a key element in our understandings of each other and the various ways in which we support each other emotionally and intellectually.

Ruth: 'Coming and Going'

After an exhausting few days at a BSA Summer School in 1990, where the language was all about 'epistemology' and 'interactionism', instead of 'phase inverters' and 'high frequency modulators', I returned to the safety of my office, only to find that the corridor had been infiltrated by no less than four sociologists who were in a room opposite mine. At first I found their presence intimidating, but also exciting. This was the first time I had had any contact with other academics since my arrival. I was looking forward to swapping notes on PhD progress, but also aware of my language, as I thought they would be terribly 'right-on'. At that time I was not 'right-on' at all. One of my first memories is being 'told off' in the pub for saying 'girls' instead of 'women'; I felt that 'woman' sounded old and sophisticated, and didn't fit my persona. In fact, I was so nervous, I knocked over my beer which poured straight into Karen's boot!

During my first year, I had become disillusioned with my department. It was there that I first encountered 'malicious sexism', unlike the 'patronizing sexism' I had encountered in engineering. The arrival of the sociologists gave me theories and a vocabulary with which to describe my experiences. I started to visit the sociology room more often. I had my eyes forcibly opened to feminist theory and methodology, which influenced both my life and my work. At some point — I don't remember when — I became a woman who was worthy of her position within an academic institution and waved good-bye to my girlhood when I could spit and swear just as well as the boys.

Although the group represents a wonderful place which both injects new understanding into my work and provides a safe buffer against the more difficult areas of working life, it would be wrong to imply a rosy and perfect world. To do so would be insulting to the others, and would suggest a characterlessness on their part. Some months ago the atmosphere became very gloomy. At first I attempted to cheer everyone up, behaving in an insanely cheerful manner. However, it became apparent that they did not want to be cheerful, so I withdrew from the group and stayed predominantly in my own room, to avoid an explosive situation. I am very intolerant of other people's moods and have only so much empathy to give when other people's spirits do not match my own. A remnant from my engineering past still sees depression as a weakness which a person should be able to 'snap out of' after they have gained the sympathy of others.

The group, and the discovery of sociology, has had an overwhelmingly positive influence both upon my work and, more especially, on my life, enabling me to feel more complete and satisfied with myself as a person. Being part of these friendships promotes a high degree of reflexivity, which has caused me to examine my relationships, my sexuality and my life-plan. I have come to realize that feminism is not equivalent to equal opportunities in the workplace, and that life is enriched by close women friends (something I had never before encountered). I have learnt that the PhD process need not be isolating even if co-workers are covering diverse topics; in fact, the diversity is definitely a strength. Although the relationships move up and down, they will never be stale. Just as our work is influenced by our friends' knowledge, so our friendships are enriched by the discoveries in our work.

Gayle: 'Being Here'

My section refers specifically to how I see the group now. Although how our relationships evolved is important, how we are now concerns me more. Our discussions are not restricted to the academic, and for me at least the personal support is at least as important as the academic, if not more so. Conversation is often fluid and slips from the academic to the personal and back again. This happens at work and socially. However, there are some things that we cannot share. At times the confidentiality that surrounds fieldwork can lead to feelings of isolation. For me this has been compounded by the re-working of my own hopes and expectations which the fieldwork has partly initiated. Also, relationships and responsibilities outside the group sometimes take precedence whether or not you want them to which can lead to feelings of disconnection. At such times it's easy to feel apart from rather than part of the group.

This group then is important to my (and I believe our) postgraduate experience. However, this is not as far as our academic social networking goes. We all have discussions, share ideas and articles and sometimes write with others both within the university and outside. Some of these people join in with the group at times, sometimes the relationships are completely distinct. The boundaries are fluid and shifting. This is also the case when one or more of us is not around for long periods of time; on fieldwork, at work, on holiday. At these times and others people are missing and missed. Yet the group revolves around who is there rather than on any particular person or combination of people. Thus, diads and triads form and reform, mingle with other people, separate and return and so it goes on.

Although I have referred throughout to the group, or myself as an individual and my relationship to the group, the word 'group' doesn't really express what this collective means to me. For me a 'group' implies a collection of people with a shared identity and shared ideas. We do clearly share many identities, as postgraduates, as researchers, as part-time teachers, as women. There is also much that we don't share: age, sexual orientation, family relationships, religious affiliation, at the very least. We do have many ideas in common and also many that are different and even in opposition to those of the others. The definition of 'group' also implies an all-inclusive and exclusive unit. As my story, and others, show, this does not reflect our realities. So perhaps collection of relationships is the best way to describe us. As individuals we all have relationships with other members of the group (I can't get away from the word) and with the group as a whole. For me the individual relationships and the group identity (which others perceive) support me. Thrown together we all attempted to be friendly; the friendship that we now have was not inevitable and was not something that we expected. It is based not so much on what we share but on the space that we are prepared to give each other. Like any relationships, these are not always easy.

Gillian: 'Being with Others'

When I discovered that the institution had allocated me a 'place' along with Gayle and Karen, we got together to organize our personal 'space' within the room. Over the next few weeks, as essential items arrived, we began to spend more time in the room, talking politely about ourselves, our research projects, our backgrounds; tentatively building up a sense of friendliness. Ruth was already 'living' in a room across the corridor; Lezli joined us, and we met Ruth's partner, and Kath, way ahead of us in her PhD.

At some point we felt safe enough to discuss the developing relationship. I only remember we thought our interaction was based on a principle of 'affirmation': it was OK for us to be 'real', to express our emotions. Imperceptibly, we moved from friendliness to friendship. There is a conceptual difference. Those who are 'friendly' share connectedness at a surface level, but continue to overtly manage the self and emotions. Within the concept of friendship lies a deeper sense of empathy not always visible to others. This is related to fundamental care for one another as human beings, incorporating respect for both difference and commonality, and a sharing of joys, sadnesses, and space.

We are all very different people, with different life experiences. My differences lie in my Christian beliefs, my role of motherhood, and my age. Sometimes I feel excluded from the others by my role of motherhood, envious of their liberty to 'socialize' together.

I am learning to be connected to other adult women, something previously outside my experience, and about which I sometimes feel ambivalent. Among these women I came to feminist epistemology for the first time, and struggled with the implications for my research, my family life, my Christian faith.

There have been changes over the past year. In September, a division of accountants 'moved into' the corridor. Rooms were appropriated by male voices that shouted to each other, laughed loudly in groups in the corridor, and, on occasions, walked uninvited into our room. For a while we felt disempowered.

Other changes occurred too. Our fieldwork phases began and now the connectedness has grown more elastic. Each time somebody goes away, there is initially a 'hole', but it quickly fills up with other relationships in the group. A recent exception happened when Karen tidied her desk just before leaving for a while. I found the unaccustomed order upsetting, and realized that an untidy desk implies a temporary absence, whereas a tidy one has a sense of permanence. I missed Karen a lot then!

Usually, though, each person is both independent and interdependent. Relationships are fluid, depending on who is 'around', often changing from hour to hour. Conflicts which occur between individuals do not extend to other relationships in 'misdirected loyalties' because each relationship is complete within itself. We are learning to be with the flow of negative emotions without feeling threatened.

The process of the PhD has been assessed as inevitably an isolating experience. It does not need to be so. Our friendship provides resources for each other. These not only facilitate my 'doing' of the PhD, but also my 'being' as a woman.

Discussion

Support

Research indicates that support for PhD students differs between institutions, between departments and between disciplines (Becher and Kogan, 1992; Becher, 1989), and varies from the excellent to the nonexistent (Carter, 1992). From our stories, two types of support emerge as significant: material and academic support.

Of the women represented in this paper, those with an academic scholarship represent the minority of research students who are materially well supported by their institution. From this advantageous position, two issues have been identified and should be commented upon. Firstly, even if the resources are available, unless they are made known to the student, they can not be utilized. Material support is often taken for granted by permanent members of the department and their existence and legitimate use may not be communicated to the newcomer. The second point is that, over and above the obvious necessity of material support, resources such as a telephone, a room, a desk, keys to cupboards, etc., symbolize belongingness. They indicate the legitimate status of the research student as a member of the department (Becher, 1989). This symbolic function of access to resources is particularly pertinent with regard to part-time and self-funded students, who do not always receive the same formal support. However, the 'informal' support of other research students can ensure that self-funded students have the same access to, and knowledge of, resources. Also, being identified with formally acknowledged research students can raise awareness of the status and role of the self-funded student in the department.

Academic support derives from a number of sources. Supervisors, other members of the department and other postgraduates can all be a source of support, as can people met through social networks, study groups and conferences.

A review of academic organization and culture with regard to the support postgraduates receive suggests two interlocking themes. One is of the Academy as a competitive, combative culture (see, e.g. Silverstein, 1974; Richards, 1986) which does not facilitate the kind of trusting relationships necessary for new or apprentice academics to comfortably risk the scrutiny of their work. Pamela Richards (1986, p. 115) claims that 'the discipline is organized in a way that undermines trust at every turn. Your peers are competing with you psychologically and structurally'. This type of competition is not efficient in facilitating academic development.

The second theme is the Academy as a patriarchal system, where women are excluded (or exclude themselves) from the male-defined culture. In this culture, women are expected to conform to traditional methods of conducting research; failure to conform is interpreted as failure to engage in proper academic work.

The paternalistic and patronizing attitudes of male supervisors and members of staff, as experienced by the women postgraduates Sue Scott and Mary Porter (1983) interviewed, or the experience of sexism and harassment discussed by Caroline Ramazanoglu (1987) created a situation where women as women or as postgraduates felt both excluded and under attack. The women in Scott and Porter's research often dealt with this by seeking out other women for support and defence in such a situation.

The portrayal of academia as a competitive and sexist institution is only a partial reflection of our own experiences. While each of us has, at some time, experienced paternalistic or sexist attitudes from male academics, we have also experienced supportive relationships with men and women, as women and as postgraduates. The relationships we have developed in our space do provide us with support in a competitive and sometimes hostile world. Our space, however, is also a place of celebration as much as it is somewhere to gain support and solace. While each of us has developed links with other people in the academic world, the room is somewhere that trusting relationships have developed slowly. These relationships have been a place in which to risk exploring original ideas and to present written work for the first time. Pamela Richards identifies this as a fundamentally important space which all academics, but especially trainees, need if they are to risk presenting work.

While the image gained of support for postgraduate students does represent part of our experience, it is a partial reflection. What is clear from our stories is that the PhD process is not inherently isolating. Nor is the marginality of postgraduate status necessarily a bad thing, as it can, if supported materially by the institution, provide a space to develop alternative support systems.

Space

Allocation of space within academic institutions has parallels in the housing market. There are decision-makers who decide where people will 'live', and this embodies a hierarchy which reflects the power and status of those competing for space. Researchers might be viewed as temporary 'immigrants' to the institution with little competitive 'clout' (Bassett and Short, 1980). Nevertheless, researchers must be provided with satisfactory accommodation in order to fulfil their function — the production of commodified knowledge which benefits the whole institution. We are given enough space to perform our tasks adequately but not enough to transgress hierarchical boundaries. However, there are benefits to be drawn from this marginalization and it seems relevant to reflect on this as a 'ghetto' (Boal, 1976). Postgraduates can be seen as an 'ethnic community' which inhabits the margins of academic space. While there may be a desire to assimilate into the academy, there are blocks to this, and advantages to maintaining our separation (Smith, 1990).

We certainly see the allocation of space in our building as reinforcing our ambiguous status. To some extent we have become ghettoized, although we feel we have turned this to our advantage. However, it seems inappropriate to end this city analogy here. Could the 'invasion' of the accountants be seen as 'gentrification' of our space (Bondi, 1992)? Certainly the accountants are of a higher status, reinforced by their male gender, and 'richer' in resources. Although we may use the common room, they have a staff room, secretarial support, and photocopying facilities, to which we are denied access.

There are other aspects of space which are relevant. The building represents a place in which we are comfortable, but there are other spaces which we inhabit, and in which we mix with others — a nearby pub, some allotments close to where Ruth and Gayle live, and staff dining facilities. Some of us are denied access to these spaces for various reasons including other commitments and distance, but, to some extent, it is possible to recreate our 'space' in other places.

Emotional and intellectual space must also be considered. It is important that there is room for individual feelings and ideas. This means that if somebody wants to talk, or be left alone, they are allowed the 'space' for this. We are also conscious of not taking up each other's space. Further, emotional and intellectual space are interwoven — talk flows unchecked between the academic and the personal. Different 'fields' and disciplines help make sense of previous experiences, as emerges in our individual accounts.

A final theme from our 'stories' is that of temporality: because of its rapid development, leaving (for example, for fieldwork) entails returning to the same place, but not the same space. As the group expands and contracts so the emotional space for each individual changes. Thus, reclaiming space involves a re-enculturation to the group. Theories of space must therefore account for emotional, intellectual and temporal dimensions.

Friendship

The term friend is often defined as a personal relationship which is both voluntary and informal, but Allan (1989) argues that it 'denotes something about the quality of the relationship you have with that person [and] is not just a categorical label' (p. 16).

Giddens states that 'proximity is ordinarily necessary for intimate relations to develop' (Giddens, 1991, p. 87) and Allan (1989) asserts that friendships typically originate from organizational bases. Although many friendships are instigated by sharing of physical space such as the workplace, this does not automatically lead to friendship. Allan also suggests that the recognition of friendship is symbolized by the time spent together outside the organizational base although other research and our own experience would suggest that this is not necessarily so. Although the friendships between us can and do extend into other areas of our lives, the shared space still remains the focal point for the relationships.

Kurth (1970) notes the distinction between being friendly and friendship and argues that many people distinguish between routine sociable ties and 'real friends'. 'True' or 'real' friendship is not sustained because of extrinsic material benefits to be gained, and therefore is not seen as instrumental. Thus, although friends may provide services to each other this is not the basis for the relationship. One of the perceived strengths of our relationships is the willingness to give support whenever this is possible while also being willing to recognize that our need for support cannot always be met. So friendship involves costs and disappointments as well as joys and satisfactions (O'Connor, 1992).

Giddens (1991) conceptualizes friendship in terms of the 'pure' relationship, which he sees as reflexively organized on an open and continuous basis, with a commitment to sustaining a balance of reciprocity. Allan (1989) also discusses this concept, but in terms of equality as an important structural characteristic, whereby the balance is kept implicit rather than explicit. He claims that to make it explicit turns the relationship into one based on extrinsic benefits, leading to its inevitable breakdown.

Our own experience of the relationships within our space highlights the inadequacy of these accounts of the ways in which friendships are sustained. Although there may be a certain amount of self-censorship when it comes to asking for support, the actual experience of this is far more complex than the literature would suggest. Support may at times be rationed; however, this is due to individual commitments and pressures rather than any attempt to maintain an equal balance of reciprocity, or 'quid pro quo' exchange of support.

Rainwater (1989) argues that a well-functioning relationship is one in which each person is autonomous, and without this autonomy the relationship will be one of co-dependency. In this sense the concept of autonomy is perceived as self-reliance and separateness and may apply to male friendships (Neuberger, 1991). However, research indicates that this is not the experience of friendships between women. A feminist critique of this argument (e.g. Miller, 1976; Gilligan, 1982; Stiver, 1984) recognizes the need to redefine autonomy as a concept based on 'the experiences of mutuality, relatedness, and the recognition of the other as a full subject' (Engel, 1980, p. 103).

In terms of our own relationships there is the recognition that we do work hard at 'getting it right' and equal recognition that we do not always succeed. Our willingness to relate to each other as full subjects strengthens, rather than weakens, the friendships between us.

Reflections

We all agree that this chapter has been very hard to write. The easiest problem to describe has been the practical organization of space. Space, in this instance, can be conceptualized in two ways. Firstly, it has not been easy to organize five separate timetables to make space for meetings. Secondly, we have all had to exercise self-discipline in reducing our verbosity!

Other difficulties involve reflexivity. Individual memories and perceptions of events and times differ; exploring these differences publicly has been hard for us. Some of these difficulties arise because of our perceptions of ourselves. Most theories use a 'group' concept, and there is no language to call upon for our 'collection of relationships'. The 'group' concept implies static identities, thus inhibiting the articulation of a collective experience, which is constantly 'becoming' but never 'is'.

Finally, writing this chapter has been another part of that process of 'becoming'. We have probably indicated the most important aspects of our experience by their absence, rather than their presence. Events, emotions and impressions which are too special, vulnerable or simply indescribable, have been placed in the absent spaces. It is necessary to read between the lines.

Postscript

Five months on things have changed. We no longer share a corridor or even a building. Ruth is at one end of the campus in a room of her own within her School whilst Karen, Gillian, Lezli and Gayle are in a building ten minutes' walk away sharing a room with six other people. . . .

Note

We would especially like to thank David Bell and Pamela Cotterill for their ongoing support and helpful comments. We would also like to thank those at the 1992 Women's Studies Network (UK) conference at Preston who showed such interest in our paper.

1 The discrepancies in the title of our institution occur as a result of a recent change in status from polytechnic to university.

References

ALLAN, GRAHAM (1989) *Friendship*, Hemel Hempstead, Harvester Wheatsheaf.

BASSETT, KEITH and SHORT, JOHN (1980) *Housing and Residential Structure: Alternative Approaches*, London, Routledge and Kegan Paul.

BECHER, TONY (1989) *Academic Tribes and Territories*, Milton Keynes, SRHE and Open University Press.

BECHER, TONY and KOGAN, MAURICE (1992) *Process and Structure in Higher Education*, London, Routledge.

BOAL, FREDERICK (1976) 'Ethnic Residential Segregation', in HERBERT, DAVID and JOHNSTON, RON (Eds) *Social Areas in Cities*, Vol. 1, London, John Wiley, pp. 41–79.

BONDI, LIZ (1992) *Sexing the City*, Paper presented at the Asociation of American Geographers Annual Conference, San Diego.

CARTER, JOY (1992) 'Making Do, Making Out! Amenities for Postgraduate Students', *Network*, 53, p. 4.

ELTON, LEWIS and POPE, MAUREEN (1989) 'Research Supervision: The Value of Collegiality', *Cambridge Journal of Education*, 19, pp. 267–76.

ENGEL, STEPHANIE (1980) 'Femininity as Tragedy: Re-Examining the New Narcissism', *Socialist Review*, 54, pp. 92–104.

GIDDENS, ANTHONY (1991) *Modernity and Self Identity*, Cambridge/Oxford, Polity/Blackwell.

GILLIGAN, CAROL (1982) *In a Different Voice*, Cambridge, Mass., Harvard University Press.

HOCKEY, JOHN (1991) 'The Social Sciences PhD: A Literature Review', *Studies in Higher Education*, **16**, 3, pp. 319–32.

HOOKS, BELL (1989) *Talking Back*, London, Sheba.

KURTH, S. (1970) 'Friendships and Friendly Relations', in MCCALL, TIM G. (Ed.) *Social Relationships*, Chicago, Aldine.

MILLER, JEAN BAKER (1976) *Toward a New Psychology of Women*, Boston, Beacon Press.

NEUBERGER, JULIA (1991) *Whatever's Happening to Women?*, London, Kyle Cathie.

O'CONNOR, PAT (1992) *'Friendships Between Women: A Critical Review'*, Hertfordshire, Harvester Wheatsheaf.

RAINWATER, JANETTE (1989) *Self-Therapy*, London, Crucible.

RAMAZANOGLU, CAROLINE (1987) 'Sex and Violence in Academic Life, Or You Can Keep a Good Woman Down', in HANMER, JALNA and MAYNARD, MARY (Eds) *Women, Violence and Social Control*, London, Macmillan.

RENOUF, JONATHAN (1989) 'An Alternative PhD', *Area*, **21**, 1.

RICHARDS, PAMELA (1986) 'Risk', in BECKER, HOWARD S. (Ed.) *Writing for Social Scientists*, Chicago and London, University of Chicago Press.

SCOTT, SUE and PORTER, MARY (1983) 'On the Bottom Rung: A Discussion of Women's Work in Sociology', *Women's Studies International Forum*, **6**, 2, pp. 211–21.

SILVERSTEIN, MICHAEL (1974) 'The History of a Short, Unsuccessful Academic Career', in PLECK, JOSEPH and SAWYER, JACK (Eds) *Man and Masculinity*, New Jersey, Prentice Hall.

SMITH, DAVID (1990) 'The Sharing and Dividing of Geographical Space', in CHISHOLM, MICHAEL and SMITH, DAVID (Eds) *Shared Space: Essays on Conflict and Territorial Organization*, London, Unwin Hyman.

STANLEY, LIZ (1990) 'Feminist Auto/Biography and Feminist Epistemology', in AARON, JANE and WALBY, SYLVIA (Eds) *Out of the Margins: Women's Studies in the Nineties*, London, Falmer Press, pp. 204–19.

STIVER, IRENE (1984) 'The Meaning of "Dependency" in Female-Male Relationships', *Work in Progress*, 83–01, Wellesley, Mass., Wellesley College.

WOOLF, VIRGINIA (1977) *A Room of One's Own*, London, Grafton.

Notes on Contributors

Sheila Brodie is an Adult Education worker at the moment employed in an Urban Aid community-based Adult Education project in one of the large housing schemes in Glasgow, as a support worker with groups. She organizes and finds the funding for courses for community groups, deals with any problems that arise and supports tutors with resources. She is lesbian, a single parent with two teenage children, Jewish and born in England though brought up in Scotland. She became involved in Women's Studies in 1986 when she attended the first Women's Studies course in Scotland at Strathclyde University.

Chris Corrin lives and works in Glasgow teaching politics and feminist thought at Glasgow University. Her main work has been with women in Hungary. Her two books are: *Magyar Women: Hungarian Women's Lives 1940s–1990s* (Macmillan, 1993) and an edited collection, *Superwomen and the Double Burden: Women's Experience of Change in Central and Eastern Europe and the former Soviet Union* (Scarlet Press, 1992). She continues to work in these fields.

Julia Hallam is teaching film and television studies in the Department of Communications, University of Liverpool. There have been considerable changes in her life recently, but she continues to be a doctoral student in Women's Studies at the University of Warwick. Her research explores the relationship between popular fictional texts and women's work, concentrating on issues of representation, identification and subjectivity in nursing. Although she is still registered as a health visitor and a general nurse, she has not practised since beginning her research in 1990.

Carrie Herbert emigrated to Adelaide, Australia as a drama teacher in 1973. She returned to study at UEA and Cambridge and then took up a post with the South Australian Government as Child Protection Officer. In 1990 she returned to Cambridge where she now runs a Consultancy in equal opportunities and sexual harassment.

Ruth Holliday is completing her PhD on the organization of production in small firms at Staffordshire University. She now lectures in OB and Business Ethics in the Business School, UCE in Birmingham. Her research interests include small firms in alternative economies, gender, sexuality and qualitative research.

Lisa Isherwood and **Dorothea McEwan** are founder members of the Britain and Ireland School of Feminist Theology. Dorothea McEwan lectures and writes on religion and politics and their impact on women. She is the editor of *Women Experiencing Church: A Documentation of Alienation* (Leominster, Fowler Wright, 1991). Lisa Isherwood lectures and writes on Christology and Ethics. They are both editors of the journal *Feminist Theology* (Sheffield Academic Press) and authors of the book *Introducing Feminist Theology* (Sheffield Academic Press, 1992).

Stevi Jackson is Lecturer in Sociology and coordinator of the MLitt in Women's Studies at the University of Strathclyde. She is the author of *Childhood and Sexuality* (Blackwell, 1982), co-editor of *Women's Studies: A Reader* (Harvester Wheatsheaf, 1993) and co-author of *Imagined Freedoms: Women and Popular Fiction in the Twentieth Century* (Harvester Wheatsheaf, forthcoming). She is currently writing a book on Christine Delphy for the Sage 'Women of Ideas' series.

Mary Kennedy is Senior Lecturer in Women's Studies in the Centre for Extra-Mural Studies at Birkbeck College, London, and currently Co-Chair of the Women's Studies Network (UK). She is co-author with Mary Hughes of *New Futures: Changing Women's Education* (Routledge and Kegan Paul, 1985), and has contributed papers on women's studies and adult education to several collections since then.

Celia Kitzinger teaches Social Psychology and Women's Studies at Loughborough University. She is the author of *The Social Construction of Lesbianism* (Sage, 1987), co-author (with Sheila Kitzinger) of *Talking with Children about Things that Matter* (Pandora, 1989) and co-author (with Rachel Perkins) of *Changing Our Minds: Lesbian Feminism and Psychology* (Onlywomen Press, London 1993; New York University Press, 1993).

Gayle Letherby is currently in her third year of PhD study at Staffordshire University. Her project is concerned to explore experiences (predominantly women's) of 'infertility' and 'involuntary childlessness'. Her research interests also include the family, women's health, bereavement and loss and all things methodological.

Joanna Liddle teaches Women's Studies at the University of Warwick and is the author of *Daughters of Independence: Gender, Caste and Class in India* (Zed Books, 1986).

Cathy Lubelska is Principal Lecturer in Social History and Women's Studies and Course Leader of Women's Studies at the University of Central Lancashire. Her current research explores interdisciplinary and experiential methodologies within feminism and women's history. She has published articles on feminist pedagogy, in which she has an abiding practical interest. She lives in Cumbria with her partner and two sons.

Dorothea McEwan's note appears with Lisa Isherwood's.

Lezli Mann is undertaking a part-time PhD at Staffordshire University. Her research explores how young people use fashion as a medium for creating and expressing identity, reflecting interests in culture, ideology, images and appearances.

Jennifer Marchbank lives in Central Region, Scotland, where she works as a Girls' Development Worker. She is currently completing her PhD in Politics on the topic 'Agenda Setting, Policy Development and the Marginalization of Women' at the University of Strathclyde where she also co-ordinates the Continuing Education Certificate in Women's Studies. Her main research issues are childcare and equal opportunity policies.

Annecka Marshall is a PhD student and part-time tutor in Sociology at the University of Warwick. She has taught feminist and anti-racist studies at the University of North London and at Birkbeck College, University of London. Interests include feminism, Black radicalism and sexual politics.

Julie Matthews is a former Foundation Studies Programme student (access route) and currently an undergraduate, studying Single Honours Women's Studies at the University of Central Lancashire. She is hoping to examine and develop new research on disabled women, after completing postgraduate study.

Louise Morley is a Lecturer in the Department of Community Studies, University of Reading, where she teaches Women's Studies, Interpersonal and Group Work Skills and Education. Her research interests include the interface between organizational policies for equality and processes of empowerment and change for individuals and groups. She has published on the subject of power, group process, difference and pedagogical approaches to work with non-traditional learners in higher education. She is currently undertaking research and consultancy in the public sector on empowerment of senior women managers.

Shirin M. Rai teaches Politics and Women's Studies at the University of Warwick. She is the author of *Resistance and Reaction: University Politics in Post-Mao China* (Harvester Wheatsheaf, 1991) and the co-editor (with Hilary

Pilkington and Annie Phizaklea) of *Women in the Face of Change: The Soviet Union, Eastern Europe and China* (Routledge, 1992).

Karen Ramsay is currently undertaking PhD research at Staffordshire University. Her project explores how disciplinary cultures shape equality of opportunity for women academics. Her academic interests include feminist methodology, sexuality and emotion in organizations.

Gillian Reynolds is in her final year of PhD study at Staffordshire University. Her research interests lie in philanthropy, charity and disablism. Her personal interests also centre on philosophy and sociology, including minority perspectives within the discipline, and theories of practice.

Lynne Thompson, having been a mature student, is now Senior Lecturer at the University of Central Lancashire. She has had wide experience in adult education, with particular reference to the needs of part-time students in non-vocational, further and higher education. She teaches History and Women's Studies, with particular responsibility for the Foundation Studies Programme, and the New Opportunities for Women Course. She is currently researching competency-based methods of assessment for access students, and the profile of part-time, evening-only students at the University of Central Lancashire and its associated colleges.

Virginia Vargas is a founder member of the Flora Tristán Women's Centre and of the Peruvian feminist movement; she is a sociologist specializing in politics. She has written several books in Spanish, including *La Participacion Economica y Social de la Mujer en el Peru* (198I); *El Aporte de la Rebeldia de las Mujeres* (1989); *Como cambiar el Mundo sin Perdernos* (1992); and numerous articles in English. She works half the year in the Institute of Social Studies, the Hague, Holland, and the other half at the Flora Tristán Centre, and is Coordinator of the International Network, 'Entre Mujeres: un diálogo sur-norte'.

Sylvia Walby was the first Chair of the Women's Studies Network (UK), 1988–90, and Director of the Women's Studies Research Centre at Lancaster University during the 1980s. She is now Coordinator of the new Gender Institute at the London School of Economics. Her publications include *Patriarchy at Work* (1986), *Theorising Patriarchy* (1990) and *Sex Crime in the News* (1991). She is currently engaged in a long-term project on the history of feminist thought.

Val Walsh started by studying Fine Art, then qualified in Sociology, followed by Women's Studies. She currently has a multiple professional identity as Course Leader for Communication Studies, Convenor for the new Women's Studies degree programme, and Equal Opportunities Consultant within the Access and Equal Opportunities Unit at Edge Hill College of Higher Education.

Ongoing research includes an Arts Council funded project, 'Women's Experience, Art Education, and Art: The Relation between Creativity, Pedagogy, and Society'. Research, writing, and conference presentations have focused on women's creativity; the position and experience of women in higher education; and developing a feminist politics/theory which articulates the interconnections between patriarchal aesthetics, ethics, and social ecology.

Sue Wilkinson is Senior Lecturer in Health Studies Research at the University of Hull, and founding editor of *Feminism and Psychology: An International Journal* and the 'Gender and Psychology' book series (both Sage Publications).

Tamsin Wilton lectures in Health Studies and in Women's Studies at the University of the West of England, and teaches lesbian studies occasionally at Bristol University. She is the author of *Antibody Politic: AIDS and Society* (New Clarion Press, 1992) and is currently writing a Lesbian Studies 'primer' for Routledge, editing an anthology of essays on lesbians and film, and co-editing *AIDS: Setting a Feminist Agenda*, to be published by Falmer Press. She lives with her son, her companion lover and her cats.

Nira Yuval-Davis is Reader in Ethnic and Gender Studies at the University of Greenwich in London. She has written extensively on women, nationalism, racism and fundamentalism in Israel and Britain. She has recently co-edited *Women-Nation-State* (Macmillan, 1989); *Refusing Holy Orders: Women and Fundamentalism in Britain* (Virago, 1992); and has co-written *Racialized Boundaries: Ethnic, Gender, Colour and Class Divisions and the Anti-Racist Struggle* (Routledge, 1992).

Index

Index

guilt 33, 59, 147–8, 170
Gurney, J.N. 115, 116

Hall, Marny 31
Hamilton, Cicely 39–40
Hanmer, Jalna 125, 174
Hansard Society 120
harassment 139, 189
sexual *see* sexual harassment
Haraway, Donna 123
Harding, S. 69, 70(n)
Hardy Aiken, Susan 125
Harrison, Brian 79
Haug, Frigga 43
Hawkesworth, Mary 21, 71
Henriques, J. 70(n)
Herbert, Carrie 93(n), 95, 102, 103
heterocentricity 168
heterosexism 74–5, 157
in academia/education 162–3
and materialist analysis of oppression 174
Women's Studies and 126, 127
see also homophobia
heterosexual imperative 39–40, 41–2, 171, 173
heterosexuality/heterosexual women 24–34, 169–70, 171
consequences 26–8
as default 26, 29, 31–2, 41–2, 172
defensiveness 126, 127, 169
equality and 40
feminists and 24–34, 168–75
guilt 33
and homophobia 164
and identity 24–34, 121, 175
leading to feminism 33
learning 46–7
and mental health 27–8, 81
political function 172, 173–4
politicization, need for 33–4
pressure towards 39–40, 84, 171, 173
problematizing 41
problems of 26–8, 47
subordination and 40, 42, 47, 172
history
backlash in context of 79–88
reconstruction in Orientalism 12–13
Hite, Shere 47
Hoagland, Sarah Lucia 25
Hochschild, A. 39
Hockey, John 180–1
Holland 5

Hollway, W. 46
home, pressure to stay in 59, 86
homophobia 75, 157, 159, 160, 170
acceptability 170
and racialization of sexuality 74
responses to 161
see also heterosexism
homosexuality
law and 86, 157, 161, 162
see also lesbianism/lesbians
hooks, bell xiv, xv, 3, 64(n), 122, 123, 124, 125, 127, 182
Hooyman, Nancy 121
Hopkins, June 27
housework 26–7

identity politics x, 5–7, 73–4
identity/identities x, 5, 121–2, 167–8
assumptions about, research and 108, 111, 115
Black 18, 68, 72–4, 121–2
class 121
contradictory 108, 123–7
default/politicized 32–4
denial of 24–6, 29–31, 34, 85
feminist xi, 85, 160
gender 44
heterosexuality and 24–34, 121, 175
lesbian 25–6, 29–30, 31, 33, 112, 167–8
multiple xiv, 70, 74, 106, 113–14, 115, 145
narrative and 46–8
psychoanalytic thought and 69–70
researchers and 64–76, 110, 111
transversalism 8–9
unexplained 108, 111, 112, 115
see also difference/diversity
ideological positioning *see under* oppression
Illich, Ivan 54
impairment *see* disability
imperialism 121–2
see also Orientalism
India 12–16, 17–18, 20
women's movement 15, 18
individualism, love and 42–3
Institute of Economic Affairs 171
intervention, feminist 121, 161
interviewing, gender and 109–10, 115
intimacy 95
see also friendship; love
Ireland 20, 163

race *see* ethnicity
racism 71, 73, 75, 121–2, 124, 158–9
  and diversity 3–4
  examples 14–15, 16
  in feminism 17, 18
  and intervention 9
  research on 66–7, 71
  researchers' response to 98–9
  unacceptability, public 170
  see also Orientalism
radical feminism 172, 174(n)
  see also feminism
Radway, Janice 44, 47
Rainwater, Janette 192
Ramabai, Pandiata 15
Ramazanoglu, Caroline xv, 26, 28, 33, 121, 189
Ranelagh, E.L. 54
rape 27
  in marriage 27, 52
  romantic fiction and 47
  and social control 58
  stereotypes concerning 98–9
Rathbone, Eleanor 14, 15–16, 18
Raymond, Janice 122
reciprocity, research and 95, 97, 100–4
Reddy, Muthulakshmi 15
reflective practice 118
Reinharz, Shulamit 32
rejection 124
relationships 192
  and identity 24–34
  see also family; friendship; heterosexuality; lesbianism; love
religion 51–62, 156–7, 158
  Goddess 54
  love and 40, 43
  Women's Studies compared to 122
  see also fundamentalism
Renouf, Jonathan 180
representation
  cultural 6
  of others 17, 20–1
research 69
  activism and xiii, xiv, 145–9, 165
  audience for 65, 70, 111
  distortion of 80–1
  emancipatory 111, 112, 115
  experience and *see under* experience
  gender and 106–16
  and manipulation 95
  requirements for 180–93
  researchers' involvement and effects xii–xiii, 97–103

risk and 112–13, 116
  self-reflexive 64–76
  subjects of 65–76, 94–5, 103–4, 106–16
  see also methodology
resistance
  lesbianism as 173, 174
  to patriarchal Christianity 57
  to suttee 17
reversal, in backlash 80–1
Rich, Adrienne 33, 164, 165, 168, 171(n), 173, 174, 176
Richards, Pamela 189, 190
right-wing politics *see* backlash; conservative politics
risk 27, 164
  research and 112–13, 116
Roach, Denise xiv
Rogers, Wendy Stainton 107
romance *see* fiction, romantic; love
Rosaldo, Michelle 39, 45
Rose, J. 44
Rowland, Robyn 25
Ruebain, D. 138
Ruether, Rosemary Radford 60, 62
Rukhmabai, Dr 15
Rushdie affair 7–8, 9
Russell, Diana 27
Russell, L. 61

Sahgal, Gita 6, 86
Said, Edward 11–12, 13, 15, 18, 21, 22
Sanday, P.R. 52
Sandoval, Chela 123
Sarsby, Jacqueline 42
Schniedewind, Nancy 123
Scotland 156–7, 163, 164
Scott, Sue 46, 110, 111, 115, 189
Scruton, Roger 173–4
Section 28 (Local Government Act 1988) 157, 161, 162
security, love and 43
Segal, Lynne 170, 174(n)
self-definition *see* identity/identities
self-determination, as right 16
self-help groups 94–5
  see also consciousness-raising
sensuality, feminist theology and 61–2
separatism 169(n)
sex (gender) *see* gender
sex (sexual activity) 169
  Christianity and 55, 56–7, 59–60
sexual abuse 103